D1534734

Prosecution Complex

Prosecution Complex

America's Race to Convict and

Its Impact on the Innocent

Daniel S. Medwed

NEW YORK UNIVERSITY PRESS

New York and London

NEW YORK UNIVERSITY PRESS
New York and London
www.nyupress.org

References to Internet websites (URLs) were accurate at the time of writing.
Neither the author nor New York University Press is responsible for URLs
that may have expired or changed since the manuscript was prepared.

Library of Congress Cataloging-in-Publication Data

Medwed, Daniel S.
Prosecution complex : America's race to convict and
its impact on the innocent / Daniel S. Medwed.
p. cm.
Includes bibliographical references and index.
ISBN 978-0-8147-9624-5 (hardback : alk paper)
ISBN 978-0-8147-9625-2 (ebook)
ISBN 978-0-8147-6435-0 (ebook)
1. Prosecutorial misconduct—United States.
2. Judicial error—United States. I. Title.
KF9640.M43   2012
345.73'05—dc23   2011038155

New York University Press books are printed on acid-free paper,
and their binding materials are chosen for strength and durability.
We strive to use environmentally responsible suppliers and materials
to the greatest extent possible in publishing our books.

Manufactured in the United States of America

For Howard Medwed who taught me to love the law;
Mameve Medwed who taught me to love the written word;
and Sharissa Jones, the love of my life.

Contents

Acknowledgments

First and foremost, I thank Sharissa Jones, my beloved wife, dearest friend, and best reader. Our daughter, Mili, deserves credit, too. When asked what her father does for a living, she has taken to telling her preschool pals that "Daddy does footnotes."

Other family members and friends played a vital role in my ability to complete this project. My parents, Howard and Mameve Medwed, provided unwavering support, not to mention great feedback on this manuscript; my brother Jono, his wife Marnie Davidoff, and their daughter Mirabelle offered much needed cheerleading throughout the writing process; and my relatives in Nebraska—Tom, Sharlane, Tod, Bryson, and Tyler Jones—treated me with their characteristic warmth. Special thanks as well to several close friends who have encouraged me for decades: John Haddad, Rich Dubois, Joel Goldberg, and Andy Sheffer. Earlier in my career, I had the good fortune to work on post-conviction innocence cases involving Fernando Bermudez, Bruce Goodman, Stephen Schulz, and David Wong, each of whom graciously permitted me to discuss their sagas in this book.

I am grateful to Hiram Chodosh, my dean at the University of Utah, and Bob Goldberg, director of the Tanner Humanities Center at the University of Utah, for a research leave to serve as a Virgil Aldrich Fellow in the fall of 2010 in order to work exclusively on this book. I also thank my former colleague at Brooklyn Law School, Will Hellerstein, for introducing me to the wonders of post-conviction innocence work and for being such a terrific mentor. Maddy DeLone, Nina Morrison, Peter Neufeld, Barry Scheck, Emily West, and their colleagues at the Innocence Project in New York City provided not only inspiration but also access to information related to several of the cases profiled in the following pages.

This book benefited greatly from a number of academics and attorneys who offered feedback on earlier drafts: Jensie Anderson, Adele Bernhard, Troy Booher, Alafair Burke, Stacy Caplow, Paul Cassell, Susan Courtney, Linda Feldman, Keith Findley, Leslie Francis, Erika George, Bennett Gershman, Lissa Griffin, Jackie Hodgson, Anders Kaye, Laura Kessler, Erik Luna, Kim Mangun, Wayne McCormack, Nancy McLaughlin, Katie Monroe, Theresa Newman, George Thomas, Debora Threedy, and Ron Wright.

I am deeply in debt to many former students for their help. Jennifer Ku, Chayce Clark, Melanie Stein Grayson, and Razvan Ungureanu devoted countless hours to assist in the research for this project. Also, several students volunteered to read drafts of the manuscript as it approached the copyediting stage: Mike Anderson, Bryan Blackwell, Frank Chiaramonte, Abby Elliott, Veronica McDougal, Natasha Naylor, Barry Stratford, Sam Sutton, and Sheri Throop. Carolynn Westenskow's administrative support was invaluable, as were my conversations with Russ Costa about certain aspects of cognitive psychology. Dan Bezdjian and Felicity Murphy helped enormously with the index. And much appreciation to the editorial team at New York University Press, particularly Debbie Gershenowitz for agreeing to publish this book, Rita Bernhard for the excellent copyediting, and Despina Papazoglou Gimbel for shepherding it through to completion.

Parts of this book build upon several of my previously published articles, most notably "Anatomy of a Wrongful Conviction: Theoretical Implications and Practical Solutions," 51 *Vill. L. Rev.* 337 (2006); "*Brady's* Bunch of Flaws," 67 *Wash. & Lee L. Rev.* 1533 (2010); "Closing the Door on Misconduct: Rethinking the Ethical Standards That Govern Summations in Criminal Trials," 38 *Hastings Const. L.Q.* 915 (2011); "Emotionally Charged: The Prosecutorial Charging Decision and the Innocence Revolution," 31 *Cardozo L. Rev.* 2187 (2010); "Innocentrism," 2008 *U. Ill. L. Rev.* 1549 (2008); "The Prosecutor as Minister of Justice: Preaching to the Unconverted from the Post-Conviction Pulpit," 84 *Wash. L. Rev.* 35 (2009); "Up the River without a Procedure: Innocent Prisoners and Newly Discovered Non-DNA Evidence in State Courts," 47 *Ariz. L. Rev.* 655 (2005); and "The Zeal Deal: Prosecutorial Resistance to Post-Conviction Claims of Innocence," 84 *B.U. L. Rev.* 125 (2004).

Justice Felix Frankfurter once wrote that "all systems of law . . . are administered through men and therefore may occasionally disclose the frailties of men." The same principles apply to law professors. Any errors in this book come from my frailties alone.

Introduction

James Giles served ten years in prison for a vicious rape he did not commit because prosecutors failed to provide the defense with evidence suggesting that a different James Giles was at fault. David Wong endured seventeen years in the penitentiary for a murder he did not commit because prosecutors relied on a dishonest jailhouse informant who received a recommendation for parole in exchange for his testimony against Wong. Bruce Godschalk wasted fifteen years of his life incarcerated for two sexual assaults he did not commit. He spent seven of those years fighting prosecutors just for the chance to subject the biological evidence retrieved from the crime scenes to deoxyribonucleic acid (DNA) testing. These three men are not the only criminal defendants who have suffered the horror of wrongful conviction due to choices prosecutors made in their cases. Why does this happen, and how can it be avoided?

I have wrestled with these questions for nearly fifteen years, ever since I accepted a job as a public defender with the Legal Aid Society of New York City. My later work helping inmates pursue post-conviction claims of innocence as assistant director of the Second Look Program at Brooklyn Law School fueled my interest in prosecutorial behavior and its impact on the innocent. Now, as a professor with some distance from the daily rigors of law practice, this book is my attempt to answer these questions.

Prosecutors and Wrongful Convictions

Since 1989 post-conviction DNA testing has exonerated more than 250 prisoners, and at least 300 other inmates with powerful innocence claims have gained their freedom.[1] But there is reason to think that these exonerations are the tip of a much larger innocence iceberg. Biological evidence suitable for DNA testing exists in only 10 to 20 percent of criminal cases; even then, it is often lost, degraded, or destroyed before any attempt to conduct post-conviction testing.[2] Without the magic bullet of DNA, prisoners struggle to overturn cases because of the difficulties involved in finding nonscientific evidence of innocence after trial and convincing skeptical judges that this evidence raises doubts about the accuracy of the verdict. As Professor Samuel Gross once put it, "the true number of wrongful convictions is unknown and frustratingly unknowable."[3]

What we do know is that specific factors cause these miscarriages of justice in the first place.[4] Prosecutorial behavior has emerged as one of those factors, a finding that clashes with our vision of the American prosecutor. Prosecutors in the United States are public officials who charge individuals with crimes and litigate those matters in court. They represent "the People" of their jurisdictions, not crime victims. Unlike defense attorneys, whose sole task is to champion their clients' interests, prosecutors are quasi-judicial officers equipped with a dual obligation. They must serve as zealous government advocates and neutral "ministers of justice." As portrayed by courts, ethicists, and Hollywood filmmakers, prosecutors committed to justice never lose a case so long as the outcome is fair.[5]

Various rationales support the idea that prosecutors should carry the weighty minister-of-justice burden on top of their advocacy responsibilities. Prosecutors are the most powerful players in the criminal justice system, capable of determining who should be charged and with what crimes. The duty to serve as a minister of justice is designed to limit abuse of this power and to compensate for the imbalance of resources that so often places the defense at a disadvantage. Demanding more of prosecutors than of other lawyers also fosters greater confidence in the legitimacy and accuracy of the criminal justice system. Anointing prosecutors as ministers of justice, in short, makes many of us feel better about the chance that justice will occur in the end.[6]

Yet reliance on "justice" as the main yardstick of prosecutorial behavior is dangerous. Few tangible rules bind prosecutors beyond the amorphous duty to do justice.[7] Even where specific rules exist—such as those concerning the evidence prosecutors must turn over to the defense before trial—courts and ethics committees seldom punish prosecutors for violating them.[8] Small wonder that the minister-of-justice ideal has not adapted flawlessly into practice.

Indeed, the idealistic image of the prosecutor as minister of justice masks a less glowing truth. Consider the following anecdote. Several years ago one of my students had a job interview with a prosecutors' office. The interview seemed to be going well until the interviewer asked whether my student had "tasted blood" in the courtroom. Silence reigned, until the interviewer explained that he wanted to hire lawyers who had already tasted blood and liked it.⁹ How did bloodlust become a prerequisite for working as a prosecutor, at least in that office?

The very source of prosecutorial uniqueness—the dual role of advocate and servant of justice—may be part of the answer, causing an "ongoing schizophrenia" about how to balance these responsibilities.¹⁰ Prosecutors are told to lock up criminals and protect defendants' rights. Although no tension should exist between a prosecutor's advocacy and minister-of-justice duties, the role of zealous advocate often takes precedence. Professional incentives and psychological pressures in most prosecutorial offices are linked with the advocate's goal of earning convictions. This creates an institutional "prosecution complex" that animates how district attorneys' offices treat potentially innocent defendants at all stages of the process—and that can cause prosecutors to aid in the conviction of the innocent.¹¹

That prosecutors sometimes contribute to wrongful convictions is troubling. Even assuming that the error rate in the criminal justice system hovers around 1 percent of felony cases, a figure smaller than many scholars estimate, that means thousands of innocent people live behind bars.¹² These cases represent far more than a series of individual nightmares; they offend our core values. Protecting the innocent is a pillar of Anglo-American criminal law, as reflected by English legal commentator William Blackstone's famous eighteenth-century maxim that it is far better to let ten guilty people go free than to convict a single innocent person.¹³ The conviction of an innocent defendant also compromises public safety. By getting it wrong at the outset, the true culprit is free to commit other crimes.¹⁴

The Structure of the Book

This book explores the role that prosecutors play in convicting innocent defendants and prolonging their incarceration. The book is divided into three parts that correspond to the key phases of a criminal case: pretrial, trial, and post-conviction. Each part begins with a representative story of a wrongful conviction, followed by chapters that fuse case narratives with evaluations of the rules and biases that permit prosecutors to assist in these injustices.

Part 1 focuses on how prosecutorial conduct before trial may result in wrongful convictions. Judicial decisions and ethical rules give prosecutors discretion to charge people with crimes, disclose evidence in their possession, and offer plea bargains. Social scientists have shown that cognitive biases may lead prosecutors early on to develop "tunnel vision" about a particular case and interpret even exculpatory evidence in a fashion that confirms their perception of the suspect's guilt.[15] Once tunnel vision becomes entrenched, a prosecutor's minister-of-justice duties all too often fade into the background and present few obstacles on the path to conviction.

Part 2 concerns prosecutorial tactics at trial that contribute to wrongful convictions. If plea bargaining negotiations falter, prosecutors normally direct their efforts toward achieving a successful outcome at trial. The upshot is that many trial prosecutors develop a "conviction psychology,"[16] an affliction that promotes the use of aggressive strategies. These strategies include the presentation of witnesses who lack credibility, the introduction of dubious forensic scientific evidence, and unfair comments on the evidence in closing arguments.

Part 3 looks at the issue of prosecutorial resistance to innocence claims after trial. Stories of post-conviction prosecutors behaving defensively fill the annals of criminal law, even when inmates put forth strong new evidence of innocence. On many occasions prosecutors confronted with the likelihood of a wrongful conviction have concocted revised theories of the case that bear scant resemblance to the approach at trial to rationalize the continued imprisonment of the defendant.[17]

Each part offers thoughts on possible reforms to add substance to the minister-of-justice concept. A number of sources shape and control prosecutorial behavior. Courts provide a check on prosecutors through constitutional doctrine and judicial opinions. Legislatures enact statutes, some of which relate to the election of chief prosecutors. Legal ethics fall into two categories that apply to prosecutors: rules and standards. Ethical rules are binding; a lawyer's violation of them may lead to disciplinary action. Ethical standards are nonbinding resolutions intended to offer guidance and encourage best practices. Prosecutors also regulate their own work through internal norms, policies, and practices.

My suggestions for reform consider all these sources. Though my recommendations vary in each section, four themes prevail: (1) that there should be greater transparency in most discretionary decisions made by prosecutors; (2) that courts and legislatures should raise the legal bar for prosecutors in justifying those discretionary choices; (3) that ethical rules should be more concrete and disciplinary agencies more inclined to penalize prosecutors for violating them; and (4) that prosecutors should construct internal review committees to evaluate major decisions to neutralize the grave effects of cognitive bias.

One theme I do not develop in much detail, despite its periodic appearance throughout the book, relates to racial bias in prosecutorial decision making. The issue of race permeates every aspect of the American criminal justice system. Other scholars have discussed this topic more capably than I ever could,[18] and I fear that any effort to cover it comprehensively here, short of a monograph-length discourse, would be incomplete.

The goal of this book is not to portray prosecutors as rogue officials indifferent to the conviction of the innocent. Such a portrayal would be misleading.[19] For that matter, drawing any generalizations about the behavior of American prosecutors, some thirty thousand strong in more than two thousand separate offices,[20] is a challenge. What seems safe to say is that most prosecutors aim to do justice, but only some hit that target consistently. This book seeks to explain and change this state of affairs.

Fair Play?

Prosecutorial Behavior Prior to Trial

State of Texas v. James Curtis Giles

Around midnight on August 1, 1982, three African American men armed with guns broke into a North Dallas apartment and terrorized the occupants. After raping a pregnant white woman, the men robbed her husband. The assailants then dragged the woman outside to a nearby field where they raped her again. It was a shocking act of brutality that local police officers did not want to go unpunished. Fortunately they had a good lead. The rape victim recognized one of her attackers as an acquaintance named Stanley Bryant who lived in her neighborhood. But the police were unable to interview Bryant before he fled Texas after the attack, and they had almost no information about the other perpetrators. The victim could only describe them in general terms, one as tall and lean and the other as short and stocky.[1]

The investigation languished for several weeks until law enforcement received a tip that "James Giles" was one of the participants in the North Dallas assault. Following up on that clue, the police discovered that a man named James Curtis Giles had a criminal record and lived thirty miles away. The twenty-eight-year-old Giles was married with a child and earned his living as a construction worker. A month after the incident, the police showed the victim and her husband an array of six photographs of men who matched the description of the perpetrators. Although the husband failed to identify anyone initially from these pictures, the woman pointed out Giles as one of her assailants, the "tall one."[2]

The case against Giles went to trial in June 1983 based on the identification. During the victim's testimony about her traumatic experience, she repeated her identification of Giles. She insisted that when she saw his photograph she was "absolutely positive that it was him."[3] She never viewed a live lineup in the case. In fact, her first in-person identification of Giles occurred during trial when the defendant was the only African American in the court-room except for a bailiff.[4]

Giles claimed he was with his wife during the time of the North Dallas incident. His wife corroborated this alibi on the witness stand. The jury nonetheless found Giles guilty of aggravated rape, and the judge sentenced him to thirty years in prison. The foreperson later explained that the jury agonized over the case but put tremendous stock in the identification.[5]

The conviction of James Giles was suspect from the start. The vicitim declared that Giles's face was inches away from her during the assault, a salient detail that reinforced the strength of her identification. But she never mentioned that her attacker had gold teeth—and Giles had two of them displayed prominently during the summer of 1982. Although police detectives denied committing any misconduct during the photo lineup procedure, a rumor surfaced that the victim had learned the name "James Giles" from a neighbor and that the police directed her to his photo.[6]

Information gathered during a police interrogation of Stanley Bryant in Indiana cast further doubt on Giles's guilt. In May 1983, two weeks before Giles's trial, the Dallas police discovered that Bryant had been arrested in Indianapolis for an unrelated crime. Dallas Detective Carol Hovey consulted with the lead prosecutor in the Giles case, Mike O'Connor, and asked police officials in Indianapolis to interrogate Bryant about the events of August 1, 1982. Indianapolis detectives obtained two statements from Bryant in which he confessed to the North Dallas crimes. Bryant attributed the entire incident to a dispute over drugs, and cited two teenagers named "Michael" and "James" as his accomplices. He described his friend Michael as the taller of the two and gave detailed information about him, including his telephone number. Bryant noted that James was a short, muscular teen who ran in the same circles. Indeed, a younger James Giles—James Earl Giles (a.k.a., "Quack")—was a known criminal associate of Bryant's who lived across the street from the victim. Bryant's wife provided a statement to the police supporting her husband's account.[7]

Dallas prosecutors withheld Stanley Bryant's statements implicating "Michael" and "James" from the defense, even though the government is required to disclose such evidence as a matter of federal constitutional law. In 1963 the U.S. Supreme Court ruled in *Brady v. Maryland* that, before trial, prosecutors must turn over all evidence that is favorable to the defense and material to guilt or punishment.[8] It does not matter whether the evidence is in the hands of the assigned prosecutor; information possessed by the police is imputed to the prosecution for *Brady* purposes.[9] Stanley Bryant's statements—as well as those of his spouse—were undeniably favorable to the defense and would have led the defense team to Quack Giles's doorstep. Dallas prosecutors knew about the Bryant statements before trial, as demonstrated by their exchanges with Detective Hovey and, through her, the Indianapolis police. Almost as worrisome as the failure to disclose the Bryant statements, prosecutors neglected to investigate the possibility that this other James Giles was one of the culprits. Bryant later pled guilty to the North Dallas crimes in return for a twenty-year sentence.[10]

James Curtis Giles, meanwhile, persisted in claiming his innocence from behind bars. Stanley Bryant viewed a photograph of him in 1985 and vowed that the man convicted of aggravated rape did not participate in the North Dallas crimes. Yet two writs of habeas corpus filed by Giles went nowhere in the 1980s.[11]

Things began to look up for Giles in 1989, when he met a man named Marvin Moore while they were incarcerated in the same prison. Moore knew a lot about the events in North Dallas. On the night of the crime, the police found Moore during a canvass of the surrounding area. The police hauled Moore down to the precinct where he was cleared by the victim and her husband (who knew him). Shaken by the experience, Moore went back to his apartment complex and visited the home of his friend Bernard Giles. During that visit he learned that Bernard's younger brother, Quack, had committed the crimes along with two others. [12]

The Dallas County District Attorney's Office conducted a cursory reinvestigation of the case in the early 1990s in response to Moore's claims but backed off after the vicitm maintained her identification and a primitive DNA test of biological evidence collected in a "rape kit" as part of the medical treatment of the victim yielded inconclusive results. Giles served ten years of his sentence before obtaining parole in 1993. In addition to living under the shadow of parole after his release, the state required Giles to register as a sex offender, a condition that subjected him to ridicule in the small Texas town where he settled.[13]

Eager to clear his name, Giles convinced the Innocence Project in New York City to take his case. The Innocence Project, founded in 1992 by attorneys Peter Neufeld and Barry Scheck, investigates and litigates post-conviction claims of innocence by inmates whose cases contain biological evidence suitable for DNA testing.[14] The Innocence Project has freed more than one hundred innocent prisoners.[15] It has also inspired the creation of numerous other groups dedicated to this work, including the Second Look Program that I helped establish at Brooklyn Law School in 2001 to handle innocence claims by New York state inmates whose cases lacked DNA evidence.[16]

In the Giles case, the Innocence Project set its sights on subjecting the biological evidence retrieved from the North Dallas crime scene to new types of DNA testing. Sophisticated DNA testing of the material from the rape kit in 2003 identified the profiles of two males, neither of which matched that of James Curtis Giles. A string of even more advanced DNA tests pinpointed the biological profiles as belonging to Stanley Bryant and a man named Michael Anthony Brown, who had died in 1985 awaiting prosecution for a different gang rape.[17]

These discoveries gave James Curtis Giles renewed hope because of the strong connection Brown and Bryant had to James Earl "Quack" Giles. Quack Giles had died in prison in 2000 while serving a sentence for unrelated crimes in Dallas. To substantiate the link between Brown, Bryant, and Quack Giles, representatives of the Innocence Project approached Michael Brown's sister. She signed an affidavit verifying that Quack Giles and her brother were good friends in the early 1980s, that their families lived in the same apartment complex in North Dallas, and that the two teenagers hung around with another neighbor named "Stan" during the summer of 1982. She also identified Quack Giles from a yearbook photo. Upon viewing a picture of James Curtis Giles, she indicated she had never seen him before.[18]

The Dallas County District Attorney's Office revived its investigation of the case in December 2006 after analyzing the evidence compiled by the Innocence Project. The prosecutors' efforts soon identified fingerprints left on a telephone at the crime scene as those of Brown. Prosecutors then dispatched an investigator to interview the victim's husband. When shown two separate photo lineups—one containing a picture of James Curtis Giles, the other featuring one of Quack Giles—he selected Quack Giles as the perpetrator. The victim also viewed a series of photographs. This time she identified neither James Curtis Giles nor Quack Giles as her attacker and acknowledged that she was not certain the man she helped convict was guilty.[19]

The final piece of the puzzle, The victim's recognition of her possible mistake, fit snugly with the rest of the evidence vindicating James Curtis Giles. The prosecution could no longer deny the compelling nature of his innocence claim and joined the Innocence Project in arguing that his conviction ought to be overturned. A Dallas judge granted the motion in April 2007. Two months later, the Texas Court of Criminal Appeals officially exonerated Giles of any role in the horrific 1982 crimes.[20]

To their credit, Dallas prosecutors took affirmative measures to right a grievous wrong. They even released documents in 2003 showing that their predecessors had withheld Bryant's statements fingering "Michael" and

"James" in the crime.[21] In 2007 new chief prosecutor Craig Watkins made investigating wrongful convictions a top priority in his administration and apologized to Giles personally for his office's missteps. Shortly after Giles's release, Watkins established a unit to review post-conviction claims of innocence.[22]

But in James Curtis Giles's mind, these belated attempts to act as ministers of justice were too little too late. They could not cleanse the stain of misconduct that had caused him nearly a quarter-century of torment. Disclosing Bryant's statements to defense counsel in 1983 would have drastically altered the trajectory of Giles's life. As Giles later remarked, the "DA shouldn't be practicing law [anywhere] in this country. They should be held accountable."[23] It appears that those prosecutors emerged from the Giles fiasco with their careers intact. The lead prosecutor, Mike O'Connor, is now a personal injury litigator in Bryan, Texas. When asked about the case in 2007, he claimed to barely remember it: "It wasn't anything unusual, it was just one of the cases we tried every month and year."[24]

The James Curtis Giles case is a grim example of how prosecutors' decisions to suppress exculpatory evidence before trial can lead to the conviction of an innocent defendant. Giles's exoneration was one of no fewer than six that occurred in Dallas County from 2007 to 2009 because of past nondisclosure of exculpatory evidence.[25] Alas, misconduct of this nature is not the only way prosecutors harm the innocent through pretrial decision making. The next three chapters examine a variety of prosecutorial choices before trial that may contribute to wrongful convictions, focusing on decisions about (1) charging crimes, (2) disclosing evidence, and (3) plea bargaining.[26]

Charging Ahead

Prosecutors enjoy vast discretion to determine which criminal charges, if any, should be filed after the police arrest a suspect. Take the following example. Assume that a man drinks a large quantity of alcohol one night, drives on a busy street, and kills a pedestrian on a sidewalk. In addition to being charged with driving while intoxicated (DWI), the perpetrator could face a litany of homicide-related crimes. This event might be viewed as criminally negligent homicide because a "reasonable person" would not have driven drunk in this manner. Alternatively, this conduct could be construed as manslaughter—a reckless homicide in which the drunk driver consciously disregarded the substantial and unjustifiable risk that an innocent citizen might be killed. But that is not the end of the possibilities. The driver might be charged with outright murder for exhibiting "depraved indifference to human life," a form of extreme recklessness characterized as murder, not manslaughter, given the abhorrence of the conduct. The differences in the definitions of criminally negligent homicide, manslaughter, and depraved indifference murder are not merely semantic. The choice between these charges could mean the difference between spending several years on probation and several decades behind bars.

Let's add a few wrinkles. Suppose the drunk driver flees the scene of the crime on foot—staggering and reeking of alcohol—and the only surviving eyewitness is an elderly white woman, Johnson. She describes the driver as a "black man, mid-thirties, medium height, medium build." The police trace the abandoned vehicle to its owner, Smith, a forty-year-old black man, and go to the owner's apartment several hours after the homicide. Smith insists he has not used his car all day and that someone must have stolen it. There is no evidence of tampering with the vehicle, but Smith explains that he has lived in the area for years and always leaves the car door unlocked with the keys in the glove compartment. Smith agrees to take a breathalyzer test. The results show that Smith has alcohol in his system, yet not enough to satisfy the legal definition of intoxication. It is possible that Smith's blood alcohol content would have surpassed the legal limit had he been tested at the time of the accident.

The police ask Smith to come down to the precinct to participate in a lineup. From behind a one-way mirror, Johnson looks at six black men standing in a row. The men are around the same age, and roughly the same height and weight. After several minutes of silent observation, Johnson points to Smith: "I think that's him, the man I saw scrambling from the car." The police officer administering the lineup asks her if she is sure. "Well, pretty much," Johnson replies. "It happened so fast." Based on this identification and Smith's link to the automobile, the police arrest Smith. May local prosecutors charge Smith with a crime?

Rules Governing the Decision to Charge

Prosecutors generally may not file a criminal charge unless it is supported by probable cause to believe in the person's guilt.[1] This standard is minimal. It requires only enough evidence for the prosecutor to believe the person more likely than not committed the crime—or possibly even less evidence.[2] Further diluting this standard are rules providing that (1) only the government's evidence is included in this calculus without reference to the defense's claims, (2) the credibility of the government's witnesses is not considered, and (3) legally inadmissible hearsay may be taken into account.[3]

Put differently, a prosecutor is not required to weigh Smith's explanation for his car's involvement in the charging decision. The prosecutor is also not obliged to consider factors that undercut Johnson's credibility, for instance, that the crime occurred rapidly at night, that this was a cross-racial identification, and that Johnson's confidence in the accuracy of her lineup identification was shaky at best.[4] Could a prosecutor charge Smith with depraved indifference murder without violating any law or running afoul of the ethics board? Yes. And could Smith quite possibly be innocent? Yes.

To be sure, the fact that a person may be charged with a crime because of the presence of probable cause does not mean that a prosecutor must do so. Prosecutors possess ample discretion in this area of their work and deservedly so. The need for individualized justice, the problem of "overcriminalization" in our criminal codes, and the finite resources of law enforcement agencies all support giving prosecutors discretion in deciding whether to charge crimes. After all, not everyone should be prosecuted for every crime he apparently committed. Such a practice would lead to an overabundance of prosecution, drain government assets, and impose penalties for outmoded or ill-defined crimes that regrettably remain on the books.[5]

Still, there must be some check on prosecutorial charging discretion as a matter of due process and basic justice. Ethics codes offer prosecutors little guidance in choosing whether to file charges in cases where the barebones probable cause standard has been met.[6] Prosecutors are urged to weigh the defendant's role in the crime, his background and criminal history, his willingness to aid the government in developing a case against another transgressor, the impact on the victim in the charging determination, and the prosecutor's individual doubts about the guilt of the accused. Prosecutors should also consider the availability of noncriminal dispositions in their decisions and need not present all charges supported by the evidence.[7] Several ethics codes forbid prosecutors from "overcharging" solely in the hopes of gaining leverage for plea bargaining negotiations.[8]

For all the lofty rhetoric in the canons of ethics, it remains unclear how charging discretion is really exercised. Empirical evidence suggests that prosecutors decline to pursue charges in a meaningful number of cases.[9] Yet charging decisions, like much of the grist of the prosecutorial mill, occur behind the scenes. This makes it impossible to know the extent to which suspect cases survive the vetting process and result in formal charges.[10] Prosecutors handle charging decisions in many different ways. In most states and local jurisdictions, the chief prosecutor (often called the "district attorney" or "state's attorney") is elected by the public and then appoints assistant attorneys to administer the office's day-to-day operations. Some chief prosecutors leave almost complete charging discretion in the hands of their assistants. Others establish specific charging guidelines and may even require assistants to seek permission from a superior before deviating from them in a particular case. On the whole, chief prosecutors tend to give significant autonomy to assistants in rendering charging decisions.[11]

Charging decisions, once made, receive limited scrutiny from those outside law enforcement. The judicial and legislative branches defer to prosecutors, their executive branch counterparts, when it comes to charging crimes. With some exceptions, charging decisions are essentially exempt from judicial review on the grounds that courts lack the expertise and access to evidence to second-guess these choices.[12] Another rationale for judicial deference relates to separation of powers; judges appear hesitant to question executive decisions before they reach fruition in court.[13] The legislative branch also provides meager oversight of charging decisions. Even if legislatures participate in the charging endeavor by defining and amending criminal offenses, legislatures in practice have abdicated responsibility for charging to prosecutors.[14] As a result, not only do prosecutors have enormous discretion in determining whether to charge a person with a crime but that discretion is also subject to token judicial review and scant accountability to the legislature.[15]

Compounding the lack of accountability surrounding charging decisions is the nature of the process by which many criminal charges wend their way to court. The procedures for filing charges vary from jurisdiction to jurisdiction but share some common features. After a person is arrested by the police, he normally must appear before a judge to determine whether he will be released or detained pending a trial date. Prosecutors in some jurisdictions file a charging document at this hearing called an "information" that outlines the nature of the accusations based on the arrest file and declares that there is enough evidence to proceed. In the federal system and in many states, serious criminal charges must first be presented to a grand jury for indictment. The main function of the grand jury is to review the evidence submitted by the prosecutor to determine whether it is sufficient to indict the suspect.[16]

It is often said that the grand jury serves as a rubber stamp to validate prosecutorial charging choices.[17] Indeed, the rules governing grand jury practice favor the prosecution. First, prosecutors dictate the flow of information to the grand jury. Second, the bulk of a grand jury's efforts occur away from judges, defense lawyers, and the media. Defense counsel is typically barred from the room. Third, the rules of evidence largely do not apply before the grand jury. Prosecutors may offer inadmissible evidence, and they generally are not required to present evidence that exculpates the defendant. Fourth, most grand juries may issue an indictment when a bare majority of its members finds probable cause to believe in the defendant's guilt.[18]

Overall, a strong presumption of deference animates the early stages of the criminal process, shrouding charging choices in a veil of secrecy that is rarely lifted for public view.[19] Even so, charging decisions involving innocent suspects do not exist purely in the world of hypothetical cases. Several high-profile cases in recent years, including the notorious Duke Lacrosse case, illustrate how criminal charges based on a one-sided probable cause determination weaken the integrity of the system. Had the flaws in the Duke case not been revealed promptly, a handful of college students might have been wrongfully convicted.

The Duke Lacrosse Case: Charging Gone Awry

The facts of the Duke Lacrosse incident merit a brief discussion to highlight the risks posed by the rules associated with prosecutorial charging decisions. On March 13, 2006, three Duke University students who were members of the school's varsity lacrosse team hosted a party in Durham, North Carolina. Most of the other students in attendance were also members of the lacrosse team. At the request of one of the party's hosts, a local escort service dispatched two African American exotic dancers, Crystal Gail Mangum and Kim Pittman, to the location. Witnesses described Mangum as being unsteady on her feet throughout the evening.[20]

The two dancers began their performance in exchange for $400 each. Sexual banter occurred throughout the routine, with one partygoer raising a broom and recommending it to the dancers for their sexual pleasure. Upset by this comment, Mangum and Pittman abruptly stopped dancing and went toward the back of the house. They were followed by several students apologizing for the broom incident and requesting a longer performance, one, in their view, more commensurate with the fee. The dancers went to the bathroom and remained there for a period of time. Some guests left at this point; others continued to decry having paid money for a brief performance; and still others were simply hanging around the house.[21]

The dancers eventually left the house and went to their car, only to return a short time later and sequester themselves in the bathroom. Within minutes, Mangum and Pittman left the house yet again. Mangum lingered outside the house and engaged in an odd pattern of behavior: banging on the front door and requesting to be readmitted, struggling to maintain her balance, trying to talk with assorted guests, and lying down on the porch. One of the guests assisted Mangum to Pittman's car. As the dancers prepared to leave, Pittman and the guests traded a series of racial epithets. Pittman drove off and placed a 911 call to report that a group of white men were yelling racial slurs at bystanders.[22]

Pittman drove to a grocery store, but Mangum refused to exit the car and appeared to be unconscious. Pittman called 911 again. At the direction of the police, Pittman took Mangum to a medical facility where she was seen by a nurse. The nurse asked Mangum, as a matter of standard operating procedure, whether she had been raped. Mangum indicated—for the first time—that she had been victimized in that fashion. She later recanted that claim at the Duke Medical Center's emergency room before reasserting that she had been raped. The police decided to treat it as a potential sexual assault and started the investigation in earnest.[23]

Durham County District Attorney Mike Nifong took charge of the case. Almost at once, he began to make public statements that cast the prospective defendants in a poor light. The investigation soon became a national cause célèbre fraught with racial and socioeconomic overtones. The media at first depicted the case as a town-gown affair—a sordid tale of spoiled, white athletes from an elite university taking advantage of an impoverished and troubled black woman. Nifong essentially positioned himself as the knight in shining armor riding roughshod over Duke royalty to correct an injustice.[24]

In early April, Mangum identified three lacrosse players—Dave Evans, Colin Finnerty, and Reade Seligmann—as her assailants. The identification comprised the main piece of evidence against the accused, but other evidence provided a measure of corroboration. The doctor who examined Mangum in the early morning of March 14 had detected vaginal swelling, and a nurse characterized Mangum's behavior at the time as consistent with that of a victim of a sex crime. Also, Evans's DNA was partially matched to biological evidence found on a fake fingernail that belonged to Mangum and that was recovered from the bathroom where she claimed the rape took place.[25]

Based on that evidence alone, could Nifong have found probable cause to believe that a rape had happened and that Evans, Finnerty, and Seligmann were the culprits? Quite possibly. But the matter gets more complicated when other evidence, most of which Nifong knew about in early April, is added to the mix. Here are the critical "bad" facts in the prosecution's case:

- Mangum had given a number of conflicting statements about the event.
- Her medical records revealed a history of severe mental health problems, including bipolar disorder.
- No DNA evidence from the rape kit matched the three alleged perpetrators.
- DNA from men other than the players was found in the rape kit.
- Pittman had on one occasion stated that Mangum's story was "a crock."
- In the first identification procedure Mangum had identified Seligmann only as a guest at the party, not a participant in the assault.[26]

Despite the conflicting evidence, Nifong earned grand jury indictments against the three men for rape. Before trial, the North Carolina State Bar filed a disciplinary complaint against Nifong concerning his inflammatory pretrial statements to the media. Nifong asked the North Carolina Attorney General's Office to take over the case while the disciplinary complaint was pending. Special prosecutors from that office investigated the case anew; by December they had concluded that Evans, Finnerty, and Seligmann were innocent and ordered the dismissal of the charges. The state bar found Nifong guilty of serious ethical lapses stemming from his improper statements to the media and his failure to disclose evidence to the defense. These findings culminated in Nifong's disbarment.[27]

One misstep by Nifong never resulted in an ethical complaint: his decision to charge the three players with rape in the first place. North Carolina, like most states, provides only that a prosecutor shall "refrain from prosecuting a charge that the prosecutor knows is not supported by probable cause."[28] This ethical rule places few demands on prosecutors, which may explain why the state bar never made allegations against Nifong under this provision.[29] In his testimony before the Disciplinary Hearing Commission, Nifong intimated that he did not know that the case lacked probable cause. He insisted that the victim's statement that a rape had occurred and that the three student-athletes had committed it was enough to bring the case to a jury regardless of any inconsistent evidence.[30] If Nifong had been accused of improper charging by the state bar, he would likely have eluded punishment given the deferential rule in this area.[31]

Mike Nifong's choice to file criminal charges in the Duke Lacrosse case and the state bar's reluctance, perhaps inability, to find ethical violations for this behavior show the failings of the current rule system governing charging decisions. On the one hand, prosecutors deserve freedom to strike individually tailored charging decisions and to channel their energies to the cases they deem most meritorious. On the other hand, this freedom should not be wholly untethered; the duty to "do justice" includes the obligation not to prosecute the factually innocent.[32]

Changing the Probable Cause Standard

Prosecutors in most jurisdictions may file criminal charges so long as they believe the allegations are supported by probable cause. Many scholars have derided this standard as woefully inadequate in protecting the innocent.[33] One possible change involves increasing the quantum of proof needed to obtain indictments and to satisfy ethical rules.[34] Professor Bennett Gershman believes "the prosecutor should engage in a moral struggle over charging decisions, and should not mechanically initiate charges."[35] Gershman has further argued that "responsible prosecutors should be morally certain that the defendant is guilty,"[36] and that prosecutors ought to proceed with charges only if they are "personally convinced of the defendant's guilt."[37] Lifting the standard from probable cause to a level that comes closer to approximating the threshold for establishing guilt at trial (proof beyond a reasonable doubt) would certainly help weed out borderline cases and spare some innocent suspects.

Another potentially beneficial reform would be to require prosecutors to consider exculpatory evidence, such as the defense's explanation of the events, as part of the charging equation. It seems illogical that prosecutors must credit only the facts that implicate the suspect in deciding whether a charge is warranted. How can a prosecutor produce a genuine charging decision while artificially excising the known "bad" facts from the equation?

Shifting the perspective from which probable cause is determined could also reap rewards. At present, the ethical standard in almost every jurisdiction is entirely subjective. As long as a prosecutor does not "know" that the charges are inadequate (namely, that they lack probable cause), he is not obliged to "refrain" from filing.[38] This creates an incentive for prosecutors to take the evidence at face value and not delve into the minutiae of a case before putting the matter in the jury's hands. Some commentators defend this standard on the basis that determining guilt is a jury function and that victims deserve their day in court.[39] Entrusting the resolution of guilt or innocence to the jury certainly appeals to populist impulses and suits our conception of democracy. Yet I have misgivings about prosecutors passing the buck in weak cases under the guise of populism.[40] For one thing, this practice allows prosecutors to become morally disengaged and ascribe odd trial results to the failings of the jury, not the office that brought the charges.[41] For another, most cases are resolved through plea bargains before trial even begins.[42] As repeat players in the field with access to vast sources of information, prosecutors could do a better job as front-end gatekeepers to prevent weak cases from entering the litigation pipeline at all.[43]

To prod prosecutors to serve as more effective gatekeepers, one might consider altering the focus of the probable cause test from subjective to objective, and asking whether a "reasonable prosecutor" would find probable cause to file charges. This change would force prosecutors to scour the evidence more rigorously prior to charging, because lack of knowledge about the weakness of the case would no longer be an acceptable excuse. Several states have added an objective twist to the subjective standard for evaluating charging decisions.[44] Prosecutors in those states, with minor variations, should "not institute or cause to be instituted criminal charges when [the prosecutor] knows or *reasonably should know* that the charges are not supported by probable cause [emphasis added]."[45] The question is when should a prosecutor reasonably know that a charge is deficient? Should a reasonable prosecutor engage in an independent investigation of each arrest file to clear this hurdle?

Although revised rules could require a "reasonable prosecutor" to investigate the facts of each case before filing charges,[46] crafting such a wholesale obligation is impractical. Prosecutorial resources are limited. A pre-charging duty to investigate cases might serve mainly to burden the already taxed coffers of these agencies and duplicate the efforts of the police.[47] Regardless of the merits of a duty to investigate, merely adding an objective part to the charging test would help.[48] It signals that prosecutors must examine the evidence in cases where an initial review has not given them an objectively reasonable sense of the case's strength. Charging decisions by prosecutorial ostriches who bury their heads in the sand, refusing to acquire the "knowledge" that a case is wanting, would no longer pass muster.

All told, the chance that innocent people will face criminal charges could be reduced by (1) raising the threshold for filing criminal charges beyond probable cause of guilt, (2) compelling prosecutors to consider "bad" facts in the decision-making equation, and (3) adding an objective prong to the charging test to deter prosecutors from ignoring the holes in their cases. The Duke Lacrosse saga may have played out differently had these rules been in place. Forced to harmonize the exculpatory facts with the inculpatory ones, Mike Nifong would have strained to reach the objectively reasonable conclusion that there was more than probable cause of guilt. Even if Nifong had nonetheless filed charges, the state bar would have been in a far better position to condemn him for that choice.

Strengthening the standards related to charging could rein in discretion without hamstringing prosecutors too much. But further checks on charging discretion are needed to address another problem: the issue of cognitive bias.

Screening Committees to Review Suspect Cases

Let's revisit the Smith drunk-driving case in a world with revised charging rules. A reasonable prosecutor, upon weighing both the "good" and "bad" facts, could find probable cause to charge Smith with, say, involuntary manslaughter. Johnson identified him with some degree of certainty; his car was involved in the fatal accident; and alcohol was present in his bloodstream at the time of his interview. A prosecutor could possibly charge Smith under a more exacting charging standard, for example, sufficient evidence to obtain a conviction. Does this seem just? Perhaps, although even a layperson might fear that Smith is innocent and that the jury system is not an adequate buffer against a wrongful conviction. To diminish the risk that questionable criminal charges will survive even with modified rules, I propose creating structures within each prosecutorial office to review charging decisions in cases that contain hallmarks of innocence.

Prosecutors and Cognitive Bias

Charging review committees are necessary because even well-intentioned prosecutors may suffer from cognitive biases that deter them from assessing the evidence against a potential suspect with perfect rationality.[49] Prosecutors usually enter a case after the police have investigated the crime and arrested the chief suspect. By that point the phenomenon of police "tunnel vision" has often reared its ugly head. Police tunnel vision occurs when detectives, after concentrating on a particular suspect, overestimate the evidence against that person and subconsciously disregard the possibility of alternative perpetrators or exculpatory evidence throughout the remainder of the investigation.[50]

What might explain this tendency? Psychologists attribute tunnel vision to a series of cognitive biases that affect how people perceive and interpret information. Professors Keith Findley and Michael Scott suggest that the foundation of tunnel vision in the criminal justice system lies in an "expectancy" or "confirmation" bias.[51] They observe that "when people are led by circumstances to expect some fact or condition (as people commonly are), they tend to perceive that fact or condition in informationally ambiguous situations. This can lead to error biased in the direction of the expectation."[52] After a person develops a theory about a topic, this bias may spur that individual to process newfound information selectively in a manner that confirms the original theory. People are inclined not only to interpret information in a way that reinforces a preexisting theory but also to seek data that validate their hypothesis and avoid evidence that undercuts it.[53] Even when confronted with information that decimates their original thesis, people may cling to their initial viewpoint, a tendency referred to in the literature as "belief perseverance."[54]

In the context of criminal investigations, once the police embrace a particular theory of a case, the detectives may view all subsequent evidence through the lens of this expectation. This can produce distorted images. The flaws in Johnson's identification of Smith in the drunk-driving matter become incidental rather than fundamental; Smith's low blood-alcohol content is chalked up to the passage of time; and Smith's tale about leaving his car keys in the glove compartment seems wholly implausible. The police may be eager to pursue avenues of investigation that substantiate their view of Smith's guilt (to interview his friends, neighbors, and colleagues about his drinking habits) and averse to following leads that support innocence (to determine if Smith's neighborhood had a high rate of property crimes or if there had been a spike in reported car thefts in the days preceding the incident). The police may discount exculpatory evidence that undermines their theory, such as signs that Smith had a credible alibi at the time of the car crash. All this occurs subconsciously. It is not as if the police normally decide to sink the chief suspect and ignore contrary evidence. One of the most horrifying aspects of tunnel vision is that those deepest in its throes may be least aware of its existence.

The cognitive biases that give rise to tunnel vision in police detectives are aggravated by external and internal pressures. Mounting calls by victims, media outlets, and government officials to make arrests do not fall on deaf ears. Detectives are mindful of the need to solve crimes and show that the community is safe. This can affect the detectives' thought processes in investigating a case. The police may also become emotionally attached to the crime victim and her version of events. The sheer volume of their workload can further provoke the police to funnel their efforts to the person they initially target as a suspect for fear of stalling the resolution of that case and the start of work on the ever increasing stack of new files cluttering the detectives' desks. Last, but not least, the method for measuring police detective performance contributes to tunnel vision. Police investigators are often assessed based on their "clearance rate," which is the percentage of crimes that are reported as solved or, in the vernacular, "closed." For obvious reasons this standard encourages overworked detectives to operate quickly, feeding into the problem of tunnel vision.[55]

The police investigation is where tunnel vision begins and where it can generate the most damage, as all later stages of the process build upon the information obtained by the police.[56] But tunnel vision is by no means the sole province of the police. Prosecutors work closely with the police and may fall prey to a comparable form of tunnel vision at the pretrial stage, especially because they usually receive only the evidence implicating the police-anointed culprit.[57] As Professor Randolph Jonakait has observed, the trial prosecutor "does not see evidence about all the possible suspects, but only the incriminating evidence concerning the defendant. Not surprisingly, the picture presented to the prosecutor almost always shows a guilty defendant."[58] This picture inevitably becomes the prosecutor's reference point, defining expectations and laying the groundwork for tunnel vision to fester. Studies show that the cognitive biases leading to tunnel vision are amplified where key information is hidden or absent in creating the initial expectation, as in the transfer of case files from the police to prosecutors.[59] At least the police have the chance to entertain evidence inconsistent with a suspect's guilt that surfaces during the investigation of a crime. Access to that information is a luxury rarely afforded to prosecutors.

The very nature of the prosecutor-police relationship also produces incentives for prosecutors to agree with the outcome of the police investigation and put on blinders to the possibility of other suspects. Prosecutors need a good working relationship with the police to do their jobs effectively. Prosecutors rely on police to investigate cases, arrest perpetrators, and track down witnesses. Police depend on prosecutors to validate those arrests by securing convictions. By collaborating repeatedly with each other over long periods, police and prosecutors can develop a shared orientation toward getting the bad guys. This creates a potent bond that bridges much of the cultural divide between the two groups.[60] Questioning the accuracy of a police investigation by declining to level charges after an arrest may jeopardize this symbiotic relationship, not to mention imperil a prosecutor's ability to perform in future cases. Research suggests that failing to display group loyalty imposes profound costs on the violator, including ostracism and outright banishment.[61] Prosecutors branded as "hard" on police all too often suffer delays in gathering updates about investigations or experience total deprivation of access to information.[62]

Like the police, prosecutors often interact closely with crime victims in the early stages of a case and trust their accounts of the event.[63] In contrast, prosecutors seldom become personally acquainted with defendants, knowing them instead through police reports and rap sheets.[64] Prosecutors may even have less exposure to criminal defendants than the police who presumably interviewed (or tried to interview) those parties during the investigation. Having crafted a personal link to the victim, and no corresponding connection with the accused, a prosecutor may overrate the inculpatory evidence and underrate any exculpatory evidence prior to trial. Many prosecutors also face political pressure to proceed with certain matters.[65] The burdens of their caseloads weigh on prosecutors as well, supplying yet another disincentive for them to critically reexamine the evidence assembled by the police prior to filing charges.[66] Finally, prosecutors may simply feel cynical about a suspect professing his innocence because they have heard similar claims countless times before.[67]

For these reasons, tunnel vision can influence a prosecutor's decision making in screening a case for potential criminal charges. The principal effect of tunnel vision in this phase is to heighten a prosecutor's belief in the suspect's guilt and lessen any suspicion that someone else may have committed the crime. In extreme situations, tunnel vision leads prosecutors to charge innocent suspects. Once charges are filed, a "sticky presumption of guilt" evolves and prosecutors tend to interpret information revealed thereafter in accord with this presumption.[68]

Recall the James Giles case from Texas. Even the chief perpetrator's revelations before trial that his accomplice was a short teenager from North Dallas were not enough to pry prosecutors from the cognitive glue binding them to their belief in the guilt of a tall, twenty-eight year-old construction worker with the same name who lived thirty miles away. It took twenty-four years for that presumption of guilt to disintegrate in the face of DNA and other evidence that undermined it.

Tackling Tunnel Vision

A number of reforms could minimize the harms caused by tunnel vision at the charging stage. Requiring the police to disclose as much information as possible to prosecutors when transferring their case files might thwart one aspect of tunnel vision: that a prosecutor's initial theory of guilt is based on incomplete information. Reviewing a complete file, as opposed to one tailored against the person whom the police have branded as the chief suspect, would help a prosecutor develop a theory of the case and prevent the prosecutor from presuming guilt where flaws in the case are apparent early on.[69] Demanding access to this information is well within the authority of a prosecutors' office.[70]

Educating prosecutors about tunnel vision also has advantages.[71] Many prosecutors' offices sponsor in-house programs offering continuing legal education; adding training workshops about cognitive bias is a particularly easy reform to achieve.[72] Coaxing people to articulate the specific reasons for their position and to offer counterarguments during role-playing exercises can decrease the effect of confirmation bias and belief perseverance. But it is difficult to get people to argue against their beliefs. Moreover, even in the best-case scenario, education and training can only reduce—not eliminate—tunnel vision.[73]

Other changes, therefore, must accompany education and training. For instance, offices could issue internal guidelines to prosecutors who make charging decisions. This allows prosecutors to self-regulate by enforcing higher charging norms than those mandated by legal and ethical rules.[74] Some prosecutors already do this. The prosecutors' office in Kitsap County near Seattle makes its general charging standard available to the public. Its policy is "to charge the crime or crimes that accurately reflect the defendant's criminal conduct, taking into account reasonably foreseeable defenses, and for which we expect to be able to produce at trial proof beyond a reasonable doubt."[75] The office goes on to explain that its charging policy is particularly demanding for "crimes against persons." Charges in those cases, such as homicide and rape, "will be filed if sufficient admissible evidence exists, which, when considered with the most plausible, reasonably foreseeable defense that could be raised under the evidence, would justify conviction by a reasonable and objective fact-finder."[76]

To supplement written policies, some offices might even designate a group of prosecutors as charging specialists devoted to filtering out weak cases.[77] Incoming Philadelphia chief prosecutor Seth Williams revamped his office's charging unit along these lines in 2010. Prior to Williams's arrival, five junior prosecutors staffed a unit with a reputation for filing the broadest and harshest charges possible. Williams changed the composition of the unit by installing eighteen experienced prosecutors to oversee the process and asked those lawyers to focus on filing charges only in strong cases.[78] Notwithstanding the question of whether veteran prosecutors are especially vulnerable to cognitive bias, Williams and like-minded district attorneys deserve acclaim for their innovative approaches to charging.[79]

The problem is that prosecutors may be reluctant to limit their charging autonomy voluntarily. Office charging guidelines are occasionally devised to be as broad and flexible as possible to provide wiggle room when defendants claim violations of them.[80] Internal guidelines need to be coupled with something else: secondary review structures that take a fresh look at charging decisions before they reach court.[81]

Charging Review Committees

The formation of an internal review committee to evaluate preliminary charging decisions could temper the effects of cognitive bias. First, a review process would force the prosecutor handling the case to verbalize the reasons for his decision, an exercise that could trigger the self-reflection needed to curb tunnel vision.[82] Even if the charging prosecutor remained gripped by tunnel vision, the review committee members would not.[83] Second, the mere existence of a review committee could improve prosecutors' decision making about whether to charge from the outset. Research demonstrates that when people know that they will later have to justify a decision to a well-informed group, they often take a more balanced and thorough approach in considering the evidence behind the decision.[84] The practice of seeking internal review of charging decisions is relatively common at the federal level.[85]

To optimize the effectiveness of an internal review committee, at least one member should play the role of "Devil's Advocate" by harping on the flaws in the prosecution case.[86] Committees may struggle to conscript employees willing and able to perform this duty without exhibiting too much deference to their colleagues' analyses. Criticizing peers' decisions is not an enviable way for a prosecutor to make a living. For that reason, Professor Alafair Burke has suggested that non-prosecutors be included in review committees. A bipartisan committee of this nature might resemble the civilian review boards that are popular mechanisms for overseeing components of police department operations.[87] At a minimum, cycling non-prosecutors through the review system would inject accountability into the process[88] and would negate any simmering "groupthink" from a body composed only of prosecutors.[89]

Establishing internal committees to review charging decisions also conforms to modern trends in institutional design theory. Professor Rachel Barkow's study of the institutional design of federal administrative agencies led her to advocate greater separation of functions within U.S. Attorneys' Offices to stamp out abuses of power more effectively. According to Barkow, federal prosecutorial agencies should detach attorneys entrusted with "investigative" tasks in a case from those focused on subsequent "adjudicative" endeavors. This model suggests that prosecutors investigating alleged criminal activity should not participate in the charging decision.[90]

Barkow's idea has the most value in the context of federal prosecutors (the focus of her study) who often engage in lengthy investigations of complex criminal activities and operate in large, hierarchical organizations. A secondary review model strikes me as more practical than enforcing a strict separation of functions in smaller county or local prosecutorial agencies, because it recognizes the efficiencies gained by having the same prosecutors involved in the investigation and charging phases of a case. Internal charging review committees embody many of the virtues of a system where there is a separation of functions—an independent assessment of a potential criminal charge by those less vested in it—without exacting too heavy an administrative toll on the average office.

The idea of housing a charging review committee within every prosecutorial office would encounter resistance. The use of non-prosecutors, in particular, would raise concerns about conflicts of interest and confidentiality.[91] The modest size of many prosecutorial agencies may also make any sort of separate review committee unfeasible in those jurisdictions.[92] Although larger offices have the resources to form internal review committees, time pressures created by the caseloads in those offices accentuate the risk that the review process will become ceremonial.[93] But regardless of the precise makeup of charging review committees and the practical barriers to their creation, there is much to recommend the concept as a tool to alleviate the effects of tunnel vision.

It would be unwise, however, to compel internal review committees to evaluate *every* charging decision. Many routine cases do not demand extensive outside evaluation. In light of efficiency concerns and resource constraints, committee review of charging decisions should be confined to cases where the risk of a wrongful conviction is most pronounced.[94] Not just high-profile or complicated matters carry such a risk but any case imbued with characteristics found in many wrongful convictions, including eyewitness misidentifications, false confessions, police and prosecutorial misconduct, dubious forensic science, jailhouse informants, and ineffective assistance of defense counsel.[95] Eyewitness misidentifications stand out as the most common variable in the conviction of the innocent. A 2010 report by the Innocence Project in New York City concluded that such gaffes occurred at trial in 76 percent of the first 250 DNA exonerations. Most of those misidentifications involved witnesses and perpetrators of different races. False confessions by innocent suspects, especially juveniles and the developmentally disabled, also take place with surprising frequency. Furthermore, informants played a role in 19 percent of the wrongful convictions cited in the Innocence Project's report, and prosecutorial reliance at trial on forensic evidence based on unsound scientific principles cropped up as a factor in about half the cases studied.[96]

Even if some of the chief factors that produce wrongful convictions are not readily identifiable prior to trial, many are. Pretrial prosecutors stand in a reasonably solid position to weigh the accuracy of an eyewitness's identification. They can gauge the conditions under which the crime occurred, discern whether cross-racial identification is an issue, and examine the photo array and lineup procedures.[97] Similarly, prosecutors can pinpoint whether the case against a suspect rests on forensic evidence and, if so, whether that evidence derives from a forensic technique susceptible to charges of inaccuracy.[98] Unearthing a false confession poses more of a challenge, but prosecutors could subject statements by juvenile and mentally deficient suspects to greater examination than other types of confession evidence. And, to be sure, prosecutors are nicely situated well before trial to assess the credibility of informants they intend to present as witnesses.

On balance, prosecutorial committees assigned to review charging decisions should steer their efforts primarily toward matters containing possible eyewitness misidentifications, false confessions, unreliable informants, or tenuous forensic findings. Offices could use charging checklists and ask prosecutors to identify whether any of these factors appear in a particular case. If any of these factors exist, and the charging prosecutor still wishes to proceed, the case file could then go to the charging committee for review.

To the extent that this cohort of cases remains too vast to tackle, I suggest aiming at charging decisions predicated on a single eyewitness and little other evidence. Those cases present the greatest hazard because of the high rate of identification error and, paradoxically, the high esteem with which jurors tend to hold eyewitness testimony.[99] Some prosecutors' offices have launched "single eyewitness" review boards. As of 2003 one such committee, operating in the Nassau County District Attorney's Office in New York, appraised about ten cases annually and dismissed an average of two per year.[100]

Although tunnel vision is an innate human trait, its worst symptoms can be treated. Forming a review committee within every prosecutor's office to take a fresh look at charging decisions in cases that possess the hallmarks of wrongful convictions would lead to the dismissal of especially weak cases prior to the submission of formal charges—and would go a long way toward making the impact of tunnel vision less fatal for the innocent. Blending this structural reform with greater individual disincentives to charge in weak cases would go even further.

Punishing Individual Prosecutors for Charging Misconduct

Encouraging disciplinary bodies to punish prosecutors for egregious charging errors might give many prosecutors—both the diligent masses hampered by tunnel vision and the few bad apples infested with rotten aims—greater pause before proceeding. Consider the Duke Lacrosse case. Noticeably absent from the raft of ethical violations alleged against Mike Nifong was one relating to the choice to charge the three students with rape. If there had been a realistic chance that the state bar would have sanctioned prosecutors for blatantly misguided charging decisions, would Nifong have wavered before making this choice? In other cases, where flaws with the prosecution's theory were not revealed in a timely fashion, would innocent suspects have avoided the agony of going to trial?

Who Should Punish Prosecutors for Outrageous Charging Errors?

Disciplinary agencies are the appropriate entities to brandish sticks to combat prosecutorial misconduct in the charging setting.[101] The other actors who might serve this function are less suited to it. Let's think for a moment about two possible players for this role: judges and prosecutors themselves.

Judges are not well positioned to detect imprudent charging decisions. Even if judges could scrutinize charging decisions effectively, they do not want to do it. Judges give prosecutors a wide berth in making all sorts of discretionary decisions. The U.S. Supreme Court has granted prosecutors absolute immunity from civil liability for activities "intimately associated with the judicial phase of the criminal process."[102] Also, when evidence of prosecutorial misconduct surfaces, appellate courts rarely refer to wayward prosecutors by name in judicial opinions and few of these cases are reversed.[103] Simply put, courts cannot be counted on to dissuade prosecutors from misconduct for many questionable exercises of their discretion. Even more, perhaps judges should not encroach too far inside the particular realm of charging because of legitimate separation-of-powers concerns. Asking courts to interfere with the initial choice to charge—a decision that is arguably the most fundamental exercise of executive power by prosecutors—may represent an unwelcome check without the requisite balance.

Nor is internal oversight by prosecutors' offices the full answer to charging misconduct. Prosecutors often contend that a variety of internal controls suffice to modulate misbehavior, including layers of supervision, training policies, internal disciplinary processes, and performance assessments.[104] Some scholars have even suggested that internal regulation of prosecutors can deliver greater benefits than any form of external regulation.[105] Internal controls certainly preempt some amount of potential misconduct. Novel charging policies adopted in Philadelphia and elsewhere show the promising possibilities of reforming prosecutorial practices from within. My recommendation in favor of internal committees to review charging decisions reflects my belief that prosecutors can play a more prominent part in achieving justice through self-regulation.

But internal disciplinary controls, even if crafted with the best intentions, may never be applied consistently and invariably lack teeth. One stark example of the failure of internal controls to halt prosecutorial misconduct came to light in the aftermath of a civil rights lawsuit related to Alberto Ramos's wrongful conviction in the Bronx, New York. Ramos, a teacher's aide at a day-care center, spent seven years in prison for allegedly sexually molesting a five-year-old girl in his care. After earning his freedom on the grounds of innocence, Ramos sued New York City. As part of discovery in that lawsuit, Ramos's attorney obtained information about prosecutorial misconduct in the Bronx. Out of seventy-two cases in which Bronx courts had chided prosecutors for misconduct, only one prosecutor received internal discipline. That prosecutor, who had been named in four of those cases, was suspended for a month and docked two weeks' salary. His superiors welcomed him with a bonus upon his return to work. They then authorized merit increases to his pay, even as his case sat untouched before the disciplinary committee. It does not appear as though this prosecutor was ever disciplined by the ethics board or that any further internal action was taken against him. Another Bronx prosecutor chastised in multiple cases for poor behavior also received merit bonuses and was never formally disciplined. This anecdote from the Bronx symbolizes a broader phenomenon across the country. Even if prosecutors assist in curbing misconduct through cultural and institutional norms as well as internal disciplinary procedures, it would be naïve to depend wholly on magnanimous self-regulation to deter and punish prosecutorial misconduct.[106]

Unlike courts and prosecutors, state disciplinary authorities are well situated to sanction prosecutors, considering that much of their daily work revolves around investigating claims of lawyer misbehavior.[107] Although their precise makeup differs from state to state, disciplinary boards are typically structured as administrative bodies that receive complaints about attorney conduct, investigate those grievances, and impose discipline where warranted.[108] The types of sanctions vary, running the gamut from censure to disbarment.

Despite their competence in this area, disciplinary boards have shown a striking reticence to punish prosecutors for even the most grievous errors. A 1999 study of 326 Illinois convictions reversed on appeal for prosecutorial misconduct over a twenty-year period showed that only two prosecutors had received sanctions from the Illinois Attorney Registration and Disciplinary Commission.[109] A more exhaustive study by Professor Fred Zacharias found a "far from staggering" number of reported cases nationwide, roughly 100, in which prosecutors had received discipline.[110]

This sobering reality about the failure of state disciplinary agencies to tangle with prosecutors differs from the approach to other lawyers. Disciplinary boards routinely sanction members of the criminal defense bar and attorneys in civil practice.[111] Just look at recent data from California. According to the *California State Bar Journal*, 4,741 public disciplinary actions were taken from January 1997 to September 2009. Only 6 of those related to prosecutors' conduct in handling criminal cases.[112]

The hesitancy of disciplinary bodies to punish prosecutors may be explained in various ways. Ethics investigations are normally instigated when a complaint is submitted against a particular lawyer.[113] That prosecutors represent "the People," and not a client per se, means that no individual has a strong incentive for filing an ethics complaint against them except for criminal defendants whose cries of injustice are understandably received with a dose of skepticism.[114] Instances of prosecutorial misconduct are also hard to spot. Discretionary decisions by prosecutors, like charging, usually occur in the interstices of the criminal process. They are not made in courtrooms or during formal negotiations with defense counsel but behind closed doors. And on occasions when the door blocking exposure to those decisions opens to outsiders, ethics codes treat prosecutorial choices with deference. Most state ethics codes are patterned after the American Bar Association's Model Rules of Professional Conduct, which contain only a single rule governing the special responsibilities of prosecutors.[115] The prosecutor-friendly nature and imprecision of ethical rules (such as the duty to "do justice") give disciplinary officials latitude to reject even a reasonably substantiated allegation of misconduct if they wish.[116] Finally, the reluctance to discipline prosecutors might be attributed in part to political considerations. Some ethics boards fear blowback from prosecutors, many of whom wield political clout.[117]

How to Motivate Disciplinary Agencies to Sanction Misbehaving Prosecutors?

Disciplinary agencies should target outrageous charging decisions, choices that fall far shy of what a reasonable prosecutor would do. To penalize prosecutors for "close calls" might lead to over-deterrence, causing some prosecutors to become too tentative and fail to charge in relatively strong cases. This is not to suggest that prosecutors should charge in borderline cases—just that legal rules and internal review committees can better grapple with those instances than the mighty stick of discipline.

Without a doubt, ethics officials would struggle to distinguish outrageous charging decisions from merely dubious ones. Over time, however, the outcomes of individual disciplinary actions would create a volume of precedents to guide future generations of ethics boards in drawing lines and defining charging misconduct worthy of sanctions. External regulation has a positive effect on attorney behavior generally, and there is no reason to doubt that more vigorous supervision of prosecutors by regulatory bodies could achieve similarly constructive results.[118]

In order for disciplinary agencies to punish prosecutors for blatantly ill-advised charging decisions, the underlying bases for those decisions must first become public with greater regularity. Next, ethical rules and standards should give disciplinary bodies more guidance in finding violations. Specific improvements might include the following:

- Given the shortage of individual complainants against prosecutors, ethics boards should be proactive in investigating potential instances of prosecutorial misbehavior that surface through media reports and local court opinions.[119]
- Requiring more extensive prosecutorial record keeping and discovery about charging decisions would give ethics boards a greater factual foundation upon which to evaluate and ultimately rest allegations of misconduct.
- The presence of internal committees to record their assessments of charging decisions would build the trappings of formality and offer transparency.
- Amending and strengthening the rules governing charging decisions—especially shifting the focal point of that test from the subjective beliefs of the charging prosecutor to the views of an objectively reasonable prosecutor—would make it easier for disciplinary bodies to detect violations and render sanctions if they are so inclined.[120]

Therein lies the rub. Changes to the rules will only help if ethics boards are keen on disciplining prosecutors at a higher rate. Providing ethics boards with increased access to information about deeply flawed charging decisions and beefing up the rules in this area would jumpstart the process of pushing them to take on prosecutors. Yet structural changes are needed to reach the finish line.

Professor Angela Davis has proposed one such structural reform: the creation of prosecution review boards geared toward evaluating claims involving prosecutors.[121] Her ideal board "would not only review specific complaints brought to its attention by the public, but it would conduct random reviews of routine prosecution decisions."[122] The board would investigate "bad practices," and the random nature of its operation would help deter "arbitrary prosecution decisions."[123]

Whether housed within a state disciplinary body or constructed as a separate entity altogether, Davis's suggested review board deserves serious consideration. A review board specializing in prosecutorial behavior would soon assemble the expertise necessary to penetrate the unique web of discretionary decisions by prosecutors. Finding capable participants for prosecution review boards might prove difficult, but strong candidates should emerge from the ranks of former prosecutors and judges—distinguished retirees with the background (and the backbone) to challenge prosecutors and little to lose by alienating the law enforcement establishment.

Inspiring disciplinary boards to investigate and discipline prosecutors for blatantly ill-considered charging decisions would complement the suggestions made earlier in this chapter. The unwillingness of state disciplinary agencies to enforce ethics codes against prosecutors can spawn disrespect for its provisions within that group. To the degree that the legal community believes there is a double standard—that prosecutors are treated better than the bulk of attorneys—this disrespect might ripple throughout the bar.[124] The presence of an invigorated disciplinary regime eager to sanction prosecutors for poor charging decisions would not only discourage prosecutors from filing charges in weak cases but could also have a far-reaching impact on the behavior of lawyers in general.

The charging decision is the tipping point for a criminal case. If the prosecutor declines to charge, the case disappears with few repercussions. If the prosecutor files charges, the state's efforts tilt toward developing a case. And once the wheels of a criminal case are set in motion toward trial, the chance of a wrongful conviction increases.[125] That is exactly why reforms to the rules and practices surrounding charging are necessary: to stop the wheels from turning at all in weak cases. The charging decision, however, is not the only pretrial weigh station on the road to a wrongful conviction where prosecutorial behavior can drive a case in the direction of injustice.

In the Interest of Full Disclosure

Discovery in Criminal Cases

Let's revisit the drunk-driving case discussed in the previous chapter. Assume a prosecutor charges Smith with manslaughter and DWI, and obtains a felony indictment from the grand jury. The case is placed on the calendar for trial. During his trial preparation, the prosecutor finds a portion of a detective's memo book buried in the bottom of a police file. The memo book contains notes revealing that the police interviewed Wiley, the man living in the apartment immediately above Smith's, on the night of the incident. Wiley reported that he believed Smith remained in his apartment all evening because he heard Smith, who tended to sing loudly when he had been drinking, rhapsodizing throughout the night. What should the prosecutor do with that information? Should it be disclosed to the defense? Must it be disclosed?

The Legal and Ethical Landscape of Disclosure

The U.S. Supreme Court has never recognized a federal constitutional right for criminal defendants to receive the evidence in the prosecution's possession before trial. Prosecutors are not even constitutionally compelled to furnish the defendant with the names of potential prosecution witnesses, let alone disclose all of the investigative information. State and federal discovery laws partially fill the void by providing defendants with the right to receive at least some of the evidence against them. But discovery rules tend to offer minimal solace to defendants. The scope of discovery in criminal cases is generally (and, bizarrely, given the stakes) narrower than in civil cases.[1]

There is one category of evidence to which criminal defendants are constitutionally entitled prior to trial: evidence that exculpates them from charges. In 1963 the Supreme Court ruled in *Brady v. Maryland* that "the suppression by the prosecution of evidence favorable to the accused upon request violates due process where the evidence is material either to guilt or punishment."[2] A prosecutor's failure to abide by his disclosure obligations under *Brady* is not subject to a good faith exception; *Brady* violations exist "irrespective of the good faith or bad faith of the prosecution."[3] The *Brady* obligation is ongoing as well. If a *Brady* violation is found during the course of trial, a mistrial may result; if it occurs after a guilty verdict, the normal remedy is a new trial.[4]

The Supreme Court later fleshed out the parameters of this obligation in four key ways. First, in *Giglio v. United States*, the Court expanded the scope of *Brady* to cover any evidence that shows the possible bias of government witnesses, such as information about promises, rewards, or inducements made in exchange for their testimony or anything else that could impeach their credibility.[5] Second, the Court modified the *Brady* rule by mandating that its disclosure requirements apply even without a specific defense request.[6] Third, prosecutors must deliver *Brady* material in a timely fashion to allow the defendant to make effective use of the material at trial.[7] Fourth, all exculpatory evidence possessed by law enforcement is classified as *Brady* material regardless of whether the specific prosecutor in charge of the case has actual knowledge of it. This suggests that prosecutors have a duty to learn about the evidence in the hands of their law enforcement colleagues.[8]

States have followed the Supreme Court's constitutional lead. State constitutional decisions, statutes, and ethical rules fortify the *Brady* doctrine— and even impose duties above and beyond it.[9] State ethical rules, in particular, usually demand more from prosecutors in disclosing evidence than is required by federal constitutional law. The American Bar Association's Model Rule of Professional Conduct 3.8(d) is typical, calling for prosecutors to "make timely disclosure to the defense of all evidence or information known to the prosecutor that tends to negate the guilt of the accused or mitigates the offense."[10] Most states have passed rules consistent with Model Rule 3.8(d) either by mirroring or emulating the "tends to negate guilt" construction of exculpatory evidence. The use of the verb "tends" in Rule 3.8(d) likely reflects a desire to create a disclosure obligation broader than that of *Brady*.[11]

Brady in Practice

The optimism felt by criminal defendants in the aftermath of *Brady* has been tempered by the application of this doctrine in practice. Most prosecutors strive to fulfill their *Brady* obligations. A great many even bend over backward to comply. They do so for reasons both ethical (to embody the minister-of-justice ideal) and practical (to avoid eventual controversies and to grease the wheels of the plea bargaining process by nurturing a good reputation with the defense bar).[12] In spite of these efforts, however, *Brady* violations take place with regularity. Prosecutors suppressed exculpatory evidence in many wrongful convictions later overturned by DNA testing, as in the James Giles case from Texas. In some of those cases, prosecutors found the evidence not to be important. In others, prosecutors eager to secure convictions willfully bypassed the disclosure rules.[13] Studies of exonerations in cases lacking DNA evidence further suggest that *Brady* violations contribute to the conviction of the innocent.[14] Worst of all, proven *Brady* errors hint at a much larger problem because most suspect disclosure choices happen in the inner sanctuaries of prosecutorial offices and never see the light of day.

Given that the *Brady* obligation is broad, ongoing, and not limited by a good faith exception, a certain number of violations are inevitable.[15] But the prospect of error is enhanced by the vagueness of the duty's doctrinal formulation. How does a prosecutor decide prior to trial whether evidence is favorable to the accused and material to guilt or punishment?

Determining whether evidence is favorable to the accused does not pose vexing problems in many cases.[16] Information pointing to James Earl "Quack" Giles's involvement in the 1982 North Dallas rapes obviously favored James Curtis Giles's defense. Similarly, notes from the police interview of Wiley in the drunk-driving example favor Smith's defense by validating a potential alibi.

Figuring out whether evidence is material to guilt or punishment is much tougher. In 1985 the Supreme Court clarified in *United States v. Bagley* that evidence is "material" only "if there is a reasonable probability that, had the evidence been disclosed to the defense, the result of the proceeding would have been different."[17] The materiality test hinges on whether the defendant can prove that the absence of the evidence undermines confidence in the verdict.[18] In analyzing materiality, courts often look at three factors: (1) the importance of the withheld evidence; (2) the strength of the rest of the case; and (3) other sources of evidence available to and used by the defense. The strength of the prosecution's case is the central variable. The stronger the government's case, the less likely an item of evidence will be construed as material.[19]

It is largely up to prosecutors alone to make pretrial decisions about the materiality of a piece of evidence. Defense lawyers lack the expertise, time, and resources to conduct the type of massive pretrial investigation needed to ferret out this evidence.[20] When a prosecutor chooses not to disclose evidence, that decision is seldom revealed to outsiders unless he has a change of heart or the evidence somehow finds its way into the hands of the defense.[21]

How, then, do prosecutors go about making *Brady* decisions guided by a nebulous legal standard of materiality and an even vaguer obligation to do justice? Specifically, how is a prosecutor supposed to apply the materiality standard before any evidence has been introduced or the defense strategy divulged?

The tension between a prosecutor's dual role of zealous advocate and minister of justice peaks in the context of *Brady* decisions, leaving prosecutors acutely vulnerable to cognitive bias. Professor Alafair Burke points out that the materiality test forces prosecutors to "engage in a bizarre kind of anticipatory hindsight review" dependent on an artificial comparison of the evidence and the still unborn trial record.[22] Cognitive biases can prompt a prosecutor who has already charged the defendant with a crime and is now conducting a pretrial materiality assessment to "engage in biased recall, retrieving from memory only those facts that tend to confirm the hypothesis of guilt."[23] The prosecutor may process information selectively, undervaluing the potentially exculpatory evidence and overrating the strength of the rest of the prosecution case.[24] Johnson's identification of Smith and the other evidence of guilt in the drunk-driving case may grow increasingly strong in the eyes of the prosecutor, while Wiley's statement seems patently weak.[25]

One's natural resistance to "cognitive dissonance" might also affect a prosecutor's evaluation of potential *Brady* evidence.[26] Having already concluded that Smith is likely guilty, a prosecutor might discount the discovery of Wiley's statement so as to shirk the uncomfortable psychic reality that he possibly charged an innocent person with a crime. As Mark Twain once put it, "a man cannot be comfortable without his own approval."[27]

Cognitive biases aside, the *Brady* materiality standard enables prosecutors to reach essentially any outcome they want. If a prosecutor withholds information to boost his chance of earning a conviction at trial, he can rationalize that choice just by weighing the evidence in a fashion that suggests it is immaterial. And since this evaluation is entirely theoretical, it is not subject to much second-guessing from others, especially defense attorneys who may never even know that the decision was made.

When *Brady* issues do come to light, the materiality test is a heavy burden for a defendant to overcome on appeal. Wiley's statement, while favorable to Smith, is not necessarily material. It does not preclude the possibility that Smith stepped out of the apartment for some period of time. It also confirms that Smith was drinking and intimates he drinks regularly, unsavory details that would not be lost on a jury. If Smith were convicted at trial, he might struggle on appeal to show that the presence of the Wiley statement would have affected the outcome. Appellate courts are frugal in doling out *Brady* reversals. One study by Bill Moushey of the *Pittsburgh Post-Gazette* waded through fifteen hundred cases and determined that prosecutors routinely withheld favorable evidence. Despite this high rate of nondisclosure, appellate courts reversed the conviction in only a handful of cases where the mistakes were so glaring and the conduct so heinous that judges had no other choice.[28] Even then, a reversal of a conviction on *Brady* grounds does not spring open the prisoner's cell. It merely entitles the defendant to a new trial with the previously suppressed evidence now available.[29]

Brady Reconceived

Is the *Brady* doctrine salvageable? Maybe. A series of reforms could address intentional misconduct and inadvertent lapses of judgment concerning prosecutors' disclosure obligations.

Carrots and Sticks

Many scholars have condemned *Brady*'s materiality standard on the premise that it lets overzealous prosecutors engage in gamesmanship to dodge their obligations.[30] It should come as no surprise, then, that some calls for reform advocate the use of sticks to beat back intentional prosecutorial misconduct and nudge prosecutors to disclose questionable *Brady* material.[31]

One popular recommendation involves persuading ethics boards to impose discipline more readily on prosecutors who purposely violate their disclosure duties. The withholding of exculpatory evidence is the most common—and most dangerous—form of prosecutorial misconduct. The ethical rules governing the suppression of exculpatory evidence are also the clearest and easiest to enforce within the pantheon of often vague admonitions such as the warning to "do justice."[32]

Yet disciplinary bodies hardly ever sanction prosecutors who disregard *Brady*'s precepts. In 1987 Professor Richard Rosen studied the entire volume of written disciplinary decisions. He dug up only nine cases in which a prosecutor had even been referred to an ethics board for suppressing exculpatory evidence. Just one of those nine disciplinary proceedings ended with a sanction, and a suspension at that. Rosen's research methodology included a survey sent to disciplinary representatives in every state. Thirty-five of the forty-one states that responded to this query indicated that no formal complaints had ever been filed alleging *Brady*-type misconduct.[33] Professor Joseph Weeks followed up on Rosen's research ten years later and discovered a similar pattern. Weeks found seven cases where prosecutors had been referred to disciplinary bodies for purported *Brady* violations. Four of these referrals resulted in sanctions, the most severe of which was a six-month suspension.[34]

These findings about the lack of discipline imposed on prosecutors for *Brady* violations, even the rarity of allegations themselves, is startling. Nothing suggests that things have changed in recent years. Data produced by groups across the country suggest that disciplinary agencies stand idly by as the tide of *Brady* violations, if not rising, continues unabated.[35]

One glaring example of disciplinary inaction took place in California in 2010. A state appellate court determined in 2007 that Phillip Cline, an assistant prosecutor in Tulare County, had improperly withheld audiotapes of interviews with state witnesses that pointed to the defendant's innocence in a capital murder case from the 1980s. It was a grisly case in which someone sexually assaulted and killed a woman before setting her on fire to destroy evidence. The appellate judges had listened to the tapes, one of which revealed that the state's star witness had admitted fabricating his story linking the defendant to the attack.[36] The judges came away from that experience shocked by Cline's callous disregard for justice. The defendant in the case, Mark Sodersten, had recently died after twenty-two years in prison, a fact that ordinarily terminates any lingering litigation in a criminal case. Angered by the severity of Cline's misconduct, the court bypassed that principle and overturned the conviction.[37]

But the opinion had no practical effect. Sodersten was dead; Cline continued to practice law. Cline had even moved up the ladder to chief prosecutor in 1992. With the appellate decision in hand, Sodersten's lawyer filed a complaint against Cline with the California State Bar. Three years later a bar official sent a letter to the attorney explaining that it was closing the investigation because it could not find sufficient proof of wrongdoing.[38] Cline remains the district attorney in Tulare County as of 2011.[39]

A renewed focus by ethics organizations on punishing prosecutors for concealing exculpatory evidence would assist in deterring the most blatant types of misconduct. It also would signal that these actions will not be tolerated. Except for the threat of discipline, there is little to dampen the spirits of those prosecutors dead-set on violating *Brady*. Keep in mind James Giles's reasonable observation that the Dallas prosecutors involved in his case should not practice law anywhere in the country. Making the threat of punishment viable—including disbarment—is perhaps necessary to stop some prosecutors from committing *Brady* misconduct.

Scholars have recommended various other sticks to goad prosecutors to turn over evidence. The proposals include relaxing the principle of absolute immunity from civil liability and criminalizing *Brady* violations themselves.[40] Simply getting appellate courts to identify the names of prosecutors who commit *Brady* violations in judicial opinions might help.[41] Several intriguing suggestions involve punishing not the prosecutor individually but the prosecution's case as a whole by either forbidding the government from retrying a defendant whose case is reversed because of a *Brady* error or otherwise putting the government in a worse position on retrial.[42] Some commentators have endorsed carrots to spur prosecutors to comply with *Brady*, for instance, the use of financial rewards.[43]

Although intentional *Brady* violations are the exception rather than the rule, anecdotes of this misbehavior surface often enough to cause concern. But focusing on bad actors obscures the bigger issue of good prosecutors who inexplicably under-disclose. Indeed, the most pressing problem relates to how well-meaning prosecutors may interpret their constitutional disclosure obligations in a way that all too often leads to withholding.

Office Policies and Practices

Some prosecutors' offices have responded to news of *Brady* violations by revamping their training programs and policies about disclosure. It is hard even for the most fair-minded prosecutor to apply a doctrine dominated by the muddled concept of materiality. A 2001 study of the Los Angeles District Attorney's Office revealed that assistant prosecutors were often confused about the *Brady* doctrine. This confusion was exacerbated by supervisors who expressed wildly different opinions about how to determine whether a piece of evidence was exculpatory. That office now has a *Brady* Compliance Division to coordinate and publicize information about the doctrine. Many other prosecutorial agencies have implemented in-house training programs and drafted office manuals that cover the topic.[44]

Internal training and guidelines to steer *Brady* decisions are admirable reforms, especially if offices set up procedures to ensure that prosecutors actually follow these directives. Offices could issue disclosure checklists that prosecutors would have to complete for each case, followed by the random auditing of case files to test whether prosecutors are using them correctly.[45] Decision-making research shows that people learn best from their mistakes if they receive explicit feedback about when they succeeded and when they failed.[46] Standardizing a feedback process to analyze what went wrong in poor *Brady* decisions would reinforce the use of disclosure checklists, guidelines, and audits.

Drawing upon practices in the medical field, Innocence Project co-director Barry Scheck has proposed the formation of Professional Integrity Programs within prosecutors' offices to oversee disclosure. Scheck envisions a horizon of "checklists and disclosure conferences, the non-punitive tracking of errors and 'near-misses,' the development of clear office-wide legal definitions of *Brady* material, the administration of audits and root cause analysis . . . and the creation of simulation exercises for training staff that builds on the lessons learned from 'near misses' and audits."[47] Critical to this type of program is convincing assistant prosecutors that higher-ups will not frown on late disclosure of *Brady* material. Without a better-late-than-never message from the top brass, a prosecutor who does not turn over evidence at the appropriate time has an incentive to keep it buried.[48]

Although these proposals make sense to me, I am less bullish on internal regulation of disclosure duties than many other observers are.[49] My pessimism does not come from distrust of prosecutors, or even doubts about getting them to carry out these changes,[50] but rather from ambivalence about the *Brady* doctrine as currently formulated. Comprehensive education and policies about what constitutes *Brady* material will fall short because the doctrine defies easy explanation. Its case-specific materiality analysis simply does not lend itself to meaningful guidelines.

Layers of Review

As in the case of charging decisions, conscientious prosecutors faced with nettlesome *Brady* issues would benefit from presenting those issues to others through a formalized review structure. Internal fresh look committees might assist in countering cognitive biases that can cause individual prosecutors to trivialize potentially exculpatory evidence.[51] Even if similar reviews already take place informally in many prosecutors' offices, those reviews occur haphazardly.[52] Institutionalizing the process would make the practice routine, and would also insert greater transparency and accountability into *Brady* decision making.

Some scholars have even called for judicial screening of prosecutors' *Brady* decisions during the discovery phase. One proposal would require that at the time of pre-trial discovery the prosecutor submit his full case file to the trial court or a magistrate for inspection. The independent adjudicator would have the authority to determine whether the file has *Brady* evidence. After the adjudicator reaches a decision, she would notify the prosecutor about the information recommended for disclosure. At this point the prosecutor could object.[53] There is already precedent for judicial involvement in the disclosure process. Massachusetts state judges must hold pretrial conferences to confirm that all discovery obligations have been met.[54] Asking courts to examine the evidence in prosecutors' files is a logical outgrowth of the pretrial conference format.

Whatever the merits of adding review structures to oversee prosecutors' *Brady* decisions prior to trial (and there are many), the reviewing bodies still would have to determine whether favorable evidence is material to guilt or punishment before the trial has occurred or the defense has even revealed its strategy. The lack of information makes the process of weighing whether the evidence would have a reasonable probability of affecting the outcome almost purely speculative.[55] The prospective assessment of materiality demanded by *Brady* and its progeny is fundamentally flawed given its vulnerability to cognitive bias even for those players—judges, prosecutorial supervisors, and others—one step removed from the heat of the litigation. It is time to rethink the very propriety of the materiality standard itself.

Materiality under the Microscope

In trying to recast the *Brady* doctrine to fulfill its early promise, let's first consider whether it can be saved by modifying the materiality test. The key question is how to calibrate the test to strike the proper balance between a prosecutor's advocacy interests and the defendant's right to a fair trial.

Making the materiality standard easier for defendants to satisfy on appeal might be one solution.[56] Changing the test from a reasonable probability of a different result to a reasonable *possibility* would make it harder for prosecutors to justify withholding borderline *Brady* information and less onerous for defendants to carry the burden of proving a violation. New York has taken this approach in certain situations. Where a defendant in New York state court makes a specific request for a piece of favorable evidence, nondisclosure of that item will satisfy materiality so long as its presence would have created only a reasonable possibility of a different result.[57]

Another possible change is to flip the burden of proving materiality on appeal from the defendant to the prosecution.[58] Defendants usually must prove that the withholding of favorable evidence affected the outcome at trial. Courts instead could force prosecutors to show that the withholding did not influence the verdict. New Hampshire has followed this course. In

1995 the New Hampshire Supreme Court held that the *Brady* test places "too severe a burden" on criminal defendants, and chose as a matter of state constitutional law to put the appellate burden on prosecutors to demonstrate "that the undisclosed evidence would not have affected the verdict."[59]

Although there are advantages to tweaking the materiality test or shifting the burden of proof on appeal, the major drawback lingers. Pretrial prosecutors who look at potential *Brady* material would still undertake the "bizarre kind of anticipatory hindsight review" described by Burke that allows selective information processing, confirmation bias, and the aversion to cognitive dissonance to flourish.[60] Telling prosecutors to consider prior to trial whether evidence would have a reasonable possibility of affecting the outcome is but a mild improvement over the reasonable probability standard. Some prosecutors might still unconsciously perceive the evidence so as to underrate the exculpatory information, overrate the inculpatory evidence, and conclude that no reasonable possibility of a different result exists. Other prosecutors might consciously subvert the modified standard by interpreting it in a manner that supports withholding, as some observers suggest is the case with the current test.[61] Likewise, giving prosecutors the burden of proof on appeal would have minimal impact on the decision to characterize evidence as material at the front end of the process.

Recognizing the difficulties any formulation of materiality poses for all actors—prosecutors in evaluating it prospectively, defendants (or even prosecutors) in overcoming it retrospectively, courts in judging it from a distance—several scholars want to discard that prong of *Brady* altogether. Courts could simply ask prosecutors to disclose all favorable evidence to comply with due process.[62] Justice Thurgood Marshall was a prominent advocate of this view. His dissent in *Bagley*, the case that produced the present version of the materiality standard, lobbied for a prosecutorial duty to turn over "all information . . . that might reasonably be considered favorable to the defendant's case."[63] In fact, well before *Bagley* and later cases developed the Court's materiality jurisprudence, the initial *Brady* decision implied that all relevant evidence favorable to the accused should be turned over.[64] With a duty to disclose all favorable evidence in place, prosecutors would no longer need to speculate about how the evidence might affect the outcome of a trial. This vision of the constitutional obligation would also more closely align it with state ethical rules that demand disclosure of all evidence that "tends to negate guilt."[65] Some jurisdictions appear inclined to go in this direction.[66]

Nonetheless, shedding the materiality prong is not the complete answer. Prosecutors would still have to determine whether the evidence is favorable, a subjective evaluation that occurs before trial without full access to information about the defense strategy.[67] Although this assessment may not raise complicated questions in many cases, it can produce tough calls for prosecutors.

Let's go back to the drunk-driving hypothetical. The Wiley statement seems favorable to Smith's defense. It solidifies an alibi defense in the form of a statement by a non-family member without any apparent interest in Smith's well-being besides neighborly concern. Suppose, instead, that Wiley said something quite different: that he heard Smith singing, as Smith is prone to do when drinking, but then heard the front door slam shut and the singing cease. Further assume that this happened shortly before the accident. At first, this evidence may appear to be inculpatory because the statement places Smith outside his apartment (and with alcohol in his system to boot) at the time of the crime. Even under a modified regime requiring the disclosure of all favorable evidence, a prosecutor might naturally feel he has no duty to hand this over.

Now add the following twist. Wiley and Smith detest each other, a facet of the case unknown to the prosecution prior to trial. Wiley hates Smith's singing and has filed countless protests with his landlord about these disturbances. Wiley wants nothing more than to see Smith vacate his apartment. Seen in this light, Wiley's statement is potentially favorable to the defense; showing that a key prosecution witness is biased against the defendant can dramatically undermine the government's case. Granted, the defense could just try to impeach Wiley when he takes the witness stand, but that is a slight consolation prize compared to the plum of having the statement upfront and being able to incorporate it into defense counsel's opening statements and the defense strategy from the start. This rudimentary example of the Wiley statement illustrates how prosecutors do not always have the knowledge required to grasp whether a particular piece of evidence is favorable. Abandoning the materiality aspect of *Brady* therefore fails to cure the doctrine's ills.[68]

Open File Discovery

The best way to guarantee that defendants receive the exculpatory evidence owed them under *Brady* is to adopt "open file" practices where prosecutors must turn over all evidence known to the government. Some commentators have pushed for a federal constitutional doctrine of open file discovery to realize *Brady*'s idealistic vision.[69] Others have urged legislators to broaden state and federal discovery laws.[70] These suggestions reflect the idea that a prophylactic rule of open file discovery is better than a case-specific standard like *Brady*.

Open file discovery certainly removes much of the subjectivity from the equation.[71] Prosecutors would not have to engage in an artificial, prospective assessment about how particular items of evidence fit within the jigsaw puzzle of a possible trial. Defendants would not have to clear the virtually insurmountable hurdle of showing that the evidence would have made a difference in the outcome. And judges could shed the chore of divining the importance of the withheld evidence. Open file discovery more generally levels the playing field by giving defendants a bird's-eye view into the government's case. Several states have endorsed far-reaching discovery regimes in recent years.[72] Mandating open file discovery as a matter of federal due process, preferably in tandem with state discovery laws and ethics rules, could rekindle *Brady*'s flickering fifty-year-old flames.

Yet open file discovery is controversial. Opponents often contend that it goes too far: that rather than leveling the playing field, compelling open file discovery would shift the balance of power in the criminal justice system in favor of the defendant.[73] Another criticism is that open file discovery could invite abuse by defendants who might intimidate witnesses or fabricate their defense strategy in reaction to the evidence against them. Judge Learned Hand summarized these concerns nearly a century ago:

> Under our criminal procedure the accused has every advantage. While the prosecution is held rigidly to the charge, he need not disclose the barest outline of his defense. He is immune from question or comment on his silence; he cannot be convicted when there is the least fair doubt in the minds of any one of the twelve. Why in addition he should in advance have the whole evidence against him to pick over at his leisure, and make his defense, fairly or foully, I have never been able to see.[74]

Although these concerns have merit in theory, lessons learned from jurisdictions that currently have broad discovery rules suggest that such fears are not borne out in practice.[75] In other jurisdictions, some prosecutors have chosen to disclose more evidence than required by law, indicating that open file practices might be in their best interests.[76] The voluntary enactment of open file discovery signals that a prosecutors' office seeks transparency and burnishes its image as an institution committed to fairness. Prosecutors can even benefit directly from open file discovery. With greater faith in the goodwill of their adversaries, defendants might embrace the notion of fair play and be reluctant to instigate protracted discovery litigation for the sake of fishing for some unknown delicacy in the deep blue sea of the prosecution's files. Defendants who are fully aware of the strength of the case against them might also be more willing to accept plea bargains than those who lack such insight. If revealing sensitive information in the file could endanger a witness or jeopardize a long-standing investigation, prosecutors can always seek protective orders to prevent disclosure of that material.[77]

Note the recent experience with open file practices in Milwaukee. District Attorney John Chisholm developed an extensive case screening and diversion program to find alternatives to incarceration for low-risk offenders. Chisholm believed that early access to information by the defense was vital to the program's success. This caused him to champion open file discovery. Not all his assistants welcomed this idea. Chisholm nevertheless plowed ahead, and in 2010 observed that open file discovery in his office had facilitated guilty pleas and enriched relationships with the defense bar.[78]

For open file discovery to succeed on a large scale, however, there must be mechanisms to enforce compliance. Even without requiring prosecutors to conduct the pretrial *Brady* materiality test that is so susceptible to gamesmanship, prosecutors still control the open file discovery process.[79] They alone have access to the precise contents of their files. Prosecutors can stretch the definition of sensitive information beyond its logical boundary and refuse to disclose an array of evidence under that justification. Open file discovery might also induce police and supervisory prosecutors to shield information from the trial prosecutor or otherwise decline to reduce their knowledge to writing in order to circumvent mandatory disclosure.[80] Skeptical defense lawyers have even derided some open file practices as "open empty file" policies.[81] At the other end of the spectrum, prosecutors might over-disclose by providing defense lawyers with a mountain of inscrutable material to sift through. In one of the Enron financial fraud cases, the prosecutors' open file discovery practice led them to turn over eighty million pages of documents without identifying or highlighting anything in particular.[82]

Several flagrant *Brady* violations have occurred in cases where prosecutors claimed to use open file discovery but withheld exculpatory evidence.[83] The behavior of Carmen Marino, the former chief prosecutor in Cleveland, offers a cautionary tale about the limits of open file discovery practices. Marino "opened" his files by asking his assistants to summon defense attorneys to the office for a conversation. During these meetings, prosecutors would read documents aloud instead of letting their adversaries look at the files. Subsequent litigation showed that these meetings were often a sham. Cleveland prosecutors under Marino's watch withheld critical exculpatory material, including evidence that would have exonerated innocent defendants in capital cases.[84]

The Duke Lacrosse case is another example of the potential failings of open file discovery. Mike Nifong enjoyed a fine reputation for giving defense attorneys open access to his evidence. Coincidentally North Carolina had enacted a liberal discovery statute shortly before the Duke Lacrosse case broke.[85] The combination of Nifong's reputation for fair play and the change in state law may have made the defense bar less vigilant in challenging his performance in the Duke Lacrosse case—and allowed Nifong to shun his *Brady* obligations by withholding exculpatory DNA evidence.[86]

Ensuring the Openness of Open File Discovery

If open file discovery were adopted nationwide, how could one verify that prosecutors' files are truly "open" to the defense? Increased oversight of discovery practices by courts and ethics boards would surely help. But greater supervision of this kind should be combined with reforms designed to bolster the likelihood that the police will turn over evidence to prosecutors at the start. Frankly, without much evidence in their possession, prosecutors honorably adhering to open file discovery do little to benefit defendants. As noted earlier, information known only to the police is imputed to the prosecution for *Brady* purposes. This means that prosecutors should root out exculpatory evidence in the hands of other law enforcement officials.[87] As noble as this component of the doctrine may be, it ignores the practicalities of the relationship between the police and the prosecution.

Prosecutors are effectively at the mercy of the police when it comes to obtaining evidence from investigations. Police agencies operate independently from prosecutorial offices and answer to different constituencies. Getting the police to turn over exculpatory evidence to the prosecutor is not a matter of authority but of negotiation and persuasion.[88] Prosecutors neither have information about the contents of investigative files without police blessing nor wield the power to access that material in the absence of such blessing. And the one entity that does have the power to pry open investigative files, the judiciary, seems unenthusiastic about monitoring police practices in the discovery arena.

How might the police be induced to turn over exculpatory evidence to the prosecution? Professor Stanley Fisher recommends legislative reforms. Fisher's statutory fixes would require the police to list and record all relevant evidence, disclose those lists to the prosecution, and provide the prosecution with all investigative materials. He would couple these changes with measures to increase the probability of compliance: the drafting of forms for listing pieces of evidence, offering training, and making particular police personnel responsible for the recording process. This is a sensible remedy, provided that the United States has the political will to supervise police activity in this way.[89]

As an alternative remedy, Fisher suggests adjustments to the ethical rules. Fisher's proposed changes include the articulation of prosecutorial duties to become familiar with police record-keeping procedures and to educate the police about the importance of revealing specific categories of exculpatory evidence. Legislative changes or amendments to the ethical rules surrounding prosecutors' obligations to learn about material possessed by the police would probably lead to the dissemination of more evidence to the accused.[90]

Even so, these reforms may not impede one of the worst threats to open file discovery, which is not the reluctance of the police to turn over exculpatory evidence to the prosecution but rather their propensity never to record such information at all.[91] Even when police officials record exculpatory information, that material might not be made available to the prosecution. Before its practices were exposed in the late 1980s, the Chicago Police Department employed a double-file system. Detectives kept two sets of books: official files and shadow "street files." Missing from the former, the contents of which were turned over to the prosecution, were any number of exculpatory items dutifully recorded and retained in the latter.[92]

Letting the defense depose prosecution witnesses in criminal cases might alleviate the fear that information will evade disclosure. Litigants often use depositions in civil cases to interrogate opposing witnesses before trial. Depositions can help in learning about the other side's case and in pinning witnesses down to their accounts. In the criminal context, subjecting investigating officers to depositions could prompt them to disclose information they failed to put into writing yet might mention at trial. Deposing other prosecution witnesses could generate information unknown even to law enforcement that aids the defense. A handful of states currently permit "discovery depositions" in criminal cases.[93]

Some observers dislike these devices, because of the perception that they are costly and risk abusing witnesses.[94] These concerns may be overstated. Florida has used discovery depositions for more than forty years.[95] According to one member of a commission that evaluated discovery depositions in Florida, these practices "make a unique and significant contribution to a fair and economically efficient determination of factual issues in the criminal process."[96] Recent decisions from the Florida Supreme Court have praised discovery depositions as important tools in unearthing new evidence and witnesses.[97]

Florida has also installed several measures to safeguard confidential information and prevent witness intimidation during discovery depositions. First, upon a showing of good cause, a court may issue a protective order restricting the disclosure of certain matters or limiting the scope of the deposition.[98] Second, the defendant may not be physically present at the depositions of other witnesses except under specific circumstances.[99] Third, state law allows for extra protections in deposing child witnesses and witnesses "with fragile emotional strength."[100]

Even assuming that discovery depositions add incidental burdens to the criminal justice system, their upside still outweighs the downside. Increasing the use of depositions across the nation would enhance the truth-seeking function of the discovery process by nicely supplementing open file practices.[101]

Training prosecutors about disclosure obligations should go along with open file discovery. While providing education for prosecutors about *Brady* bears limited fruit in light of the subjectivity of the doctrine, training about open file discovery is much easier—just instruct prosecutors to turn everything over unless an item endangers a witness or impairs a current investigation. Open file discovery does not rest entirely on the ethical judgment of a prosecutor embroiled in the adversary system to make discretionary choices, and for good reason. Prosecutors have not proven themselves up to the task of reliably making the correct choice.[102]

The initial promise of the *Brady* doctrine has not been realized. When the Supreme Court handed down *Brady v. Maryland* in 1963, it elevated the United States above all other nations as the first to mandate the disclosure of exculpatory evidence by prosecutors. Despite this head start, much of the Western world has outpaced the United States in the depth and breadth of the discovery rights granted to criminal defendants.[103] Various alterations, even alternatives to *Brady* must be considered to reach the doctrine's potential to advance justice.

Whether *Brady* remains unchanged, experiences modifications, or is replaced with open file discovery, decisions regarding the disclosure of evidence to the defense will still depend to some extent on the ethical compasses of prosecutors. Patrick Fitzgerald, now the U.S. Attorney in Chicago, believes that "culture shapes behavior" in prosecutorial agencies.[104] Fitzgerald tries to hire people who already have good values and then train them to be ethical lawyers. He looks for lawyers who, upon finding exculpatory evidence while sitting alone in the office on a Saturday before a Monday trial, will turn it over without hesitation.[105] The Dallas County District Attorney's Office shares this view. That office sends case law on disclosure duties to job applicants and tells them to come to their interviews ready to discuss the ethics of disclosure.[106] What a wonderful idea. Crafting disincentives to deter the withholding of evidence and incentives to promote obedience to disclosure rules work on the outer edge of prosecutorial behavior; forming an ethical environment where disclosure is the accepted cultural norm works at the core.

Plea Bargaining Pitfalls

Assume that manslaughter and DWI charges are pending in the Smith drunk-driving case discussed in the previous chapters. At this point the prosecutor might give Smith the chance to plead guilty to a reduced charge. The state's case is by no means a slam dunk; Smith could avoid conviction if even one juror buys his alibi. The prosecutor also has a full helping of other cases on his plate, which makes the prospect of going to trial in the Smith matter even more unappetizing. Given the chance of losing at trial and the time involved in trying the case, the prosecutor is motivated to offer a plea bargain attractive enough to entice the defendant yet not too lenient as to seem out of line with offers in similar cases or appear disrespectful to the memory of the victim.

So, imagine the prosecutor offers Smith the following deal: plead guilty to criminally negligent homicide and the state will recommend the minimum sentence to the judge. Further suppose the disparity between the minimum sentence for criminally negligent homicide and the maximum sentence for manslaughter is significant, say, fifteen years in prison.

The prosecutor describes the deal to Smith's defense attorney, who later relays it to her client. Smith may find the offer tantalizing. His defense is not especially strong. An eyewitness has placed him and his car at the crime scene. He had alcohol in his system when tested several hours after the incident. And, most important of all, an innocent bystander died. The jury will want someone to pay for that injustice, with the likely target of their animus being the lonely figure sitting at the defense table. Along with the possibility of losing, Smith might fear the publicity that could accompany a trial.

Smith could stand his ground and hope for a better deal as the trial nears, perhaps to DWI alone, but that is no surefire bet. As the state invests effort during the run-up to trial, a prosecutor could just as easily retract his offer as extend a more favorable one. Smith may also know that judges seldom take kindly to defendants who turn down fair plea offers. If Smith is convicted at trial of the same crime to which he declined to plead guilty, he may be subject to what some observers call the "trial tax" and receive a higher sentence than the one in the plea offer.[1] Weighing the costs of going to trial (a stiffer sentence) against the benefits (the chance of an acquittal), Smith might agree to the deal—even if he is innocent.

This scenario plays out every day in courthouses across the United States. Plea bargains occur in more than 95 percent of criminal convictions. If anything, the rate of dispositions through guilty pleas is climbing.[2] Many plea bargains are negotiated by prosecutors and defense attorneys in a matter of minutes, and then pitched to the accused by harried defense lawyers who steer their clients to accept the offer all the while proclaiming, "It's your decision." Once a deal is struck, it is presented to a judge who has a packed court docket and no incentive to second-guess the agreement so long as there is a sliver of a factual basis to support the conviction.[3]

A strong presumption of correctness attaches to plea agreements. Defendants who plead guilty are represented by counsel. Judges must notify defendants about the rights they are waiving during the entry of the plea at a hearing called a plea allocution or colloquy.[4] The plea colloquy, the final act in the plea bargaining drama, generates a record of the defendant admitting guilt in open court. There may be curtain calls in the form of appellate and post-conviction challenges to the plea—claims the plea was not knowing, voluntary, and intelligent—but for the most part these attacks are futile. The case moves from center stage to somewhere off-off-Broadway, making it unlikely anyone will revive it for a second run of analysis. That is the point of plea bargaining: to achieve a quick, tidy, and final resolution. An enduring question, however, is whether plea bargaining harms the innocent.

Innocent Defendants and the Temptation to Plead Guilty

Many scholars have explored (and often deplored) the rise of plea bargaining, attributing it to the demands imposed by the surge of cases in our criminal justice system. As Professor Albert Alschuler observed more than forty years ago, "the guilty-plea system has grown largely as a product of circumstance, not choice."[5] My goal here is not to critique the ramifications of this circumstance but to home in on one troublesome offshoot: that some innocent defendants will rationally forgo their right to trial and plead guilty. A portion of them may be risk-averse or want to get on with their lives as soon as possible. Others are wooed into pleading guilty by the plain truth that prosecutors offer the best pleas in the *weakest* cases. And the weakest cases, of course, are those with the highest chance of implicating an innocent defendant.

It is unclear how many defendants succumb to temptation and plead guilty to a crime they did not commit. Commentators traditionally downplayed the chance that the innocent might plead guilty, deeming the risk so microscopic that no systemic analysis of the problem was ever called for. But a large amount of anecdotal evidence suggests that some innocents do accept plea bargains. Thirty-one of the thirty-nine convictions obtained in the Tulia, Texas, scandal—in which a rogue white undercover narcotics officer fabricated evidence against black men and women in a small town—came from guilty pleas. After the officer was wholly discredited, all those convictions were overturned on the basis of actual innocence.[6]

Chris Ochoa's case paints a graphic picture of why an innocent person might plead guilty. In 1988 the manager of a Pizza Hut restaurant was raped and murdered in Austin, Texas. The police investigation led to the arrest of Richard Danziger and Chris Ochoa, two employees of a different Pizza Hut in the vicinity. The police threatened Ochoa with the death penalty during their interrogation of him, and even pointed to the vein in his arm where prison officials would administer the lethal injection. Dazed by these tactics, Ochoa wrote a "confession," pled guilty, and received a life sentence in exchange for testifying against Danziger. Ochoa's testimony proved integral to Danziger's conviction at trial. Eight years later a man serving a life sentence for other crimes, Achim Josef Marino, contacted state officials and confessed to the Austin rape-murder. It took another four years before the authorities located biological evidence from the crime scene. Subsequent DNA tests confirmed that Marino was the perpetrator.[7]

Empirical data support the proposition that innocent defendants accept guilty pleas at a rate that is far from microscopic. The Innocence Project determined that defendants had pled guilty in 19 of the first 250 cases in which post-conviction DNA testing resulted in an exoneration.[8] Professor Samuel Gross's research echoes these findings. He concluded that the convictions in 20 of 340 documented DNA and non-DNA exonerations from 1989 to 2003 derived from guilty pleas.[9] These figures are alarming when one considers how hard it is to reverse a guilty plea. Courts and legislatures, quite understandably, restrict a defendant's ability to challenge a conviction on appeal that he voluntarily accepted at the beginning. Moreover, it is often hopeless to obtain biological evidence for post-conviction DNA testing in cases that never made it to trial. If the evidence was even collected at the outset, it may well be long gone.[10]

All signs point to the likelihood that a sizable number of innocent defendants plead guilty, especially in less serious cases. The peculiar nature of our plea bargaining process in which the best offers are made in the weakest cases ensures that this is the case and that it has been for some time. A study from half a century ago asked prosecutors which among a series of factors might prompt them to plead out a case. Every respondent answered affirmatively to only one of those factors: case weakness.[11]

Innocent defendants who resist the lure of a generous plea offer do so at their peril. Consider the following New York case that I investigated and litigated during my tenure with Brooklyn Law School's Second Look Program. A large white man entered the El Classico Restaurant in the Long Island town of Brentwood one evening in February 1999. The man ordered food from a cook. While the cook was preparing the meal in the kitchen, the man robbed a waitress at knifepoint; she was the only other person present in the dining area at the time. The waitress screamed. The cook rushed out but caught only a glimpse of the culprit as he fled.[12]

Both the cook and the waitress identified Stephen Schulz as the perpetrator from a photo array. Schulz was a tall white man who lived nearby, weighed 250 pounds, and had a prior criminal record. The cook later identified Schulz in a lineup—the waitress never participated in any identification procedures beyond the photo array—and prosecutors charged Schulz with first-degree robbery. The prosecution made Schulz an offer before trial: plead guilty to a lesser crime with a three-year prison sentence. Schulz rejected the deal on the grounds that he was innocent.[13]

At trial, the cook maintained his belief in Schulz's guilt despite a series of inconsistencies in his testimony and reason to question his credibility.[14] Then the waitress took the stand. At a key juncture in her testimony, when asked whether the man who had robbed her was present in the courtroom, she answered no. She insisted that the perpetrator was taller and heavier than the defendant, characteristics not easily conveyed through a photograph. The jury nevertheless found Schulz guilty of robbery in the first degree. The court sentenced him to eleven years in prison.[15]

In 2001 my students and I began to follow a lead that Schulz's trial attorney had not comprehensively pursued. Anthony Guilfoyle, a white man who was both taller and heavier than Schulz, had pled guilty to six robberies that occurred in the Brentwood vicinity between January and March 1999. The modus operandi of these crimes resembled that of the El Classico robbery. We located the waitress in 2002. Upon viewing a photograph of Guilfoyle, she identified him with 90 percent certainty as the man who had robbed her. Neither the police nor anyone else had ever shown her Guilfoyle's picture. We also interviewed Schulz's roommate, a disabled mechanic with no criminal record. He declared that he was home with Schulz watching television when the robbery took place, but he never testified as an alibi witness at trial.[16]

After amassing affidavits from the waitress and the roommate, as well as other materials, we filed a motion with the judge before whom Schulz was tried and convicted, asking for a new trial on the basis of newly discovered evidence. The judge denied our motion without so much as holding an evidentiary hearing. That decision was affirmed by two state appellate courts. After several years of post-conviction litigation, a federal court judge issued Schulz a writ of habeas corpus, releasing him in 2007.[17] Happy ending notwithstanding, Schulz would have been released much sooner had he accepted the three-year plea offer prior to trial.

Why Do Prosecutors Offer Generous Pleas in Weak Cases?

It may seem strange that prosecutors, if they take their minister-of-justice role to heart, would make attractive plea offers in weak cases. Here are some thoughts about why a fair-minded prosecutor might offer a desirable plea in a case that lacks strong evidence of guilt.

Tunnel Vision

Prosecutors gripped by tunnel vision and personally convinced of the defendant's culpability often perceive a weak case as a problem of proof rather than innocence.[18] In other words, a prosecutor who has already categorized the case as suitable for charging might attribute evidentiary holes to faulty police investigation, the defendant's intimidation of witnesses, or pure bad luck. From that foundation, it follows that a prosecutor might extend good plea offers. If the case is a poor one based on the evidence, the risk of acquittal is huge. A prosecutor seeking to convict someone he believes to be guilty in a weak case needs to submit an extremely favorable deal to bring the defendant into the fold. A light sentence, if not optimal, becomes tolerable to the prosecutor. It avoids the vagaries of litigation, metes out punishment to a transgressor, and frees government witnesses from the anxiety of testifying.[19]

Loss Aversion

The social science concept of "loss aversion" explains how people seek to lock in results they frame as gains and avoid losses. Prosecutors may frame plea bargains in weak cases as gains—victories earned without the cost, effort, and uncertainty of trial—and make appealing offers to those defendants.[20]

Passion

Prosecutors may feel passionate about a specific case and tailor their plea bargaining tactics to match those sentiments, however irrational. They may adopt a hard line in cases they want to take to trial (refusing to make a plea offer at all in a murder case with gruesome facts) versus a soft stance in cases they feel ambivalent about (offering a sweetheart deal to a defendant charged with marijuana possession). A prosecutor's outlook on plea bargaining in an individual case may even be shaped by strong feelings about the other cases on his roster, because a guilty plea would open up time to pursue those more vigorously.[21]

Closure

Statistics compiled by the U.S. Department of Justice suggest that the average state assistant prosecutor closes about ninety felony cases per year.[22] Prosecutors straining under the pressures imposed by their caseloads have a heightened practical and psychological need for closure. This need may cause prosecutors to take mental shortcuts in processing information, quickly conclude that a defendant is guilty, and offer a plea bargain without much reflection.[23]

Concern with Public Perception

Prosecutors may worry about the ripple effects of appearing overly compliant to defendants. Word that a prosecutor has expressed openness to a defendant's innocence claim before trial by dropping charges could invite copycats, triggering a raft of crocodile tears and trumped-up tales of innocence.[24]

Work Experience

A violent crime tends to arouse more intense feelings in a novice prosecutor than in a veteran prosecutor accustomed to sordid cases. As a consequence, the two lawyers might take different approaches to constructing a plea offer in the matter.[25]

Career Goals

Given that a prosecutor's conviction rate is a key variable in earning promotions, attorneys who wish to ascend the office hierarchy may take a plea bargaining position informed by a preference for any sort of "win" over a potential "loss."[26] By offering irresistible pleas in weak cases, a prosecutor can pad his conviction rate and hide flaws in those cases, perhaps even those of his own making, from public view. Going to trial could produce acquittals, marring the prosecutor's record. Also, prosecutors typically have fixed salaries and lack any financial motivation to try difficult cases.[27]

Yet some prosecutors may have incentives to take cases to trial, especially lawyers who think that gathering trial experience will impress potential employers in the private sector.[28] For politically minded prosecutors seeking to parlay their litigation record into elected office or a judgeship, the decision to try a particular matter could reflect an effort to gain publicity by winning a high-visibility case.[29] Working as a prosecutor is a well-trodden road to the bench. A 2007 study concluded that three-quarters of all felony court judges in Cook County, Illinois, were former prosecutors.[30]

Office Policies and Idiosyncrasies

Some offices have guidelines that forbid plea bargains in certain categories of cases or restrict an individual prosecutor's discretion in offering a deal. Others place emphasis on pleas and give assistants autonomy to strike bargains as they see fit. An organization's plea bargaining policies may not be driven by ideology alone. Busier offices could view plea bargains more charitably than those with the time to consider taking a greater number of cases to trial. Similarly, financially strapped agencies might favor plea bargaining more than offices with greater capacity to absorb trial costs.[31]

Regardless of a prosecutor's motives in structuring a plea offer, innocent defendants often encounter a vexing choice: plead guilty now or possibly undergo a worse fate later. The chance that innocent defendants will plead guilty is exacerbated by the legal doctrines and ethical rules governing the plea bargaining process.

The Failure of Legal Doctrines and Ethical Rules to Protect the Innocent during Plea Bargaining

Courts have given prosecutors limited guidance about plea bargains. Although prosecutors may not obtain a guilty plea through torture or threats of physical harm, the U.S. Supreme Court authorizes techniques that some might find implicitly coercive. A prosecutor usually may impose time limits on the availability of a plea offer, condition an offer upon the defendant's willingness to withdraw pretrial motions, and propose a harsher sentence after trial than the

one entertained during plea negotiations.[32] Courts are not passive participants in a plea bargaining regime that empowers prosecutors and enfeebles defendants. The judiciary has directly shaped this regime through the trial tax.[33]

In addition, judges have interpreted the *Brady* doctrine in a way that does not help defendants much during the plea bargaining phase. In 2002 the Supreme Court held in *United States v. Ruiz* that federal constitutional law does not compel prosecutors to disclose information that could be used to impeach the credibility of witnesses (so-called *Giglio* material) prior to a guilty plea.[34] Favorable impeachment evidence may be withheld by prosecutors as part of plea negotiations, signifying that a lower court may "accept a guilty plea . . . despite various forms of misapprehension under which a defendant might labor."[35] *Ruiz* did not answer the question of whether impeachment evidence that supports the factual innocence of the defendant merits pre-plea disclosure.[36] *Ruiz* also left unclear whether the Court might treat non-impeachment *Brady* evidence any differently. Nevertheless, the Court offered some hints about how it might resolve these issues. It noted throughout *Ruiz* that *Brady* is a trial-related right, intimating that its role in plea bargaining is minimal. The upshot of the Court's failure to enforce constitutional disclosure rules during plea bargaining is that, in a system where more than 95 percent of criminal convictions result from pleas, defendants hardly benefit from the *Brady* doctrine.[37]

Like the courts, ethics boards have neglected to provide safe haven to innocent defendants in the area of plea bargaining. The chief American Bar Association rule on prosecutorial ethics, Model Rule of Professional Conduct 3.8, is silent when it comes to the prosecutor's plea bargaining role. Rule 3.8 indirectly affects plea bargaining through its prohibition on interaction with unrepresented defendants. A prosecutor may not engage in plea discussions with a defendant unless and until he has received the opportunity to retain counsel.[38] Other ethical rules limit a prosecutor's discretion in the plea bargaining context but normally only in instances of brazen misconduct. Prosecutors who misrepresent the facts of the case to induce a guilty plea run afoul of general ethical rules that ban lawyers from "conduct involving dishonesty, fraud, deceit or misrepresentation" or making false statements to a tribunal.[39] All things considered, ethics canons fail to navigate prosecutors through the murky waters of plea bargaining, much less confine their options in deciding which route to take and where to dock.[40]

Even without robust oversight by courts and ethics boards, internal regulation by prosecutors themselves does provide a measure of constraint on plea bargaining strategies. As mentioned above, some prosecutors' offices have guidelines describing factors that prosecutors should consider in choosing whether to offer a plea bargain and how to structure it. But those factors are often vague and suffer from the defects intrinsic to self-regulation.[41]

A New Plea Bargaining World

The prevailing image of plea bargaining is that of a marketplace where the defendant barters his right to a jury trial and the government its right to pursue the highest sentence possible.[42] In an ideal world, market dynamics create efficient bargaining that arrives at a fair result. Numerous scholars have debated the market theory of plea bargaining in which rational actors negotiate in the shadow of anticipated trial outcomes.[43] Diving into those deep, well-charted waters is not something I am inclined to do, except to note that markets work best when the negotiating parties are relative equals. This does not occur in the criminal justice system; the balance of power during the plea bargaining stage slants heavily toward the prosecution to the point where prosecutors effectively possess the power of "adjudication."[44] Prosecutors decide what to offer, what conditions to impose on those offers, and what information to reveal. Defendants entertaining a plea offer are not well positioned to assess the strength (or weakness) of the government's case. Defendants who balk at an offer run the risk of losing at trial and facing a worse outcome on sentencing day.[45]

Some observers find this state of affairs acceptable, ascribing possible imperfections in a particular plea bargain to the cost of doing business in the crowded corridors of criminal courts. I disagree. The current mode of plea bargaining in the United States places pressure on innocent defendants to plead guilty, a societal cost that is impossible to quantify and that cannot be justified by the benefit of efficiency. Stephen Schulz's case exemplifies the dilemma experienced by innocent defendants. He gained his freedom, yet only after serving many more years in prison than he would have if he had accepted his plea offer.[46] What about those defendants who resisted the temptation to plead guilty and incurred the trial tax but have not managed to obtain their release? Or those who yielded to the pressure to plead guilty and whose cries of innocence remain unheard based on the misconception that the innocent do not accept pleas?

Many of the proposals mentioned in chapters 1 and 2—the need to educate prosecutors about wrongful convictions, to set up internal review systems, and to embolden disciplinary agencies to sanction prosecutors for ethical lapses—apply with equal force in the plea bargaining context. But additional changes are required here given the ubiquitous nature of plea bargaining. Guilty pleas are far and away the primary vehicles through which convictions are obtained in the United States; trials are becoming relics of the past, observed so rarely on the highway of our criminal justice system as to cause bystanders to gawk. Speedy and nimble, guilty pleas often escape critical examination by judges, even by members of innocence projects. It is difficult to detect whether an innocent person has pled guilty because the case record is usually so barren, the evidence so sparse, that one cannot lift up the hood and see what went wrong.

Although banning plea bargaining altogether would stop innocent defendants from pleading guilty, abolition is too blunt an instrument. The criminal justice system would grind to a halt without a financial commitment of epic proportions to boost the supply of court personnel and facilities to meet the soaring demand for trials.[47] And let's not lose sight of the reality that most criminal defendants are guilty. Plea bargaining allows for the timely resolution of those cases, conserves resources, helps ensure that similarly situated defendants are treated similarly, and saves crime victims from testifying in open court.[48] Assuming that plea bargaining is here to stay and that it *should* stay in some form, the question then becomes whether anything can repair the most glaring flaw in the engine of plea bargaining practices: that some innocent defendants plead guilty to avoid the uncertainty of going to trial and receiving a higher sentence upon conviction.

Trial Tax Reform

There is a stark sentencing differential in the American criminal justice system depending on whether a defendant pleads guilty or is convicted after a trial. Defendants who reject a plea offer customarily receive a steeper sentence upon conviction on those charges after trial than the one contained in the plea offer.[49] The Federal Sentencing Guidelines illustrate how this practice can play out. Accepting responsibility through a guilty plea triggers a sharp cut in the defendant's federal sentence. Defendants considering a plea offer presumably know they will receive a much longer sentence if they lose at trial in a federal case.[50]

Some observers think the trial tax unduly burdens a criminal defendant's Sixth Amendment right to trial by skewing the process in favor of waiving that right and accepting a plea bargain.[51] The practice of differential sentencing encumbers a defendant's right to trial, but is that burden heavy enough to make the practice constitutionally infirm? Differential sentencing serves some valid purposes. Guilty pleas save scarce resources, and the trial tax encourages defendants to plead guilty. Also, a guilty person who accepts responsibility is conceivably a better candidate for rehabilitation than one who denies culpability and insists on trial, and therefore may deserve a lighter sentence.[52]

The trial tax actually works well in cases involving guilty defendants who possess frivolous defenses, occasions where taking the case to trial is a folly for all parties. A defendant will likely lose and suffer at sentencing, while the prosecution and court will exhaust resources. The trial tax minimizes the chance such a folly will occur; it effectively becomes a "plea discount" to induce the clearly guilty to dispose of the case in short order.[53] Granted, invoking the right to trial even in those instances has symbolic value that should not be dismissed out of hand. Society benefits to some extent whenever a case is tried in open court, a defendant's guilt weighed by a jury of his peers, and a verdict pronounced for all to hear. That said, I suspect a pyrrhic victory provides cold comfort to a guilty inmate mired in prison on a lengthy sentence after turning down a reasonable plea and blowing trial.

The fundamental problem with the trial tax is not its effect on the guilty— for whom it provides a helpful, if paternalistic, incentive to act in their best interest—but on the innocent. Consequently, modifying as opposed to abandoning differential sentencing might be the best approach.

One idea is to tinker with the trial penalty to narrow the disparity between post-plea and post-trial sentences. Italy has put a strict cap on the price defendants must pay to forego trial. Under the procedure of "party-agreed sentences" in Italy, the prosecutor and defense may reach a pretrial accord about the appropriate sentence, but final punishment may not exceed two years in prison.[54] The Italian practice of "abbreviated trials" is another way of resolving cases without conducting a full trial. It requires the prosecutor's consent and provides for a statutorily mandated plea discount equal to one-third of the defendant's sentencing exposure.[55]

The innocent might be less prone to acquiesce to a plea in the United States if legislatures imposed statutory caps on the trial tax like those in Italy.[56] But reducing the penalty could also inspire the guilty to roll the dice and proceed to trial with greater frequency. And adjustments of this sort would treat the symptoms of the illness rather than offer a cure. Some innocent defendants who are risk-averse would still plead guilty even if the sentencing differential is smaller.

Professor Daniel Givelber has suggested a sliding scale of trial penalties based on the merits of the case. Under Givelber's proposal, sentencing judges would engage in reviews of each conviction achieved through trials and enhance the defendant's sentence *only* in cases where (1) the government's case was overwhelming, and (2) the defense was frivolous. In all other cases, where either the state's case was weak or the defense meritorious, judges would refrain from imposing an increased sentence.[57] Although this suggestion may not be a full antidote—judges are imperfect, defendants might still make irrational decisions about their prospects at trial, and factual disputes could arise about the specifics of the plea offer—it has potential. Sentencing judges are accustomed to reviewing trial proceedings. It should not be too much to add this type of assessment to their portfolios.[58]

Givelber's proposal would allow innocent defendants to make plea bargaining decisions unfettered by the fear they will be penalized for going to trial. This assumes that innocent defendants have access to information about the government's case and can accurately gauge their trial prospects. This assumption is far from the truth.

Disclosure Rules and the Plea Bargaining Process

For plea bargaining to work better, even in a world without a hefty trial tax, the parties must be able to appraise their prospects at trial with a semblance of accuracy and then negotiate in response to their sense of the probable outcome. Prosecutors are largely able to do this. Not so with criminal defendants, who often lack access to information about the government's case because of the Supreme Court's reluctance to enforce the *Brady* doctrine in the plea bargaining setting. Even where defendants benefit from state laws compelling some pre-plea disclosure,[59] many jurisdictions allow prosecutors to ask defendants to waive their discovery rights as a precondition to a plea. The prevalence of discovery waivers ensures that many defendants never receive information about government witnesses whose reliability might be attacked or other evidence that could help in estimating the chance of acquittal.[60]

The information asymmetry created by pre-plea disclosure rules means that a prosecutor's ability to predict the result at trial in any given case far exceeds that of the defendant. This is a formidable advantage in hammering out a plea. Worse yet, barriers to information can lead the innocent to plead guilty because of a misimpression that the government's case is much stronger than it actually is.[61] Many innocent defendants have *less* information about the case against them than the guilty. If Smith did not kill the pedestrian in the drunk-driving hypothetical, he probably has no clue whether there were any witnesses at the scene who could testify on his behalf. Ironically, Smith might be better positioned to build a defense and anticipate the government's trial strategy if he were the perpetrator. In some cases, defendants might not even know if they are innocent. Smith could have been so intoxicated during the evening in question that he does not remember whether he drove at all, let alone hit someone.[62]

Expanded discovery rules are one way to rectify the information imbalance. The position of innocent defendants before trial would radically improve if state legislatures endorsed open file practices and made disclosure available immediately after the charging decision, especially if accompanied by bans on discovery waivers.[63] An obvious shortcoming of this approach is that it would produce a patchwork quilt of statutory protections across the country riddled with holes in its coverage. This may match up with our view of federalism, where states serve as laboratories for policy experimentation, but it would not manufacture the blanket protection of the innocent that studies of wrongful convictions cry out for.[64]

The Supreme Court could offer more comprehensive protection to the innocent if it chose to extend the federal constitutional right to receive certain evidence to the pre-plea stage.[65] The effectiveness of this remedy presupposes that the flaws in *Brady* are corrected, as discussed in chapter 2. It also presupposes the Supreme Court's reversal of *Ruiz*—or at least the refusal to apply *Ruiz*'s holding to favorable, non-impeachment evidence.[66] A federal constitutional right to broad discovery after the filing of criminal charges could go far in boosting a defendant's ability to negotiate just plea bargains.[67]

Another way to bolster an innocent defendant's plea bargaining posture is through ethical rules. Model Rule of Professional Conduct 3.8(d) obliges prosecutors to "make timely disclosure" of all evidence that "tends to negate the guilt of the accused or mitigates the offense."[68] This rule does not clarify whether "timely disclosure" encompasses disclosure prior to a plea bargain. Rule 3.8(d) and state rules of its ilk should make plain that they apply in the pre-plea setting.[69]

Judicial Monitoring of Prospective Pleas

Even if the trial tax was altered and prosecutors were compelled to disclose more information prior to plea discussions, some innocent defendants would still plead guilty. Tunnel vision and selective information processing would lead prosecutors to offer attractive deals in weak cases; risk aversion and disdain for the publicity associated with a thorough airing of criminal charges in open court would lead innocent defendants to accept them. Establishing structures within prosecutors' offices to review plea offers could prevent some wrongful convictions by having other sets of eyes pore over proposed bargains.[70] Yet some innocent suspects will pass through even elaborate screening systems devised by prosecutors and plunge into the pool of defendants who will receive offers to plead guilty.

One means of enhancing oversight is to ask judges to play a more active role in reviewing plea deals. The Federal Rules of Criminal Procedure and several states expressly limit judicial involvement in plea discussions. This practice differs from civil litigation where judges often take the lion's share of responsibility in brokering pretrial settlements. In criminal cases, judges typically only enter the plea process at the very end. Given that the prosecution and defense have already reached a compromise, those parties have no incentive to disclose anything to the judge that might disturb the agreement and usually stipulate to a barebones account of the facts for rote presentation to the court. Judges likewise have little reason to probe into the facts of a privately arranged agreement because unraveling it could burden trial dockets without any assurance of a more equitable outcome.[71]

Assorted rationales explain the minor role played by judges in plea bargaining. If plea discussions were to fail after a judge's intervention, the parties might fear retaliation on the part of the judge at trial and sentencing. This could pressure defendants to accept a plea early on. Also, judges may not know the facts of the case, potentially making their involvement in plea discussions less than helpful. Finally, greater judicial oversight of plea bargaining could clog up the process.[72]

Despite these concerns, there is a modest trend to encourage judicial input into plea bargaining. In states where courts are allowed to monitor pleas, the evidence is heartening, suggesting that judges aid the efficiency and fairness of the process.[73] Professor Jenia Iontcheva Turner has analyzed plea bargaining practices in Connecticut and Florida, two states that allow for meaningful judicial involvement. In 2006 she concluded that "a judge's early input into plea negotiations can render the final disposition more accurate and procedurally just."[74] That judges do not know the minutiae of a case is not necessarily a disadvantage. Judges can be more objective than prosecutors in analyzing the merits of a plea because they have fewer preexisting beliefs.[75] Judicial involvement also limits the risk of coercion in a system where the trial tax flourishes. Judges can give defendants an accurate sense of the distinction between the likely post-plea and post-trial sentences—surely a more reliable impression than the one created by prosecutors.[76]

Greater judicial participation in plea bargaining might also muffle some of the worst prosecutorial tactics that induce the innocent to plead guilty. Prosecutorial threats and bluffing, even if sanctioned by the Supreme Court, will not fare well before trial judges. Mindful of this, prosecutors might tone down their rhetoric. Even where an innocent defendant is enticed by a prosecutor's plea overtures, a judge's early involvement makes it more probable that any discrepancy between the genuine facts of the case and those presented at the plea colloquy is exposed.[77] To address fears about retaliation, judges who actively participate in plea discussions that do not result in an agreement could be forbidden from presiding at trial.[78]

On balance, asking judges to oversee the plea bargaining process to some extent holds promise. Instilling more transparency in plea bargaining alone strengthens the legitimacy of the process. It also helps justify plea deals to crime victims who are often annoyed by the secretive nature of the negotiations and decry their outcomes as too lenient.[79]

A Word about No Contest and *Alford* Pleas

Two variations from the typical guilty plea deserve comment here. With the court's consent, defendants in many jurisdictions may plead *nolo contendere* or "no contest" to a criminal charge, which is simply an assertion that the accused will not fight the charges. The absence of a mea culpa appeals to many defendants facing a subsequent civil case because a party's past statements of guilt ordinarily may be admitted as evidence at later trials.[80] In 1970 the U.S. Supreme Court endorsed another version of a plea in *North Carolina v. Alford* by upholding a state practice in which defendants were permitted to accept the charges against them but simultaneously *deny* that they committed the crime.[81]

Although I am loath to speed full-throttle into the academic debate about no contest and *Alford* pleas,[82] it appears safe to say that some innocent defendants are seduced by these options. Twelve defendants entered either no contest or *Alford* pleas to child molestation charges in Wenatchee, Washington, in the mid-1990s. Two of those defendants later found evidence that the purported victim had falsely accused them because of coercive police interrogation tactics. That child recanted, opening the door for those two defendants to withdraw their pleas. The media later revealed that the police investigator had prodded children to fabricate literally *thousands* of sex abuse charges, hurling scores of convictions into a state of flux.[83]

The basic problem with no contest pleas is that the process through which they are produced seems indifferent, at best, to whether the defendant committed the crime. A judge entering a traditional guilty plea must become convinced that there is at least a factual basis for the conviction. Judges need not undertake that endeavor with no contest pleas.[84]

Before condemning no contest pleas too harshly, I should note that they are rare and occur primarily with low-level offenses. Prosecutors are reluctant to offer them; even if offered, judges do not always consent to their entry.[85] No contest pleas are nonetheless deeply troubling. They increase the danger that an innocent defendant will accept a conviction, especially since the process does not demand any admission of guilt as a prerequisite.[86]

The threat posed by no contest pleas pales in comparison with that of *Alford* pleas. In *Alford* cases, courts are formally put on notice that the plea is flawed—that there is a good chance the pleading party is innocent. Still, this practice exists in almost every American jurisdiction for reasons that remain puzzling.[87] One possible justification is the idea that criminal defendants are autonomous beings entitled to choose whether to take a plea while maintaining their innocence and avoid the unpleasantness of trial.[88] Another alleged rationale is that *Alford* pleas are the lesser of the other evils facing the innocent: either damn oneself with phony words of guilt through a regular plea or persevere to trial and confront the trial tax.[89]

I am unmoved by these arguments. The meager benefits wrought by *Alford* pleas hardly come close to making up for the cost of innocent defendants accepting criminal convictions. I feel the same way about no contest pleas. Equivocal plea bargaining should be banned.[90]

Part 1 of this book has explored the chief ways in which prosecutors contribute to the conviction of the innocent through tactical decisions made prior to trial. The decision to charge someone with a crime puts in motion a sequence of events that may lead to a wrongful conviction. Flaws in discovery rules accelerate this process by depriving defendants of evidence that could aid their cases. And the nature of the plea bargaining regime further corrodes the innocent's chance for vindication by perpetuating a system where defendants in the weakest cases—those most likely to involve an innocent—receive the best plea offers from prosecutors.

I have presented a series of reforms to guard against the problems created by charging, discovery, and plea bargaining practices. Altering the standards for determining whether there is sufficient evidence to charge someone with a crime, establishing prosecutorial review committees to screen charging decisions, and spurring disciplinary agencies to subject charging choices to greater scrutiny can mitigate the risk that an innocent defendant will be placed in the criminal justice system at all. Even if an innocent suspect is charged with a crime, open file discovery could diminish the odds that the charge will result in a conviction. Plea bargaining practices that make it harder for prosecutors to offer generous plea bargains in weak cases might embolden more innocent defendants to fight the temptation to plead guilty.

But even if pretrial practices are revised along these lines, tactical decisions by prosecutors before trial are not the only points in the criminal process that can set an innocent defendant's case on the course to conviction. Prosecutorial behavior at trial can build upon pretrial missteps and facilitate the conviction of the innocent.

PART II

Beyond a Reasonable Doubt?

Reasons to Doubt Prosecutorial Conduct during Trial

People of the State of New York v. David Wong

Kin-Jin "David" Wong, an illegal Chinese immigrant from Fujian Province, worked in New York City in the early 1980s.[1] In 1984, after his conviction for participating in a robbery, Wong began an odyssey through the prison system that led him to Clinton Correctional Facility in upstate New York.[2]

Wong was in the Clinton prison yard on a snowy afternoon in March 1986 when someone stabbed an African American inmate named Tyrone Julius to death. The yard contained six hundred to seven hundred inmates at the time, most of them dressed identically in state-issued green clothing. Richard LaPierre, a white corrections officer, was manning his post in an observation tower located roughly 350 feet from the scene. LaPierre claimed that, just prior to the murder, he saw a group of inmates clustered together. He observed one inmate, wearing a hood, walk past the group. He then noticed another inmate leave the group, approach Julius from behind, and strike him in the lower neck or shoulder. LaPierre raised his binoculars to track the assailant's path. While LaPierre informed his colleagues by radio that an inmate was down, he tried to watch the perpetrator wind his way through the throngs. Following LaPierre's communication, corrections officers detained two Asian inmates in the yard, Tse Kin Cheung and David Wong. Wong soon became the chief suspect.[3]

Wong seemed an unlikely perpetrator from the start. No weapon or blood was found on him, even though the type of wound inflicted on Julius would have "spurted" blood, according to subsequent statements by the medical examiner. Furthermore, LaPierre's description of the stabber immediately after the incident failed to match Wong in several crucial respects. LaPierre claimed that the stabber at first "appeared to be white." LaPierre also neglected to mention the presence of dark gloves, which Wong was wearing when he was apprehended in the yard.[4]

Still, LaPierre confirmed his identification by choosing Wong's picture out of a photo array. Prosecutors later obtained an indictment of Wong for murder based mainly on LaPierre's appearance before the grand jury where he admitted "it was hard to tell" the perpetrator's race. After acknowledging that it was initially difficult to identify the race of Julius's assailant, LaPierre testified at trial that the culprit was "Oriental."[5]

Eyewitness testimony from Officer LaPierre was a key piece of the prosecution's case at trial, especially when corroborated by another witness who claimed to have enjoyed an even better view of the stabbing. Peter Dellfava, a white prisoner, stated he was fifteen feet away when the murder occurred. According to Dellfava's trial testimony, he was walking with another inmate that afternoon "when I had seen an incident in the yard with another inmate . . . and what looked like he was hitting him. . . . I saw this man right here [Wong] doing the hit."[6] Dellfava expressed certainty about the perpetrator's identity, alleging that he had seen Wong many times and talked with him often.[7]

By the time he testified, Dellfava was out on parole. The Clinton County District Attorney had evidently contacted the New York State Division of Parole on Dellfava's behalf, resulting in a successful appearance before the Board. This was no small feat. Dellfava had a prior record for attempting to escape from prison—a circumstance normally frowned upon by parole commissioners.[8]

Entrusted with the task of cross-examining LaPierre and Dellfava were two local lawyers assigned to represent Wong as indigent defense counsel, a duo that overlooked several promising investigative leads. Contrary to New York state law, only a fraction of the Department of Correctional Services' Bureau of Criminal Investigation (BCI) report completed after the stabbing was ever disclosed to the defense. The disclosed portions alluded to an alternative perpetrator. The document revealed that Otilio Serrano, a prisoner at Clinton, "advised that an inmate named Gutierrez was the subject who had stabbed the inmate in the yard" before noting that Serrano recanted this allegation in a second interview. In a third interview, Serrano stated that Wong could not have committed the stabbing. Despite these statements, the defense attorneys never spoke with Serrano before trial.[9]

Compounding matters from Wong's perspective was his inability to contribute much to his defense because of his limited English proficiency at the time of trial. The interpreter appointed to his case did not even speak the regional Chinese dialect with which Wong was most familiar. She only spoke Mandarin, a language Wong barely understood. The defense attorneys did not recognize the barrier this distinction posed for their client and never asked for a new translator even in the face of ample opportunities to do so.[10]

In July 1987 an all-white jury convicted Wong of murder in the second degree. He eventually received a sentence of twenty-five years to life in prison to be served consecutively with the term imposed for his robbery conviction.[11] A juror later observed that "the jury put a lot of stock into both" LaPierre and Dellfava as witnesses.[12] Even crediting LaPierre's and Dellfava's testimony—and discounting the effect of the defense's paltry investigation and the translation issue—a gaping hole emerges when reflecting on this trial: the lack of any motive for the crime. The trial generated no evidence of a previous dispute between Wong and Julius or any gang rivalries implicating them. Why would Wong seek to kill Julius, an African American inmate who had only recently arrived at Clinton?[13]

Fits and Starts: 1987–2000

Soon after Wong's murder conviction, Tse-Kin Cheung wrote to prominent Asian and Asian American leaders on his friend's behalf. New York City activist Yuri Kochiyama took an interest in the case and formed the David Wong Support Committee (DWSC). Part political action committee and part personal support network for a prisoner whom its members believed to be innocent, the DWSC worked throughout the 1990s to aid Wong's defense. As lawyers came and went—by 1999 fourteen attorneys had tried, without success, to free Wong—the organization remained steadfast, keeping the case on the front burner in New York legal circles (or at least keeping it from being extinguished on the backburner).[14]

The losses mounted. A state appellate court rejected Wong's direct appeal in 1990, concluding that "the evidence is legally sufficient to support [the] defendant's conviction."[15] A state post-conviction motion filed back in the trial court in 1997 claimed that newly discovered evidence warranted a new trial and contained seven affidavits from inmates, each of whom asserted that he had witnessed the stabbing and that Wong had not committed it. The affidavits went so far as to insist that a Latino inmate had carried out the assault. Not only did the trial court reject the motion but also a panel of judges unanimously affirmed this decision on appeal. Lawyers filed two other motions in the late 1990s, but neither had been thoroughly resolved by the time the case took an important turn.[16]

New Evidence: 2000–2003

Jaykumar Menon, a young lawyer at the Center for Constitutional Rights in New York City, inherited the Wong case in 1999, assuming the mantle previously held by experienced attorneys like fabled civil rights activist William Kunstler. Menon pledged to focus on the factual background of the incident—to reinvestigate the case from the bottom up. Assisted by a private investigator, Menon located Peter Dellfava in upstate New York. During an initial interview in December 2000 and later in written and videotaped statements, Dellfava recanted his trial testimony. Dellfava swore that he did not witness the stabbing of Tyrone Julius and that "the first time I ever saw David Wong in person was in court." Dellfava recalled that he was friendly with some corrections officers and that a sergeant approached him after the stabbing, saying "it was an Oriental guy, wasn't it?" Sensing an opportunity to improve his own situation in exchange for cooperating in the Wong case, Dellfava asked for a transfer to a facility closer to his family and a recommendation for parole, both of which materialized. In explaining his choice to come clean, Dellfava claimed, "I need to do the right thing."[17]

Dellfava's recantation, as vital as it was to the defense, represented only the start of the reinvestigation. Recantations are viewed with skepticism by the courts and seldom supply the basis for overturning a conviction on their own.[18] Shortly after Dellfava executed his affidavit, Menon sought assistance from the Second Look Program, which William Hellerstein and I oversaw at the time. We agreed to join Menon as co-counsel in 2001. The entire defense team realized that we had to find details about the actual killer.[19]

By that stage, journalist David Chen of the *New York Times* had found inmates willing to describe the culprit as a Hispanic male who limped. Many of these witnesses were reluctant to identify the killer by name because of concerns about being branded as "snitches." Further investigation by Menon and Second Look ultimately pointed to former Clinton prisoner Nelson Gutierrez as the perpetrator, reinforcing the hint that Otilio Serrano had provided fifteen years earlier when he told officials that an inmate named "Gutierrez" had stabbed Julius. What prompted several prisoners to take the step of attaching Gutierrez's name to the general description of the assailant was the circulation of news that the killer had died in the Dominican Republic. Incidentally, Gutierrez was known as "Chino" by virtue of his Asian facial features.[20]

No longer frightened of snitch status, seven inmates representing a cross-section of the racial and ethnic makeup of the prison community signed affidavits stating that Wong had not committed the crime. These prisoners received *no* tangible benefits from the defense team in return for this assistance. A new, more viable story of the stabbing began to take shape: that the incident was retribution for a beating Gutierrez had suffered from Julius while at a New York City jail.[21]

Teofilo Fernandez signed an affidavit stating that in 1984 he was incarcerated at Rikers Island, a detention facility in New York City, awaiting his trial for murder when he befriended a fellow inmate named Nelson Gutierrez. Gutierrez had a cast on his leg at the time and informed Fernandez "that he had a fight with black people over the telephone—that the black people had the phone and that they didn't want to give it to the Dominicans." After Fernandez's arrival at Clinton Correctional Facility in the spring of 1986, he again ran into his friend. Gutierrez confided in him: "I got the guy who broke my leg in Rikers Island and a Chinese guy paid for it. I didn't pay for it." Another inmate, Santo Valdez Cuello, recounted in an affidavit how he and Gutierrez became so close when they lived in the same dormitory at Fishkill Correctional Facility in the early 1990s that Gutierrez one day confessed to having killed the man who had injured his leg at Rikers.[22]

An affidavit from Sharon Julius, the wife of the victim, confirmed the account of the Rikers Island scuffle as well as Tyrone Julius's role in it. Mrs. Julius stated that someone stabbed her husband a few days after his arrival at Clinton and that she believed her "husband died as the result of an altercation that he had with a set of Hispanic brothers in prison in New York City." Sharon Julius learned from one of Tyrone's closest friends that her husband "had run afoul of two or three brothers who were Dominican or Colombian" and that he had died as a result of a hit put out on him.[23]

Corroborating the bookend accounts provided by Fernandez, Cuello, and Sharon Julius—which described the preceding tangle in Rikers and the post-stabbing confessions by Gutierrez—were a series of eyewitness statements from inmates present in the Clinton prison yard at the time of the stabbing. Two of Gutierrez's Dominican friends executed affidavits detailing the incident. Three inmates who lacked any personal relationship with Gutierrez also signed statements for the defense.[24]

Affidavits from these inmates and Sharon Julius made up the crux of a post-conviction motion filed by the Wong defense team with the trial court in August 2002. After two judges recused themselves from hearing the case, the motion landed on the desk of Family Court Judge Timothy Lawliss. In January 2003 Judge Lawliss ordered an evidentiary hearing to explore the defense allegations. The defense called ten witnesses. These witnesses included Peter Dellfava, who repudiated his trial testimony; six prisoners who testified about having witnessed the stabbing, three of whom identified the killer as Nelson Gutierrez and two of whom described the killer in a manner that matched Gutierrez's features; and the victim's widow, Sharon Julius, whose testimony substantiated many inmates' characterization of the attack as revenge for a beating that Gutierrez had sustained at Rikers. The prosecution presented no witnesses.[25]

Judge Lawliss denied Wong's motion in September 2003. He termed the inmate testimony "preposterous" and "unreliable." Dellfava's testimony at the hearing, in Lawliss's view, was "particularly unreliable." Perplexed as to why Dellfava had not come forward earlier, or at least after his parole expired in 1995, Lawliss failed to mention any number of logical explanations for Dellfava's delay, for instance, worries about perjury charges or the triggering effect of the private investigator's sudden arrival on his doorstep. Lawliss scoffed at the claims by Cuello and Fernandez that Gutierrez had confessed, and disparaged the credibility of the other witnesses. Lawliss also questioned the statements by several prisoners that knowledge of Wong's innocence—and Gutierrez's guilt—was widespread within the Clinton inmate population.[26]

In "stark contrast" to the inmate witnesses, according to Judge Lawliss, stood the trial testimony of Officer LaPierre. Citing the lack of evidence to "demonstrate that Mr. LaPierre was anything other than a disinterested, unbiased and credible witness," Lawliss dismissed the defense argument that LaPierre was simply mistaken. The judge stated that "any individual, particularly any individual who works in the correctional facility, would have to understand the significance and enormous responsibility of identifying another human-being as a murderer." Notable for their absence from Lawliss's opinion were virtually any references to Sharon Julius and the Rikers Island incident, pieces of the evidentiary puzzle that for the first time offered a motive for the slaying.[27]

Justice Served: 2004

The Wong defense team appealed Judge Lawliss's ruling. In October 2004 the appellate court reversed the decision. The appellate court deemed Dellfava's recantation believable, considering his possible exposure for perjury prosecution, and suggested the "recantation further acquires an aura of believability because of the testimony of the other witnesses at the hearing and the lack of trial evidence connecting [the] defendant with the commission of the crime or establishing a motive for him to commit the crime."

As for the other witnesses, the court discounted the significance of "minor inconsistencies" in their hearing testimony. The court instead noted that the prisoners "uniformly stated that they would not have testified against Gutierrez while he was alive because a reputation as a 'snitch' would place them in a position of peril in any prison population." Moreover, the court emphasized the existence of a motive attributable to Gutierrez and the partial corroboration of that account by Sharon Julius. In light of the newly discovered evidence, the discrepancies in LaPierre's statements, and the limited evidence against Wong, the court sent the case back for a new trial.[28]

It remained uncertain for several weeks whether the authorities would retry the case. Judge Lawliss even scheduled jury selection before recusing himself from any future proceedings to avoid "the appearance of partiality." Eventually, and apparently with a great deal of reluctance, the Clinton County District Attorney filed a motion to drop the charges, remarking that "I think a jury will have a difficult time finding beyond a reasonable doubt that David Wong committed the murder." The murder case against David Wong had reached an end. Understanding what had transpired in his wrongful conviction had only just begun.[29]

Despite all the case's quirks, *People v. Wong* is not as unique as it may seem. Rather, several patterns emerge from this case that mesh with broader themes from studies of wrongful convictions. First, the way in which Wong gained his freedom through the combined efforts of the media, political activists, public interest lawyers, and an innocence project is, if not a roadmap for success, a trail blazed in the past. Second, even though DNA exonerations tend to make headlines, many wrongful convictions, as in Wong's case, lack biological evidence that could be subject to DNA testing. Such cases are difficult to litigate given the absence of a method to prove innocence to a degree of scientific certainty. Third, the factors that led to Wong's conviction crop up repeatedly in the scholarly literature: eyewitness misidentification, ineffective assistance of counsel, and racial bias.[30]

At bottom, however, dubious prosecutorial behavior constituted the most significant factor in the Wong case. The prosecution's reliance on a jailhouse informant, Peter Dellfava, reinforced the shaky eyewitness identification of Officer LaPierre to hammer the final nail in the coffin of Wong's trial.[31] Prosecutors also exhibited a classic case of tunnel vision; after targeting Wong, law enforcement officials consistently disregarded exculpatory evidence as it surfaced over time.[32] The failure of the prosecution to disclose the entire BCI report may also have affected the outcome, but one cannot be sure—the missing portions have never seen the light of day.

Flawed prosecutorial trial tactics, like those used in the Wong case, have contributed to wrongful convictions across the country. The U.S. Supreme Court has demanded that trial prosecutors proceed with earnestness and vigor but "refrain from improper methods calculated to produce a wrongful conviction."[33] A litany of trial tactics might be categorized as improper methods, including the preparation and presentation of unreliable witnesses, the use of shady forensic scientific testimony, and unfair comments on the evidence in closing arguments. Proper methods used by prosecutors can also prompt a jury to convict an innocent defendant. The following three chapters explore the tactics employed by prosecutors at trial that contribute to the conviction of the innocent as well as the various rules and doctrines that fail to stop these practices from flourishing.

Preparation and Examination of Witnesses

Assume that plea bargaining negotiations reach a standstill in the Smith drunk-driving case. The prosecutor could dismiss the case, but chances are strong that Smith will go to trial. The prosecutor has already filed criminal charges, adhered (more or less) to his discovery obligations, and entertained plea discussions. Although these efforts could be written off as "sunk costs," the prosecutor is unlikely to do so. In his mind, the defendant's refusal to play ball through a plea bargain may be ascribed not to actual innocence but to foolhardiness. A prosecutor afflicted with tunnel vision can now shift his myopia to the end game: a guilty verdict at trial.

The Conviction Psychology

After plea bargaining has failed, a host of institutional, political, and psychological forces converge to pressure prosecutors to strive for convictions at trial. In an occupation where job performance is difficult to gauge, prosecutors are often evaluated based on their individual conviction rates.[1] Stories abound of supervisors using motivational devices to push trial prosecutors to secure convictions. Examples include publicizing individual conviction rates in the form of batting averages or listing attorneys on a bulletin board with stickers next to each name, green for wins and red for losses.[2] In 2010 the Arapahoe County District Attorney's Office in Colorado used a different green item (cash) to reward lawyers with high conviction rates; it gave year-end bonuses to felony prosecutors who tried at least five cases and earned convictions in 70 percent of them.[3] The desire for—or, rather, the *expectation* of—a conviction as the result of a criminal trial has become so entrenched within prosecutorial agencies that, in at least one office as of 2000, any assistant who tried a case that yielded an acquittal had to file a report with the chief prosecutor explaining "what went wrong."[4]

Political considerations reinforce the institutional emphasis placed on conviction rates. Chief prosecutors at the local and state levels ordinarily must be elected by the public without any term limits. Federal prosecutors are appointed in a process that has political overtones as well. The president of the United States appoints the attorney general, who supervises the Justice Department and selects chief prosecutors (known as U.S. Attorneys) in each of the federal districts. All these appointees must receive confirmation from the Senate, a painstaking endeavor that exposes their backgrounds to public scrutiny. Assistant prosecutors in state, local, and federal offices must also be cognizant of the political ramifications of their work because they serve at the pleasure of their bosses and might suffer in the event of regime changes. Trial outcomes, in particular, have politically charged ripple effects.[5]

Aware of these political realities, candidates vying for chief prosecutor tend to campaign on tough-on-crime themes. Broad messages about public safety impress eligible voters, most of whom see themselves as prospective crime victims rather than defendants. Many candidates have experience as assistant prosecutors, allowing them to tout their conviction records in support of their public safety platforms.[6] Political considerations may even distort choices about *which* cases to prosecute. A 2009 study suggests that concerns about maintaining a high batting average heading into an election cycle can cause prosecutors to reduce their number of "at bats," that is, to pursue cases only where they have a strong chance of hitting a home run with a conviction.[7] Taking a case to trial that ends in an acquittal is not usually worn as a badge of honor by district attorneys on the campaign trail, notwithstanding any inclination to trumpet the minister-of-justice concept.

Once elected, chief prosecutors regularly cite their office's trial record in seeking to justify their budgets and earn additional resources.[8] An office's passion for convictions does not necessarily have a negative fiscal impact on its operations. Although the cost of prosecuting crimes is borne by each local office, the costs of incarceration stemming from those efforts are not. Most prisons subsist through state funding. This split funding of the criminal justice system disperses the financial burden between state and local coffers.[9]

Along with institutional and political forces, psychological factors may push individual prosecutors to view convictions as the coin of their realm. Prosecutors who work in organizations that prize convictions may internalize the emphasis put on conviction rates and treat their win-loss record as a sign of self-worth. By classifying convictions as wins, prosecutors may become dependent on those outcomes to bolster their confidence. A healthy ego is an especially valuable tool for trial lawyers whose jobs hinge on the ability to show poise before an audience. A trial prosecutor's mind-set may also be shaped by the ideology that draws many lawyers to district attorneys' offices: a wish to protect the public. This impulse can inject an element of personal morality into a prosecutor's approach. Dedicated to safeguarding the community, and fueled by self-righteousness, some incoming prosecutors adopt a gung ho persona targeted at cleaning up the streets.[10]

One product of these institutional, political, and psychological pressures is that many trial prosecutors develop a "conviction psychology," a term Professor George Felkenes invented in 1975 that remains as apt today as it was then.[11] Adding the conviction psychology to the mix of biases formed prior to trial—tunnel vision, belief perseverance, loss aversion, and so on—is a dangerous cognitive concoction for prosecutors. And, for the innocent, it is a recipe for disaster.

The immense pressure to gain convictions clashes with the minister-of-justice concept.[12] Aspiring attorneys are trained in the art of zealous advocacy during law school with little attention paid to the one ethics rule aimed solely at prosecutors, the admonition to "do justice."[13] The vagueness of the do-justice mandate gives much room for prosecutors to interpret it.[14] All too often, this skirmish between the ill-defined goals of justice and the blatant benefits of conquest within a prosecutor's psyche results in the triumph of the latter. Justice William Douglas of the U.S. Supreme Court once observed that "the function of the prosecutor under the Federal Constitution is not to tack as many skins of victims as possible to the wall."[15] But it is hard for young prosecutors to shun the hunt mentality of an aggressive institutional culture and pursue justice.[16] That the object of the hunt is considered a threat to society fans the flames of many a prosecutor's indignation.

Believing in the wisdom of the chase, some prosecutors feel justified in using the most potent weapons available at trial. Prosecutors know that they carry a heavy burden; they must prove the defendant guilty beyond a reasonable doubt. A single juror holdout can produce a hung jury. Prosecutors also know that they have just one shot at a conviction because of the Supreme Court's interpretation of the Double Jeopardy Clause, which generally prevents the government from retrying a defendant after an acquittal.[17] For many prosecutors, losing track of their prey is simply unacceptable.

The notorious "Two-Ton Contest" in Illinois shows the hunt mentality taken to the extreme. More than a decade ago a group of prosecutors in Chicago developed a game to enliven things around the office. The rules were quite simple: the first prosecutor to convict four thousand pounds of defendant flesh won. Predictably, competitors angled for assignments to cases involving the heaviest criminal defendants.[18] The sense that a prosecutor's primary goal in practice is to obtain guilty verdicts through zealous (and possibly carnivorous) advocacy techniques defies the minister-of-justice ideal.

Questionable Witness Preparation and Examination Tactics

The hunt at trial begins with an evaluation of the evidence and the preparation of witnesses. The chief government witnesses in the Smith drunk-driving case are the eyewitness, Johnson, and the upstairs neighbor, Wiley. Johnson's eyewitness identification is the heart of the case. In preparing Johnson for trial, the prosecutor might want to shore up her testimony by coaching her so as to minimize inconsistencies or downplay any residual uncertainty. Johnson might even be discouraged from speaking with the defense.[19]

Are these appropriate witness preparation techniques? It depends on how they are implemented. Witness preparation is crucial to effective trial practice. Meeting witnesses early on permits prosecutors to gauge whether they have information that will advance the government's position at trial. These meetings also allow prosecutors to determine whether there is a factual basis to the case, figure out a logical sequence for the presentation of evidence to make the material most accessible to the jury, and notify witnesses about evidentiary rules so they may avoid revealing prejudicial information that could contaminate the trial. The best prosecutors pursue all these ends while remaining objective and demanding the truth from their witnesses.[20]

But some witness preparation tactics go too far. A prosecutor may not counsel a witness to testify falsely.[21] Conduct short of telling a witness to lie is also looked down upon. The practice of "horseshedding" a witness, recommending that he slant his testimony in a certain manner and rehearsing that script, is considered unethical.[22] In fact, prosecutors are limited in their ability to compel witnesses to appear at preparation sessions at all. Prosecutors in most jurisdictions may not use subpoenas to ensure witnesses' compliance with their interview requests. As a corollary to this rule, prosecutors should not advise a witness to neglect defense overtures for an interview.[23]

There are also restrictions on the scope of a prosecutor's examination of witnesses during the actual trial. Knowingly presenting perjured testimony violates due process.[24] If a prosecutor is aware of a witness's intention to testify falsely, he must persuade him to do otherwise or else decline to put the witness on the stand. If a prosecutor learns after the fact about a witness's perjury, he must take remedial action to correct the misrepresentation.[25] A prosecutor also may not pose a question on cross-examination of a defense witness unless there is a good faith ground for the factual predicate behind the inquiry. For instance, asking a witness whether his wife left him because of his infidelities—without any factual basis to the question—may leave an indelible blemish on the jury's perception of that witness, even if the witness responds with a stern "no." When it is sufficiently damaging to the defense, this prosecutorial tactic of launching an unsupported question on cross-examination infringes upon the defendant's right to a fair trial.[26] Prosecutors have a "special duty" not to mislead the court, jury, or defense counsel. Failure to honor this duty can lead to the reversal of a conviction.[27]

Yet there is a gray area that prosecutors can exploit between directing witnesses to do something and subtly leading them down that primrose path. Guiding (rather than telling) witnesses to emphasize particular facts during their testimony does not automatically violate the canons of ethics, provided the prosecutor acts in good faith.[28] Instructing Johnson to "just let the jury know what you saw that drunk do that tragic night" reinforces the need to put a bad person behind bars without insisting she skew the facts in any particular direction. Memory retrieval is a complicated process. The use of certain language by prosecutors can telegraph to witnesses how they ought to testify; it can even alter a witness's highly malleable recollection of the facts.[29] After a witness embraces an adulterated version of a story, that version can harden into the true account in the mind of the witness.[30] Asking Johnson whether "the guy was really staggering, just tripping all over himself when he got out of the car" could reshape her view of the event and cause her to overstate her impression of the driver's intoxication during her testimony.

Also, if Johnson shows reluctance to meet with the defense team and asks the trial prosecutor for his thoughts, the prosecutor's ensuing silence or bare recitation of the correct law on that score (that Johnson is not required to do so) may seal her decision. That behavior does not strike me as counseling a witness to turn down a defense request for an interview. And as long as there is a smidgen of factual support for a question on cross-examination, a prosecutor may feel he is on firm footing. Would a prosecutor be derelict in asking Smith if he drinks too much? If he drinks every day? Wiley's statements to the police may have given prosecutors an adequate factual foundation upon which to rest those questions—and upon which to poison the jury against the defendant. A judge may preempt the questioning as prejudicial, but a prosecutor is likely safe from an ethical standpoint.

Improper witness coaching by prosecutors is one of the dirty secrets of the adversary system, a pervasive practice that subverts the search for truth during trials. Prosecutors normally prepare witnesses in closed-door sessions where no notes are taken. The participants in these encounters seldom disclose what happened, and cross-examination has limited utility in prompting such revelations.[31]

The murder case against one of my former clients, Fernando Bermudez, shows the dangers of improper witness preparation and examination. Bermudez's saga began at a New York City nightclub in August 1991. A group of African American teenagers inside the club traded taunts with some young Latinos. The insults escalated into punches. One of the black teens slugged a Latino nicknamed "Shorty" in the face. Less than an hour later, Shorty approached a man in the nightclub, explained he had been punched, and pointed to Raymond Blount as his assailant. Outside the club, the man asked Shorty yet again to identify the person who had hit him; Shorty indicated that Blount had done it. The man then shot and killed Blount.[32]

Investigating detectives rounded up a handful of eyewitnesses that night. The eyewitnesses worked together at the local precinct to develop a description of the shooter and the Latino teenager who had directed him to Blount. The police quickly identified Shorty as Efraim Lopez, a sixteen-year-old Puerto Rican. Identifying the shooter proved more difficult. In an unusual procedure, the police let the eyewitnesses trade notes as they sifted through photographs of suspects. They ultimately settled on a photograph of Fernando Bermudez, a Dominican known as "Most."[33]

With Bermudez labeled as the chief suspect, the police hauled Efraim Lopez in for questioning. During a lengthy interrogation, in which an experienced felony prosecutor participated, Lopez admitted that the perpetrator was an acquaintance from his neighborhood. He referred to this acquaintance intermittently as "Lou" or "Luis" and his street name as "Woolu." (In the early 1990s portions of crack cocaine packaged in tobacco cigarettes were called "wools.") Lopez insisted that he did not know anybody who went by "Most."[34]

Indeed, there was little to suggest that Lopez had any connection to Bermudez whatsoever. They had different ethnic backgrounds and hung out in different neighborhoods. This did not stop Manhattan prosecutors from charging Bermudez with murder. Meanwhile, a Puerto Rican named Luis Munoz, who was known as "Woolu" and lived near Lopez's grandmother, left the jurisdiction.[35]

The case against Bermudez went to trial. Lopez testified as part of a cooperation agreement stipulating that in exchange for his testimony he would not face any charges related to the shooting. The same prosecutor who participated in the police interrogation of Lopez examined him at trial. Lopez identified Bermudez at trial as the "Woolu" who had committed the murder. When asked point-blank by the trial prosecutor whether he knew the shooter's real name, Lopez maintained he did not. The prosecutor failed to correct this, even though he knew that Lopez had referred to the shooter as "Luis" and "Lou" shortly after the incident. Had this information come out at trial, the defense team would have had a lead about another suspect. The jury found Bermudez guilty of murder.[36]

Bermudez pined away in prison. Many lawyers over the years—including William Hellerstein and me at the Second Look Program in tandem with Marjorie Smith, a dedicated solo practitioner—filed state and federal petitions on Bermudez's behalf. It was all to no avail until 2009, when a new team of lawyers, led by Lesley Ringer and Barry Pollack, convinced a state court judge to hold an evidentiary hearing on Bermudez's case. The judge reversed Bermudez's conviction partly on the basis that the prosecution had introduced key trial testimony from Lopez that it knew or should have known was false.[37]

Reining in Improper Witness Preparation and Examination

What should be done to deter unwelcome conduct by prosecutors in this area of trial practice? Professor Stephanos Bibas suggests that cultivating an office environment where convictions are not the be-all and end-all is a good start.[38] Chief prosecutors can shift the organizational focus away from an emphasis on convictions through various techniques—championing the general concept of justice, praising attorneys who dismiss cases for lack of evidence, discouraging bragging about conviction rates, awarding promotions based on criteria other than "wins," and giving high status to ethics mavens from whom other attorneys are expected to solicit guidance. Junior attorneys take their cues from above. Rhetoric from high-level supervisors matters in forming an ethical office that rejects the hunt mentality. Systematically hiring new prosecutors who fit within this culture and training them to embrace it are essential to preserving an ethical culture over time.[39] As for more concrete reforms, offering internal training on non-suggestive interviewing techniques could help well-intentioned prosecutors from straying into foul territory during witness preparation and examination.[40]

Greater documentation of witness interviews could also assist in finding instances where prosecutors veer out of bounds. The private nature of witness preparation conferences deprives courts, not to mention defense attorneys, from any insight into whether prosecutors crossed the line. Forcing prosecutors to put witness interviews in writing would add much needed transparency to those conferences. Better yet, *videotaping* all witness interviews with prosecutors would allow outsiders to pick up on subtle signals that written reports cannot convey.[41]

Recording requirements should come with provisions that call for the timely delivery of this information to the defense. Let's briefly go back to the Bermudez case. The police had actually videotaped the Lopez interrogation—but prosecutors dragged their feet in turning over the tape to the defense, delivering it only on the cusp of trial, and the judge denied defense counsel's request for a continuance.[42] One can only wonder whether the trial outcome would have differed had defense counsel received the tape with enough time to analyze it.

Defendants would also benefit from rules that authorize courts to inspect recordings of prosecution witness interviews. A judge could hold a pretrial hearing when there is some basis for thinking that a prosecutor's preparation techniques unduly tainted a witness's testimony. To ensure that courts are not overwhelmed with this procedure, defense attorneys could bear the initial burden of showing grounds to believe prosecutorial interview tactics have compromised witness testimony.[43] Finally, stronger and more explicit ethical standards could prompt some prosecutors to refrain from conduct that might unintentionally bring about false testimony.[44]

Improper witness preparation and examination techniques by prosecutors can affect the result of a criminal trial. These techniques are particularly risky when the prosecution has already promised benefits to the witness in exchange for testifying against the defendant. Like Efraim Lopez in the Bermudez case and Peter Dellfava in the Wong prosecution, cooperating witnesses and informants have played leading roles in many trial dramas that put the innocent in prison.

The Use of Jailhouse Informants in Criminal Cases

In a broad sense, the term "informant" applies to any civilian who gives information to the police, such as jailhouse informants, criminal accomplices, and concerned citizens. Informants typically expect to receive tangible benefits for their assistance. These benefits include monetary payment and immunity from prosecution. Some people may seek intangible rewards. The mere prospect of receiving attention from the police, exacting revenge

against a rival, or eliminating a criminal competitor can motivate individuals to act as informants.[45]

Jailhouse informants tend to be the most peculiar and problematic witnesses.[46] Informants who are already in prison may offer to provide evidence incriminating another inmate—often to the tune of how that other prisoner "confessed" in private—in return for leniency on a pending charge or favorable treatment of another form.[47] The specific kind of benefit can border on the absurd. In one San Diego case, prosecutors were so keen on convicting four gang members that they gave a jailhouse informant a cell equipped with a color television, and allowed conjugal visits to take place in a prosecutor's office.[48]

Jailhouse informants have a nearly irresistible incentive to fabricate statements against other criminal defendants.[49] What makes jailhouse informants especially dangerous, according to one commentator, is that they "claim no insider knowledge of the crime; rather, their ticket to freedom or other rewards is based entirely on the alleged confessions made to them by defendants, which in an information-friendly world may be spun from whole cloth."[50] In trying to punch their tickets, informants have tapped into a bevy of pipelines to make their information sound credible.[51] Sometimes the informant may have good reason to know details about the crime; in at least three DNA exonerations a witness who received favorable treatment for testifying against the defendant at trial turned out to be the *actual* perpetrator.[52]

Trial prosecutors, eager as they are to present damning evidence against a defendant, are often primed for manipulation by jailhouse informants. After prosecutors fuse the information into their cases, they develop a stake in its accuracy. One former prosecutor likened the relationship between informants and their handlers to "falling in love with your rat."[53] In spite of inherent reliability concerns, the use of informants received the U.S. Supreme Court's blessing in 1966.[54]

The hazards of jailhouse informants were on full display in the 1989 investigation into informant practices in the Los Angeles County jail. As part of that investigation, informants admitted to perjury in dozens of felony convictions. An alarming fact that emerged was that detectives hoping to bolster a case occasionally arranged with jail officials to put the chief suspect in a sector of the facility brimming with informants, so that one of his neighbors might overhear (or more likely contrive) a confession from the suspect and later repeat that account on the witness stand. Many informants were implicated in the scandal. Yet only one of them faced perjury charges—Leslie Vernon White, the whistle-blower who exposed practices in the jail and discussed his own aptitude for snitching on the television program *60 Minutes*. During one thirty-six-day period, White provided evidence about three murders and one burglary to Los Angeles prosecutors. All this information supposedly came from fleeting jailhouse exchanges where inmates volunteered details about their crimes.[55]

Many prosecutors ward off the temptation to use informants. A memorandum authored by Stephen Trott, a former prosecutor and current federal judge, became lore in U.S. Attorneys' Offices. The document gave two lessons about the use of informants: "One. Don't do it unless you have to. Two. Corroborate, corroborate, corroborate."[56] Some prosecutors feel they have to rely on informants in certain kinds of cases. Informants figure prominently in prosecuting conspiracies and official corruption cases where the criminal activities by their very nature are covert and difficult to penetrate by law enforcement. Supporters of the use of informants often justify the practice on utilitarian grounds, the ugly means defended as necessary to convict sophisticated criminals.[57] Advocates of the practice also point out that defendants are well positioned to refute false informant testimony. Constitutional law requires that prosecutors alert the defense prior to trial about the nature of any inducements provided to government witnesses in exchange for their testimony.[58] This puts the defense on notice about witnesses who have incentives to commit perjury.

But the rationales for using informants are belied by prosecutorial practices on the ground. Prosecutors do not depend on informants solely in cases where they have few alternatives.[59] Even worse, prosecutors who rely on informants may follow creative detours to circumvent their constitutional disclosure obligations. Prosecutors have led witnesses to testify that no prearranged deal was made as a condition of their appearance at trials where details of their cooperation agreement later surfaced. Prosecutors may even broker the deal with the informant's *attorney*, purposely leaving the informant oblivious to the nuances of the deal and allowing him to testify honestly that "he" has not been promised any inducements. Although prosecutors should negotiate through the informant's attorney when they know the witness is represented by counsel, that rule does not mean those communications should be structured to sidestep disclosure duties.[60] Courts have treated these subterfuges as constitutional violations.[61] Another ploy used to dodge disclosure involves prosecutors offering leniency to a witness through "a wink and a nod" without verbalizing the arrangement, a technicality countenanced by some courts.[62] Formal agreements are rare—and when they do exist, they typically capture only the broadest parameters of the cooperation.[63]

Aside from deliberate efforts to bypass disclosure rules, the mere practice of relying on jailhouse informants without taking precautions to ensure truthful testimony brings up ethical issues for prosecutors. These issues include previously mentioned prohibitions against knowingly presenting perjured testimony and misleading the tribunal. The habit of using jailhouse informants at the very least undercuts the minister-of-justice mantra because of the strong chance of false testimony.[64] Perjured testimony surfaces in many wrongful convictions, as evidenced by Professor Samuel Gross's 2005 study finding "at least one sort of perjury" reported in over 40 percent of all exonerations.[65] Other studies validate this data.[66]

The presence of inmate Peter Dellfava in the David Wong murder prosecution was hardly unusual, then, especially since the stabbing took place *within* a prison. Nor was it odd that he received a recommendation for parole from the district attorney. The most curious and commendable part of the Dellfava saga is that he admitted to lying.[67] Assuming that most jailhouse informants who perjure themselves are reluctant to own up to their machinations in the end, and that they are bona fide, if maddening, weapons in the crime-fighting arsenal,[68] it is important to focus on reforms that might decrease the likelihood of perjury at the outset.

Micro-Level Change: Enhancing the Reliability of Jailhouse Informant Testimony in Individual Cases

As Justice Robert Jackson of the U.S. Supreme Court observed in 1952, "the use of informers, accessories, accomplices, false friends, or any of the other betrayals which are 'dirty business' may raise serious questions of credibility."[69] Cleaning up this dirty business could involve banning jailhouse informant testimony altogether or excluding it from specific cases.[70] But most jurisdictions are leery of adopting blanket exclusionary rules because of the perceived benefits provided by informants. Many crusaders for reform instead seek to enrich the process for testing the reliability of individual informants.[71] Let's explore these possibilities.

Discovery

Several states have endorsed greater discovery in cases involving jailhouse informants.[72] In 2000 the Oklahoma Court of Criminal Appeals noted the unique dangers presented by jailhouse informants and instituted special discovery rules to prevent them. Oklahoma prosecutors now must disclose any information relevant to an informant's testimony at least ten days before the start of trial, including his full criminal history, any "deal, promise, inducement, or benefit that the offering party has made or may make in the future to the informant," and "the specific statements made by the defendant and the time, place, and manner of their disclosure."[73] The government must also reveal "all other cases in which the informant testified or offered statements against an individual but was not called."[74] The Illinois legislature adopted similarly vast discovery measures in 2004 for jailhouse informant testimony in capital cases.[75]

For these rules to have any impact, however, there must be something concrete to discover. To that end, prosecutors should memorialize wink-and-nod arrangements and turn them over to the defense. This is standard practice among federal prosecutors.[76] Professor Robert Mosteller has recommended even greater precautions: recording "first drafts" of informant stories and documenting the full scope of promises made to or assumed by the informant. Preserving first drafts would dissuade snitches from modifying their accounts over time as they gather more knowledge about the defendant's case. Equally vital, these documents would provide a yardstick against which to compare their trial testimony.[77]

Depositions

To add flesh to the bones of discovery rules, courts could permit defendants to depose jailhouse informants before trial. As discussed in chapter 2, discovery depositions might allay the fear that certain information eludes disclosure and might even dig up details unknown to prosecutors. The informality of depositions lets defense lawyers expose flaws in informant testimony before trial to an extent impossible to achieve through cross-examination in court. By then, the witness may have been coached or, at a minimum, be resistant to impeachment with his promised benefits so near at hand.[78]

In-Court Safeguards

Judges could also offer in-court protections to neutralize the impact of informant testimony on trial outcomes. Here are three suggestions:

First, trial judges should hold pretrial reliability hearings to assess the credibility of informant testimony before admitting it at trial.[79] Testimony from informants may carry persuasive power with jurors, which is reason enough to subject it to careful pretrial review.[80] Illinois authorizes pretrial hearings specifically to test the reliability of jailhouse informants. A smattering of case law suggests that trial judges in other jurisdictions may also conduct such hearings.[81]

Second, judges should require independent evidence that corroborates an informant's account before allowing an informant to testify at trial. That corroboration should not consist of statements from *other* informants.[82]

Third, after an informant testifies, courts should provide jury instructions that outline the dangers involved with this evidence and urge the fact-finder to view the testimony with a skeptical eye.[83]

Macro-Level Change: Revamping the Informant System

Many proposed reforms target the systemic role of jailhouse informants in the United States. Scholars have recommended restrictions on the types of crimes that can be mitigated via cooperation.[84] Others have pressed for caps on the number of cooperators who may receive sentence mitigation to force prosecutors to use informants selectively.[85] Some observers seek to increase accountability through public registries of informants that would effectively blacklist perjurers and recidivist snitches.[86] Professor Alexandra Natapoff has taken this goal of publicizing informant practices a step further. She wants law enforcement agencies to produce compilations of redacted informant profiles or even aggregate statistics on an annual basis.[87]

Some of the large-scale reforms mentioned in previous chapters also apply here. A one-two regulatory punch—external oversight by courts and disciplinary agencies accompanied by internal monitoring by prosecutors themselves—might not knock out informant perjury but could put the practice on the ropes.[88]

Judicial Oversight

Courts could do a better job of deterring prosecutors from the misuse of jailhouse informants. A due process violation exists under Supreme Court precedent when perjured testimony is the responsibility of prosecutors or is known to them, as in the Bermudez case.[89] If judges were to be consistently vigilant in finding due process violations when prosecutors did not actually know but *should have known* about the perjury, then prosecutors might have a powerful incentive to subject jailhouse informants to exacting pretrial scrutiny.[90]

At the risk of digressing, I should note that holding prosecutors accountable when they should have known about perjury could improve the criminal justice system beyond keeping some dishonest jailhouse informants off the stand. Perjury by police officers is considered so rampant (particularly at pretrial suppression hearings regarding whether the seizure of contraband was constitutional) that this conduct has earned its own moniker: *testilying*.[91] If the police are correct, virtually every drug dealer in the United States suffers from acute clumsiness given the pervasiveness of "dropsy" cases in which police officers claim that narcotics suddenly fell out of a person's hands and into plain view.[92] Few observers accuse prosecutors of encouraging these deceits, just of treating them with benign neglect.[93] Prosecutors might clamp down on this practice if they could be taken to task for eliciting incredible police testimony.

Ethics Boards

Ethical rules should bar prosecutors from presenting jailhouse informants without factors that signal truthfulness.[94] Adding a concrete rule of this nature would make it easier for disciplinary agencies to sanction prosecutors for misusing jailhouse informants. That presupposes, of course, that ethics boards are willing to monitor prosecutorial behavior more thoroughly than has been the case.

Prosecutorial Self-Restraint

A host of internal remedies could persuade prosecutors to rely on jailhouse informants only in rare circumstances. Crafting strict office policies on the use of jailhouse informants would provide much needed guidance to trial prosecutors, create a level of uniformity within the organization, and increase compliance with best practices. Forming review committees to assess decisions by individual prosecutors who want to introduce informant testimony would offer a fresh look to thwart cognitive biases.[95] Getting prosecutors to take perjury more seriously could cause jailhouse informants to hesitate when contemplating whether to lie at the start. And demanding that prosecutors receive training in how to detect deception and avoid tipping off informants about the manner in which the government wants them to testify would assist on the margins. Compared to other institutional players, prosecutors are in the best position to test the veracity of informant testimony before trial. They should do so.[96]

The response of the Los Angeles District Attorney's Office in the wake of the 1989 county jail scandal offers a ray of hope in an otherwise grim landscape. That office developed policies, procedures, and training regimens related to jailhouse informants. Office policy now requires Los Angeles prosecutors to introduce evidence that strongly corroborates an informant's account. Even then, an in-house jailhouse informant committee must grant prior approval of the informant's appearance at trial. This process is by no means perfunctory. In 2007 the California Commission on the Fair Administration of Justice reported that this committee had claimed to approve only twelve in-custody informants in the previous four years. Attorneys and investigators from the Los Angeles prosecutors' office must also record all interviews with jailhouse informants, and a central index is maintained to track the use of these witnesses over time.[97]

The role played by a jailhouse informant in the David Wong murder case highlights the flaws in this part of the U.S. criminal justice system. The havoc wreaked by witnesses such as Peter Dellfava can only be avoided by strengthening the procedures through which informant reliability is tested, reducing any systemic inducements to lie, and warning juries about the suspect nature of testimony by jailhouse informants. The reforms proposed in this chapter are mainly of the "sunshine" variety, measures aimed at bringing the opaque relationship between jailhouse informants and their prosecutorial handlers into the open.[98] Putting the spotlight on informant practices can better prepare defendants for trial—and better protect the innocent from being burned by perjured testimony.

Test Tubes on Trial

Prosecutors and Forensic Evidence

A tough trial lies ahead for the prosecution in the Smith drunk-driving case. There is solid circumstantial evidence implicating Smith but also a shaky eyewitness who is vulnerable to attack on cross-examination. What the prosecutors would love to find is evidence establishing a direct link between Smith and the crime scene, at least one stronger than Johnson's eyewitness identification. Suppose there is the potential to forge such a connection. Assume the driver of the vehicle stepped in mud while leaving the accident on foot. An intrepid crime scene investigator documented and preserved the boot prints. After arresting Smith, the police confiscated his boots and sent them to the state crime laboratory. A forensic analyst visually compared the boot prints to the treads in Smith's footwear, declaring them a match. This "scientific" evidence could clinch the prosecution's case. Similar evidence has done so in many trials—occasionally to the detriment of innocent defendants.

A Brief Look at the Forensic Sciences

Many forensic science disciplines have emerged over the years to assist the prosecution of crime. Some, like fingerprinting, are well known. Others are less so, such as the field of forensic odontology, which measures bite marks made in human skin against a suspect's dental records, or hair microscopy, which compares hairs retrieved from a crime scene against those obtained from the suspect.[1]

Juries tend to believe in forensic science and to expect its appearance in every case, a phenomenon possibly influenced by the television program *CSI*.[2] Yet juror reliance on scientific evidence predates the popularization of crime scene investigative techniques through the mainstream media. One study from 1987 found that nearly "one quarter of the citizens who had served on juries which were presented with scientific evidence believed that had such evidence been absent, they would have changed their verdicts—from guilty to not guilty."[3] Ill-equipped to second-guess the science, jurors all too often accept forensic evidence at face value. Prosecutors know this and regularly rely on forensic evidence to cement their cases when it is available. At the same time, that evidence could rest on a flimsy scientific foundation.[4]

Take boot print evidence. Although the imprints left by the fleeing driver could very well belong to Smith, it may be hard to tie them to his shoes with any degree of accuracy. Without clear protocols for determining a match, different boot print examiners can reach dramatically different conclusions. This occurred in an Illinois case involving the murder of a ten-year-old girl in 1983. The evidence against Stephen Buckley, Rolando Cruz, and Alejandro Hernandez included a boot print supposedly left on the front door of the victim's house when Buckley kicked it in. Adamant that they had the right men, prosecutors submitted the boot print to several crime labs for analysis. Various county, state, and out-of-state experts were unable to identify Buckley's boot as the origin of the print. Undaunted, prosecutors pitched the case to Dr. Louise Robbins, a controversial examiner known as the "Cinderella" expert for her penchant to make the print fit the shoe by using a unique grid format to spot multiple points of shape. Robbins testified that there was a match and, for her trouble, received a fee of $10,000. Despite the fact that the jury deadlocked and someone else confessed to being the perpetrator, Buckley languished in prison for two extra years. Cruz and Hernandez were not so fortunate. They were convicted of the rape-murder, miscarriages of justice that took a decade to unravel.[5]

Forensic science often surfaces in studies of wrongful convictions. In fact, 52 *percent* of the first 250 DNA exonerations included the presentation of forensic evidence at trial.[6] Even fingerprint evidence, long hailed as the gold standard of forensic science, has contributed to the conviction of the innocent. In 2004 Stephan Cowans was exonerated based on post-conviction DNA testing after he had served six and a half years incarcerated in Massachusetts for shooting and injuring a Boston police officer. A crucial piece of evidence at trial consisted of fingerprints that allegedly connected Cowans to the crime.[7] DNA testing is also not immune from the virus of unreliability; defective DNA comparisons at trial have led to wrongful convictions on at least five occasions.[8] Methodologies less refined than DNA and fingerprinting are even more susceptible to error.[9]

Arson science is a discipline now under siege. In one much ballyhooed capital case, Cameron Todd Willingham was convicted in 1992 of murdering his three young daughters, all of whom died in a fire in his Texas home. Two local arson experts testified at trial that Willingham had set the fire intentionally. In the ensuing years, reports by journalists and forensic scientists debunked the arson testimony from Willingham's trial. Even an expert hired by the State of Texas to reexamine the case concluded that there was no scientific basis whatsoever for classifying the fire as arson. Those reports came too late. Willingham was executed in 2004—five years before investigations into his case ripened and set in motion a cascade of efforts to clear his name.[10] These efforts have drawn national attention. Arizona, Nebraska, and Oklahoma recently passed resolutions demanding statewide review of questionable arson cases, and a number of other jurisdictions reopened specific cases.[11]

What might explain these disturbing findings about the use of forensic science at trial? Professor Jane Moriarty attributes unreliable forensic science to a slew of factors: "fraud and negligence in the laboratory; the failure to use blind testing procedures; the lack of meaningful standards to judge the validity of a given theory; inadequate or nonexistent proficiency testing; and inadequate or nonexistent databases from which to draw comparisons."[12] A common theme in the forensic science disciplines is that they blossomed within the corridors of government crime laboratories rather than those of universities. As a consequence, they have not faced the rigorous validation tests applied to "hard" sciences like biology, chemistry, and physics. Creatures of the crime lab, not the academy, forensic scientists operate in offices lacking a scientific culture—environments that may value the ends of the process (ideally, a match) far more than the means.[13] Many crime labs are also unregulated and underfunded. Even where regulated, these organizations often neglect to adhere to proper scientific standards that could reduce error rates.[14]

Some forensic scientists have aggravated dormant flaws in their disciplines by testifying inaccurately at trial. In a 2009 study of trial transcripts from 137 DNA exonerations, Professor Brandon Garrett and Innocence Project co-director Peter Neufeld concluded that forensic analysts called by the government offered invalid testimony in 60 percent (82) of those cases. The scientific testimony in this dataset typically consisted of either references to erroneous empirical population data or conclusions unsupported by statistics. These instances were not the handiwork of a few scientists who testified repeatedly. Seventy-two experts employed in twenty-five states participated in these wrongful convictions.[15]

The lack of external regulation and internal scientific rigor has led to scandals within crime labs. One notable scandal took place in Houston. In 1998 the victim of a rape identified sixteen-year-old Josiah Sutton as one of her two assailants. To prove his innocence, Sutton requested a DNA test on evidence preserved from the crime. The Houston Police Department Crime Laboratory (HPDCL) determined that Sutton's DNA matched that of the profile procured from the victim's rape kit. Sutton was convicted after trial. Several years later, an exposé by a Houston television station alleged that the DNA/Serology Unit of the HPDCL had done shoddy work. It turned out that for more than a decade the unit had used inappropriate experimental controls in its DNA tests and mischaracterized the statistical significance of DNA findings at trial. Inquiry into the Sutton matter proved that the HPDCL had erred in that case, and a follow-up DNA test confirmed Sutton's innocence.[16] The brouhaha concerning the DNA/Serology Unit was not the last of the Houston crime lab's troubles; a 2009 probe found irregularities in over half the lab's fingerprinting cases taken from a randomly audited sample.[17]

In the summer of 2010 news broke of a far-reaching crime lab scandal in North Carolina. The exoneration of Greg Taylor, who spent seventeen years in prison for a murder he did not commit, prompted the North Carolina Attorney General to commission a review of the State Bureau of Investigation (SBI). As part of the review, an SBI analyst admitted that he had failed to report test results showing that a substance on Taylor's SUV was not blood and that he had done so at the behest of his bosses. The statewide audit verified the analyst's account, disclosing that the SBI had systematically withheld or misrepresented results in more than two hundred cases. Three of the botched cases involved defendants who had already been executed before the audit's release.[18]

Some scandals are the fault of individual scientists as opposed to widespread incompetence within a particular crime lab. The New York State Inspector General issued a report in 2009 blasting fiber analyst Gary Veeder for substandard work during his fifteen-year tenure with the State Police's Forensic Identification Center in Albany. Investigators uncovered testing errors in nearly 100 of the 322 cases in which Veeder oversaw the examination of trace evidence. Veeder routinely neglected to conduct required tests when examining fibers, and then later claimed he had performed them. It appears that Veeder was unable even to use a microscope properly. Although there is no evidence that anyone else was complicit in Veeder's fraud, supervisors perpetuated his deception through scanty review of his work.[19]

Trial prosecutors have added to these scandals by relying on expert testimony that was quite obviously flawed.[20] Consider the careers of forensic scientists Fred Zain and Joyce Gilchrist.

Fred Zain was the chief serologist in West Virginia for many years. Forensic serology involves testing bodily fluids to detect the presence of antibodies and antigens in order to identify the source of crime scene evidence. Serology served as a key forensic science tool in the decades prior to the growth of DNA testing in the late 1980s. Zain frequently testified about the certainty of serological findings that, in truth, were far from certain. During one stretch, from 1979 to 1989, he falsified test results in more than one hundred cases. Most troubling is the revelation that West Virginia prosecutors depended on him above all his colleagues, even going so far as to send evidence to him after he had moved to Texas because his replacements had not yielded the "right" results in pending cases.[21]

Joyce Gilchrist worked as a chemist in the crime lab of the Oklahoma City Police Department. Infamous for her ability to convince juries with evidence only she could divine, she became a favorite of local prosecutors even as courts and fellow members of the forensic science community denigrated her work. She consistently failed to distinguish between her personal and scientific opinions, overstated the nature of her conclusions, delayed in disclosing evidence required to be turned over to the defense, and drafted incomplete reports. In one case, her testimony helped convict Robert Miller of raping and murdering several women. DNA testing eventually exonerated Miller while implicating another suspect whom Gilchrist had *excluded* as the perpetrator before Miller's trial. Long after Gilchrist's reputation had plummeted, prosecutors persisted in soliciting her testimony until the controversy became impossible to ignore.[22]

In response to these and other scandals, the National Academy of Sciences (NAS) conducted a comprehensive study of the forensic sciences. That undertaking produced a scathing 2009 report that advocated a slate of reforms to keep flawed forensic science out of courtrooms. The NAS Report recommended the creation of a National Institute of Forensic Sciences to establish best practices, set standards for the mandatory accreditation of labs, and promote peer-reviewed research in forensic science. The institute would also craft standard terminology for use in forensic reports and testimony.[23]

The NAS Report's proposed changes to the forensic science community are much needed. Improving the quality of forensic science is a critical step on the path away from the presentation of unreliable forensic evidence at trial. Another step involves understanding why prosecutors have contributed to this phenomenon and how they can be kept from doing so in the future.

Prosecutors and Forensic Science

The deliberate misuse of forensic evidence by trial prosecutors, though rare, does occur. A 1967 U.S. Supreme Court case, *Miller v. Pate*, provides perhaps the most egregious documented example of this misconduct. That case concerned the sexual assault and murder of an eight-year-old girl. The prosecutor extracted trial testimony from a chemist employed by the state crime lab to the effect that a pair of men's underwear, purportedly belonging to the defendant and found near the crime scene, was stained with the victim's blood. The prosecutor capitalized on this testimony during his closing argument by asserting that the shorts were found with the girl's blood type on them. More than ten years elapsed before a chemical microanalyst testified at a habeas corpus hearing that the stains consisted of *paint*—and that the trial prosecutor knew this.[24]

Short of blatant misconduct, prosecutors have propped up feeble forensic scientific evidence in three main ways. First, prosecutors have concealed or belatedly provided the defense with information about scientific evidence that they plan to introduce at trial.[25] Because of the complicated nature of this evidence, most jurisdictions have specialized discovery laws that require prosecutors to turn over test results, reports, and statements by experts well before trial. These rules often impose an additional duty on prosecutors to furnish samples of the evidence to the defense to allow for independent testing.[26] Without access to this material in a timely fashion, defense counsel may be unprepared to penetrate the cloak of invincibility that swaddles expert witnesses. This exposes some defendants to "trial by ambush."[27] An unsettling theme in many of these cases involves prosecutors stalling the disclosure of lab reports, even encouraging experts never to compile full reports at the start.[28]

Second, prosecutors have introduced forensic expert testimony that any reasonable prosecutor should know is unfounded at best. The prosecutors who depended on Joyce Gilchrist and Fred Zain have plenty of company. During Jimmy Ray Bromgard's 1987 rape trial in Montana, the prosecution introduced testimony from forensic scientist Arnold Melnikoff indicating that head and pubic hairs retrieved from the crime scene matched those of the defendant. Melnikoff estimated the possibility that he was wrong at 1 percent. He went on to claim that there is "a multiplying effect," as head and pubic hairs differ, meaning the risk of misidentification would be "1 chance in 10,000." There never has been any statistical basis for asserting the probabilities of hair comparison, let alone for Melnikoff's self-proclaimed multiplying effect. His testimony so lacked scientific validity as to leave little doubt that

Montana prosecutors were aware of its inadequacy.[29] Misleading scientific testimony in many cases springs from witness preparation sessions where prosecutors telegraphed their desire for the expert to testify in a certain manner.[30]

A third fishy practice relates to prosecutors improperly bolstering an expert witness's credibility on the stand. Prosecutors have presented an expert as a neutral witness when that person has worked hand-in-glove with the prosecution in numerous cases. On other occasions, prosecutors have suggested that the witness belongs to a group that is particularly trustworthy and exaggerated the extent of the expert's credentials.[31]

As jarring as these accounts of wayward prosecutors may be, a more common story is of otherwise conscientious prosecutors who fail to screen out weak scientific evidence at the front end of the process. Why might this happen? As discussed in chapter 4, prosecutors stand to gain professionally and psychologically by "winning" convictions.[32] Forensic science can help achieve this goal. The presence of an obliging forensic scientist also relieves pressure on overworked police detectives and prosecutors to investigate those cases further.[33] Moreover, the bulk of prosecutors are ill-trained to distinguish good forensic science from bad.[34] Last, but not least, one cannot discount the effect of cognitive biases on prosecutorial perceptions of forensic science. As a case approaches trial, prosecutors may experience an "escalation of commitment" to their theory of guilt and a diminution in their capacity to view complex scientific evidence with objectivity.[35]

As a result, even well-intentioned prosecutors—overwhelmed by the demands of their caseloads, perplexed by the idiosyncrasies of science, and intent on convicting the guilty—may present forensic evidence at trial without always questioning its legitimacy. Prosecutors can justify this behavior by pointing to other safeguards built into the system to prevent so-called junk science from infiltrating the courtroom. Judges in most jurisdictions play a gatekeeping role in scrutinizing scientific evidence before trial to guarantee that it is both relevant and reliable.[36] This diffuses the responsibility for evaluating forensic science between judges and prosecutors. One side effect is that prosecutors can deny being wholly responsible when junk science does taint a trial.[37]

Reforms to Counter Prosecutors' Misuse of Scientific Evidence
Structural Change

States should reconfigure the association between law enforcement officials and forensic scientists. Given that the majority of forensic scientists work at crime labs affiliated with law enforcement agencies, it is hard to say that those experts operate independently of the prosecutors for whom they so often develop evidence. This close interaction can lead crime lab analysts to support prosecutors' theories even if the science is inconclusive.[38] As the U.S. Supreme Court observed in a 2009 case, *Melendez-Diaz v. Massachusetts*, "a forensic analyst responding to a request from a law enforcement official may feel pressure—or have an incentive—to alter the evidence in a manner favorable to the prosecution."[39] Proponents of institutional design theory often contend that establishing a separation of functions within organizations can advance best practices and protect against unchecked power.[40] Forming truly separate crime laboratories would serve as a bulwark against forensic fraud.[41] Building on this concept, prosecutors should establish internal protocols governing the use of scientific evidence at trial and add a layer of review to inspect cases that turn on scientific evidence.[42]

No More Trial by Ambush

Legislatures should expand discovery statutes to target scientific evidence with greater precision. Revised discovery rules should specify that the contents of all laboratory reports, electronic data, and case notes must be disclosed prior to trial.[43] Statutes could also require that all laboratory protocols and procedures be made available, and that each stage in the testing of evidence and the interpretation of results be recorded. As a key complement to these laws, prosecutors should bear responsibility to instruct crime labs about the disclosure obligations surrounding scientific evidence.[44] These changes could partially correct the information deficit that prevails in many cases: situations where defense counsel has neither the capacity nor the opportunity to examine the bases for the proposed scientific evidence before the expert takes the stand.[45]

Ethics and Experts

The most elemental of each lawyer's ethical obligations is the duty of competence. The very first rule in the Model Rules of Professional Conduct provides that "a lawyer shall provide competent representation . . . Competent representation requires the legal knowledge, skill, thoroughness and preparation reasonably necessary for the representation."[46] Attorneys keen on trying criminal cases must have some understanding of forensic science; otherwise, they may lack the "knowledge" and "skill" to perform competently.

The American Bar Association agrees with this assessment. That organization recommends that training about forensic science become accessible at minimal cost to criminal law practitioners and that lawyers ought to develop competence in any aspect of forensic science that is relevant to a case or consult with other attorneys who are.[47] In short, every prosecutor should receive forensic science training. If that proves too burdensome, prosecutors' offices could train a select squad of lawyers as specialists in the forensic sciences and assign them to the trial team in cases where those issues arise.[48]

The compulsory training of prosecutors about forensic science, however laudable, does not thoroughly protect against the later misuse of forensic testimony at trial. Although ethical rules forbid prosecutors from instructing witnesses to testify falsely, knowingly presenting false testimony or improperly bolstering the credibility of witnesses, the rules are silent on the topic of unreliable testimony.[49] This silence speaks volumes and permits the coaching of experts to flourish. Lawyers and their experts often engage in a subtle negotiation prior to trial to reach a middle ground where both sides are comfortable with the proffered testimony.[50] The main ethical guidepost directed at prosecutorial use of expert testimony, found in the American Bar Association's Standards for Criminal Justice, cautions that "a prosecutor who engages an expert for an opinion should respect the independence of the expert and should not seek to dictate the formation of the expert's opinion on the subject."[51] This provision carries a further warning: "to the extent necessary, the prosecutor should explain to the expert his or her role in the trial as an impartial expert called to aid the fact finders and the manner in which the examination of witnesses is conducted."[52] This language strikes the right tone on the surface but lacks substance. Absent structural changes in the relationship between crime laboratories and prosecutorial agencies, the image of the "impartial" and "independent" forensic scientist is woefully naïve.[53]

In light of the vagueness of the rules governing prosecutorial use of expert witnesses, some scholars have proposed amending the canons of ethics to tackle this issue head-on. Professor Jane Moriarty advocates changes to ethical standards that would require prosecutors to ensure that only reliable expert evidence is admitted at trial.[54] Professors Paul Giannelli and Kevin McMunigal also recommend alterations to ethics codes. They home in on the problem of willful blindness: situations where prosecutors neglect to investigate the holes in their expert's testimony, allowing them to escape the ethical proscription against presenting evidence they "know" to be false. To ameliorate this problem, Giannelli and McMunigal press for an addition to the Model Rules demanding that prosecutors "refrain from knowingly, recklessly, or negligently offering false scientific evidence."[55] This amendment "would create an affirmative obligation on the part of the prosecutor to take reasonable steps to assure the soundness of the scientific evidence she offers."[56] The reasonable steps requirement would compel investigation by prosecutors beyond simply relying on the expert's own assertions about the field and her skill.[57] Prosecutors who engage in expert shopping to find a favorable witness whose conclusion might not be duplicated (see Exhibit A, the Cinderella Expert) would risk violating this proposed ethical rule. A trend of inaccurate laboratory results would likewise provide prosecutors with knowledge of the failings in the forensic testimony.[58]

Amending ethical rules and standards is a worthwhile endeavor. At the very least, prosecutors in cases like Bromgard's trial in Montana could no longer ignore the obvious unreliability of expert testimony without subjecting themselves in theory to sanctions. Indeed, for these modified ethical rules to have any impact, disciplinary agencies must express greater willingness to punish prosecutors for their indiscretions, a clarion call voiced throughout this book.

Daubert Redeemed

One way to keep unreliable science out of court—and prosecutors in check—is for judges to improve their screening of forensic evidence. Before 1993 the admission of scientific evidence hinged mainly on whether a particular discipline had gained general acceptance in the relevant scientific community. This was a boon for the forensic sciences. As long as a discipline had achieved general acceptance, it frankly did not matter whether its scientific underpinnings were untested or poorly supported. It also gave judges an out. Courts did not have to examine the underlying science with any rigor; they merely had to determine whether the discipline had achieved acceptance and then swing the door open to its admission.[59]

A 1993 Supreme Court case, *Daubert v. Merrell Dow,* appeared to usher in a new era where judges in most jurisdictions would scrutinize the reliability and relevance of any proposed scientific evidence before trial.[60] Although *Daubert* suggested that judges should consider general acceptance, the opinion indicated that this factor took a backseat to the validity of the science itself and the procedures guiding its production.[61] Only the most meritorious forensic evidence would seemingly survive this gate-keeping by the courts. This provoked renewed attacks on handwriting evidence, hair comparison, fingerprinting, and bite mark analysis.[62]

Yet the promise of *Daubert* remains unfulfilled in criminal cases. While judges appear to be circumspect in evaluating scientific evidence in civil cases in the post-*Daubert* world, a similar level of scrutiny is missing in the criminal context. Weak forensic science continues to pour, not drip, into criminal trials. This may be attributable to a number of variables, among them judicial inertia and the failure of the criminal defense bar to mount effective challenges to scientific evidence.[63] Whatever the underlying reasons, this pattern needs to end. The judiciary should serve as the ultimate safety valve, looming behind the prosecution to keep junk evidence away from the jury.

How, then, might trial judges become inspired to review forensic evidence with greater care in criminal cases? Inspiration might come from (1) educating judges about the connection between weak forensic science and wrongful convictions, and (2) offering greater assistance and resources to judges to perform the gate-keeping exercise. The time required for a judge to gain a basic grasp—much less evaluate the reliability—of intricate scientific evidence is enormous. To make this process easier, states could empower judges to appoint independent, neutral experts to educate them about complex scientific disciplines at *Daubert* hearings. Judges in some jurisdictions have the authority to do this, but they seldom take advantage of this option. Judges should be encouraged to do so.[64]

I admit that the use of independent panels of experts to assist judges is not a complete solution. For one thing, it is costly. For another, there is no assurance that any individual or group of experts will "get the science right."[65] On balance, I am not optimistic that judges will ever exercise their gate-keeping function as thoroughly as they should in criminal cases.

Given the uncertainty surrounding whether judges can rise to the task of consistently fulfilling their *Daubert* duties, it may be unwise to depend too much on the bench to filter out bad science from criminal trials. This is all the more reason to implement the changes suggested above that would occur "upstream" from the trial itself—separating crime labs from law enforcement, revamping discovery laws, and fine-tuning ethical rules and standards to ask more of prosecutors. If the science is purified upstream in the process, then there is less risk that bad science will flow down and contaminate criminal trials at the expense of innocent defendants.

Closing the Door on Innocence

Improper Summations by Prosecutors

Suppose that both the prosecution and the defense have rested in the Smith case. The evidence is in, the witnesses long gone. Only closing arguments remain. The prosecutor goes first. Rising slowly, he dons an air of solemnity befitting the occasion.

"Ladies and gentleman of the jury, the state has presented evidence proving beyond all reasonable doubt that, on the night in question, someone drank too much alcohol, got behind the wheel of a car, and killed an innocent bystander. There is no question about the identity of that person: the man sitting right there."

The prosecutor pauses, and then points at the defendant.

"First, Ms. Johnson, whom I found to be a completely unbiased and credible witness, saw this tragedy with her own two eyes. She watched the defendant dash off into the night, leaving his victim to die on a cold sidewalk.

Second, the vehicle that rammed into the bystander belonged to Mr. Smith.

Third, a breathalyzer test performed on the defendant right after the incident confirmed the presence of alcohol in his system, a fact corroborated by his neighbor, Mr. Wiley, who told us about the defendant's drunkenness that fatal night.

Fourth, we heard from a forensic scientist who compared boot prints left at the crime scene with those obtained from Mr. Smith's footwear and concluded they were a match.

Ladies and gentlemen of the jury, I implore you: if the boot fits, you cannot acquit. The streets would be far safer with this menace behind bars."

Now it is the defense attorney's chance. She emphasizes the weakness of the boot print evidence and the uncertainty of Johnson's identification. Over and over, defense counsel proclaims: "Reasonable doubt, reasonable doubt. If you have a doubt about my client's guilt that you can give a reason for, then you cannot convict." The prosecutor waives his right to rebuttal. The jurors then begin their deliberations in secret, the prosecutor's admonition—and the defense attorney's plea for mercy—ringing in their ears. Was the prosecutor's closing argument appropriate?

The Boundaries of Proper Summation by Prosecutors

Prosecutors enjoy wide latitude to comment on the evidence during summation. The rationale is that prosecutors bear the burden of proof and therefore should not be unduly constrained at the end of the proceedings in arguing the merits to the jury.[1] In some states, the defense gives its summation before the prosecution's turn.[2] But, in many jurisdictions, prosecutors present their closing argument first, followed by the defense, and then may rebut the defense attorney's summation.[3] The ability to speak both first and last during this phase is a formidable advantage, a potent one-two punch based on the psychological principles of primacy and recency.[4] By going first, prosecutors can frame the issues and anticipate the defense's arguments. This initial crack at the jury puts the defense on its heels. The chance for rebuttal allows prosecutors to inflict a knockout blow by reinforcing its themes as well as responding to unforeseen defense arguments just before the jurors go off to deliberate. Studies indicate that last words are long remembered by listeners.[5] And prosecutors can choose these last words essentially as they see fit.[6]

Yet prosecutors can abuse this freedom. Aware that jurors put tremendous stock in closing arguments, many prosecutors conclude with rhetorical flourishes that pull at the heartstrings.[7] Scholars dating back to Aristotle have warned that the most persuasive arguments often contain an appeal to emotion—and that emotionally laden rhetoric can distract people from making rational choices.[8] This risk is heightened during a prosecutor's summation. Juries may trust and respect prosecutors due to their positions as government officers. Certain tactics by prosecutors can exploit this trust and respect so as to tilt the scales of justice unfairly against the defendant. For this reason, courts and ethicists have paid special attention to prosecutorial misconduct during summations, spending decades parsing the distinction between "hard blows" versus "foul ones."[9]

Delineating the full range of prosecutorial misconduct that crops up during closing argument exceeds the scope of this chapter. Still, it is useful to highlight the "cardinal sins"[10] of summation misconduct:

- A prosecutor may not offer his personal opinion about the guilt or innocence of the defendant. This behavior invades the province of the jury. More troubling, it may imply that the prosecutor has access to information not presented at trial that substantiates guilt. A prosecutor may argue *why* a defendant is guilty but must stop short of interposing his personal belief.[11]
- A prosecutor may not assert his personal view about the credibility of a particular witness. This is known as vouching for a witness. Just as the determination of guilt or innocence is assigned to the jury, so is the assessment of credibility. When a prosecutor vouches for a witness, the statement carries the weight of his role as a government official and may give the impression that the government has knowledge about the witness that the jury has not heard. It is acceptable (and common practice) for a prosecutor to argue that certain witnesses should or should not be believed. In making that point, prosecutors should steer the jurors to objective criteria—witness demeanor, motivations to testify, and consistencies or inconsistencies in their testimony—and not to the prosecutor's own sense of the witness.[12]
- A prosecutor may not argue facts that were excluded at trial or misstate the nature of the evidence. For instance, a prosecutor may neither misquote the words offered by witnesses nor embellish the testimony introduced into evidence.[13]
- A prosecutor may commit a constitutional due process violation by engaging in inflammatory arguments geared toward rousing jury passions or prejudices. Examples include appealing to jurors' sense of patriotism, urging jurors to preserve public safety by convicting the defendant, and introducing racial or ethnic bias into the decision-making dynamic.[14]
- A constitutional violation may occur when a prosecutor comments on a criminal defendant's refusal to testify at trial. Defendants enjoy a privilege against self-incrimination under the Fifth Amendment. This means that a defendant has no obligation to testify at trial. Any reference by a prosecutor during summation to a defendant's failure to testify insinuates that the defendant has something to hide, thereby compromising the privilege and undermining his choice not to take the stand.[15]
- A prosecutor may not encroach upon a defendant's Sixth Amendment right to counsel by mocking or impugning the integrity of the defense attorney.[16]

Did the prosecutor commit any of these sins in the Smith case? It appears as though he did. The prosecutor vouched for the credibility of Johnson by saying "I found [her] to be a completely unbiased and credible witness."

Outlining the reasons why Johnson was unbiased and credible (perhaps that she had no preexisting relationship with the defendant and no reason to implicate him falsely) would have been appropriate. The prosecutor's final remark—"The streets would be far safer with this menace behind bars"—was a bald appeal to the passions of the jury. The admonition that "if the boot fits, you cannot acquit," though seemingly benign on its own,[17] likely exacerbated this paean to prejudice given that it mimics Johnny Cochran's phrase from the much maligned O. J. Simpson case. Finally, the prosecutor may have laid it on too thick in describing the forensic evidence, depending on whether the expert witness testified that the print indeed matched the sole of Smith's boot.

The Link between Summation Misconduct and Wrongful Convictions

Prosecutorial overreaching during summation is among the most common forms of error in criminal cases and has contributed to a rash of wrongful convictions.[18] Specifically, scholars have detected eighteen DNA exonerations where prosecutors exaggerated the implications of forensic scientific testimony during closing argument.[19] Here is one of them:

In August 1988 a man wearing a nylon mask demanded money from a night manager finishing her shift at a McDonald's restaurant in Duquesne, Pennsylvania. The assailant then chased her into the parking lot and shot her to death. Another McDonald's employee identified Drew Whitley as the culprit.[20]

The Whitley case went to trial based primarily on the eyewitness identification and some forensic evidence. The police had retrieved a trench coat, hat, and nylon stocking from the parking lot. A technician from the county crime lab testified at trial that the hairs found in the stocking were similar to those of Whitley but did not declare them to be a match. During closing argument, however, the prosecutor insisted that the hairs were identified as belonging to Whitley. The jury found Whitley guilty of murder. Many years later Whitley's attorney petitioned the court to have the hairs from the crime scene subjected to DNA testing. Those tests excluded Whitley as the source of the hairs, prompting the prosecution to drop all charges against him in 2006.[21]

Overstating the nature of forensic evidence is merely one of the ways in which prosecutorial tactics during summation might hurt the innocent. Prosecutors have also aided in producing wrongful convictions by advancing novel theories that were wholly unsubstantiated by the evidence presented at trial. Consider the case of Jeffrey Deskovic.[22]

On the morning of November 17, 1989, the police found fifteen-year-old Angela Correa dead in a wooded area of a park in Peekskill, New York. She had been beaten, raped, and strangled. She had last been seen alive on November 15, and the medical examiner estimated that her time of death was between 3:30 and 4:30 that afternoon. Next to her body the police found three different hairs, plus a note written from Angela to "Freddy" dated "11/15/89." Over the next two months, the police interviewed many of Angela's classmates at Peekskill High School, including Freddy Claxton, who was presumed to be the "Freddy" referred to in the note. Claxton had a solid alibi for the entire afternoon of November 15.[23]

Jeffrey Deskovic, a sixteen-year-old student at Peekskill High, did not have an alibi. He was absent from school that afternoon, and witnesses described him as strangely distraught over Correa's death; they observed him crying and attending all three of her wakes. This conduct piqued the curiosity of law enforcement, leading detectives to interview Deskovic eight times. Deskovic behaved oddly during these encounters. He even tried to assist the police by conducting his own investigation and sharing his thoughts about possible suspects.[24]

Deskovic allegedly confessed to the crime at the end of a grueling interview session in January 1990. Curled up in the fetal position under a table, Deskovic gave a bizarre account of the incident, noting that he "sometimes hears voices and they make [him do] things [he] shouldn't" and that he had "realized" he might be responsible for the crime. This interrogation was not recorded despite the availability of an audiotape recorder. The police arrested Deskovic that day. Even without any eyewitnesses or scientific evidence connecting Deskovic to the crime scene, prosecutors later filed charges against him for rape and murder.[25]

The police continued their investigation after Deskovic's arrest by subjecting the evidence collected from the crime scene to forensic tests. In March 1990, just days after the prosecution had obtained an indictment against Deskovic, the police received DNA test results on the seminal fluid from the rape kit. The results excluded Deskovic as the source. Other tests found no link between Deskovic and the hairs found next to Correa's corpse. Yet the police did not drop the case against Deskovic. And neither did Westchester County prosecutors.[26]

The case proceeded to trial. The prosecutor acknowledged the "wrinkles" posed by the biological evidence but used hard-hitting strategies to clear them up. The government advanced alternative theories of the case, vacillating between arguing that (1) Deskovic had acted with an unknown accomplice, and (2) that the semen had been supplied by a consensual sexual partner (most likely Freddy Claxton) and that jealousy had propelled Deskovic into a murderous rage. These theories did not make much sense. The accomplice theory clashed with the core hypothesis that Deskovic was an awkward loner fixated on Correa; the consensual partner story had no evidentiary support in the record. After the close of evidence, the court criticized the accomplice theory, spurring the prosecutor to withdraw his request to argue it during summation.[27]

That did not prevent the prosecution from elaborating upon its consensual partner theory, which is precisely what it did. The prosecutor argued during closing that "in all probability" Freddy Claxton was the source of the semen; the note to Freddy, in effect, was characterized as a love letter. The problem was that this hypothesis was unproven—and contradicted by the evidence:

- The prosecution had mapped out Correa's movements throughout November 15, a time line that left little room for Correa to have engaged in sexual activity. Although the prosecution hinted that Correa had had sex before the 15th and that the semen had stayed in her body, that theory seems dubious at best, especially given that it hinged on the proposition that she had not bathed in the interim.
- There was no evidence that Correa was involved in a consensual sexual relationship with *anyone* in November 1989, much less Freddy Claxton. Police interviews with Claxton, other Peekskill High School students, and Correa's family members failed to suggest that Correa was sexually active at the time.
- Even assuming that Claxton and Correa had a clandestine sexual relationship, Claxton had an alibi for November 15. From the time that school let out until well after Correa's death, Claxton and *four* friends were playing basketball.[28]

The prosecutor's summation in the Deskovic case apparently violated one of the gravest cardinal sins: the prohibition on arguing facts not presented at trial and misstating the nature of the evidence. But the prosecutor's efforts to attribute the semen to Claxton likely sounded reasonable to the jurors. In the end, the jury found Deskovic guilty of rape and murder, and his conviction was affirmed on appeal.[29]

Deskovic maintained his innocence from his prison cell. Prosecutors ignored his pleas to run the DNA samples through state and federal databases to check for the true perpetrator. Only in 2006 did his luck change. The Innocence Project accepted his case that year and persuaded Janet

DiFiore, the newly elected chief prosecutor in Westchester County, to conduct the requisite DNA tests. Tests performed on the semen from the Correa rape kit produced a match to the biological profile of Steven Cunningham, a convicted murderer imprisoned for strangling a woman to death. When confronted with this evidence, Cunningham confessed to raping and killing Correa by himself.[30]

The First Deputy District Attorney for Westchester County sought to dismiss the case against Deskovic in November 2006 on the grounds of actual innocence. She apologized to Deskovic on behalf of her office and the Peekskill Police Department. The court expressed remorse as well. Those apologies, even if heartfelt, could not turn the clock back to 1989. By the time the court overturned his conviction, Deskovic was thirty-three years old. He had spent half his life in prison for a brutal crime he did not commit owing in part to the trial prosecutor's behavior during closing argument.[31]

Explanations for the Prevalence of Prosecutorial Misconduct during Summation

Why might a well-meaning trial prosecutor strike foul blows during closing argument? The cognitive biases that infect prosecutorial decision making throughout the pretrial and trial stages of a criminal case come to a head in summation. By closing argument, a prosecutor consumed by tunnel vision has a conviction within sight. A conviction not only validates the initial decision to pursue the case and expend scarce resources but also boosts a trial prosecutor's standing in the office.[32] With the end of the case so near at hand, and having already devoted one's heart and soul to the adversary process, the temptation for prosecutors to overdo it during closing argument—to be "spectacular" in the words of the legal scholar Roscoe Pound—is almost irresistible.[33] A time-honored axiom is that spectacular performances by prosecutors during summation have greater sway with jurors than more measured approaches. Sadly an element of truth lies in this belief. One study from the 1970s concluded that prosecutors who were "rude, ungrammatical, tough and direct" had higher conviction rates than peers who shunned such behavior.[34] Yet these psychological, institutional, and practical factors do not tell the full story. Courts and disciplinary agencies deserve some of the blame, too.

Courts have long bemoaned the high rate of prosecutorial misconduct during summation. Nearly every state and federal appellate court at some point has denounced the "disturbing frequency" and "unheeded condemnations" of flagrant misbehavior in closing argument.[35] These reprimands, however, have not translated into action. Many judges instead have shown compassion for prosecutors who engaged in overzealous behavior. In 1897 the U.S. Supreme Court acknowledged that "in the heat of argument" attorneys occasionally get "carried away." If every such remark resulted in a reversal, the Court went on, "comparatively few verdicts would stand."[36] The New Jersey Supreme Court struck a similarly conciliatory chord over a century later: "criminal trials are emotionally charged proceedings. A prosecutor is not expected to conduct himself in a manner appropriate to a lecture hall."[37]

Judicial ambivalence toward summation misconduct manifests itself in case outcomes. Appellate courts may chastise prosecutors for errors during closing argument but seldom reverse those cases because of the "harmless error doctrine." Under this doctrine, an error from a criminal trial only yields a reversal of the conviction if the mistake was not harmless.[38] Put differently, proving that an error occurred at trial is usually not enough to trigger reversal on appeal. That error must have affected the result. If the evidence of guilt presented at trial was strong, it is doubtful a court will overturn a conviction based on misconduct during summation.[39]

The harmless error doctrine rests on the idea that guilty defendants should not receive new trials due to minor blunders. And it has served that purpose. Empirical studies show that in the overwhelming majority of criminal cases where appellate courts find a trial error, that error is characterized as harmless.[40]

While the harmless error doctrine has succeeded in depriving the guilty of new trials, it has also kept the innocent in prison. A 2010 study released by the Innocence Project reported that in 65 of the first 255 DNA exonerations in the United States, the defendants had claimed prosecutorial misconduct during the appeal of the conviction or a civil suit.[41] Relying on harmless error analysis, courts reversed convictions in only 12 of the 31 cases in which they acknowledged the existence of prosecutorial misconduct.[42] The Innocence Project's study suggests that courts are particularly stingy when it comes to claims of summation misconduct. The report cited 45 DNA exonerations where the defendants had raised "improper argument" as an issue.[43] Courts found error in more than half those cases but deemed the error not harmless in just 4 of them.[44] Although the report did not identify which of these cases involved improper *closing* argument in particular, a look at the underlying data reveals that inmates alleged summation errors in at least 22 cases; none of those allegations resulted in appellate reversal.[45] These statistics send a dangerous signal. Prosecutors can play fast and loose with the rules during closing argument, because the chance of reversal on appeal is so small.

The chance of personal and professional shame is equally small. As noted in chapter 1, appellate court decisions that discuss instances of prosecutorial misconduct hardly ever refer to the individual attorney by name.[46] Professor Paul Spiegelman studied forty-five federal court opinions over a ten-year period in which a conviction was overturned and improper prosecutorial summation was a key ground for the decision. Judicial opinions mentioned the prosecutor's name in only six of those cases.[47] Other data support Spiegelman's findings. California state appellate courts identified the prosecutor in approximately 10 percent of 707 cases from 1997 to 2009 in which they found misconduct.[48] This courtesy may be extended to prosecutors because of their role as quasi-judicial officers; judges do not want to discourage attorneys from taking on this public-service function. A more distressing explanation is that many judges are former prosecutors who empathize with the demands of that occupation and cut their brethren some slack.[49] Whatever the reason, the reluctance of courts to disclose the names of prosecutors who engage in misconduct—especially when combined with the harmless error doctrine—makes the judiciary a meager check on prosecutors inclined to overreach during closing argument.[50]

Ethical rules also provide little deterrent. The Model Rules of Professional Conduct offer no real direction to prosecutors. Rule 3.4 generally advises that,

> [a] lawyer shall not . . . in trial, allude to any matter that the lawyer does not reasonably believe is relevant or that will not be supported by admissible evidence, assert personal knowledge of facts in issue except when testifying as a witness, or state a personal opinion as to the justness of a cause, the credibility of a witness, the culpability of a civil litigant or the guilt or innocence of an accused.[51]

The American Bar Association (ABA)'s Standards of Criminal Justice add further warnings, proclaiming that criminal law practitioners "should not make arguments calculated to appeal to the prejudices of the jury" and "should refrain from argument which would divert the jury from its duty to decide the case on the evidence."[52] The Commentary to the ABA Standards, moreover, notes that,

> prosecutorial conduct in argument is a matter of special concern because of the possibility that the jury will give special weight to the prosecutor's arguments, not only because of the prestige associated with the prosecutor's office, but also because of the fact-finding facilities presumably available to the office.[53]

Singling out prosecutorial conduct in argument as a matter of special concern is admirable. Nevertheless, the Commentary gives only "broad guidelines" about summation misconduct by prosecutors, and prefaces its discussion by observing that "to attempt to spell out in detail what can and cannot be said in argument is impossible since it will depend largely on the facts of each case."[54] Without defining the contours of what is permissible, the Model Rules and ABA Standards fail to offer much practical guidance to prosecutors—or ethics boards.[55]

Confronting the Problem of Improper Closing Arguments

Many of the reforms proposed in previous chapters concerning prosecutorial self-regulation might reduce the rate of misconduct during closing arguments. Chief prosecutors should:

- Provide training about what constitutes a "foul blow" during summation.
- Change the office incentive structure to counter the conviction psychology.
- Boost supervision of junior prosecutors in their first few trials.
- Create review committees to serve as sounding boards for prosecutors to present dry runs of proposed closings.
- Develop and enforce a sliding scale of sanctions for summation misconduct.

These proposals could help. Forgive me, however, for echoing an oft-repeated refrain: self-regulation alone is inadequate. Some prosecutors will get caught up in the emotionally charged final stage of a trial regardless of training, supervision, and office review. Even the prospect of internal discipline may not dampen the ardor of a zealous prosecutor bent on "winning," vindicating what he perceives to be the best interest of the victim, and polishing his credentials as a skillful advocate. Better self-regulation of prosecutorial closing arguments, then, must come equipped with better external regulation.

Monitoring by Trial Courts

Trial courts could more effectively monitor summation errors by prosecutors as they occur. Judges could intervene during closings more often (even without an objection) to stop improper argument at the point of inception, and then instruct the jury to disregard the offensive comments. As a follow-up, trial judges could refer the errant prosecutor to local disciplinary boards. And for the most egregious of prosecutorial errors, there is always the option of granting a mistrial.[56]

Although calls for trial judges to better police the summation process have merit, they seem unrealistic in practice. Keep in mind the leeway afforded to litigants during closing argument. An offshoot of this leeway is that judges are wary of interrupting summation. In fact, attorneys themselves are reluctant to interfere with an adversary's closing argument by raising an objection; many lawyers worry that the jury might perceive these efforts as intrusive.[57] Moreover, by the end of a criminal trial, judges have a stake in seeing it through to its expected end. Just as sports referees hesitate to call penalties in the waning minutes of close games—preferring to let the combatants' talents dictate the result—trial judges are also loath to meddle in summations.

Harmless Error Reconsidered

Far removed from the hubbub of trial, appellate courts are theoretically well positioned to address the problem of summation misconduct. Appellate judges could reverse any conviction tainted by improper closing argument tactics, publicly reprimand the offending lawyer, and even report that attorney to the ethics board. In truth, appellate courts fare poorly in restraining prosecutorial excesses during closing arguments because of the harmless error doctrine. Canvassing the case law on summation errors reveals not just widespread misconduct but a large amount of recidivism. The same prosecutors and the same offices are committing the same kinds of trial misconduct despite repeated scoldings in judicial opinions.[58]

A federal appeals court cited the U.S. Attorney's Office for the District of Puerto Rico twenty-four times for improper closing argument between 1987 and 1998. The court used an array of methods to communicate its displeasure. These ranged from criticizing the behavior in the particular case; warning the individual prosecutor involved; condemning supervisors for providing lackluster oversight; and suggesting discipline of the offending prosecutor.[59] Yet constrained by the harmless error doctrine, the court overturned these convictions only three times, the last of which occurred in 1993.[60] The continuation of misconduct after 1993 suggests that federal trial prosecutors in Puerto Rico were not deterred by the threat of reversal.[61]

This tale of the U.S. Attorney's Office in Puerto Rico shows the failings of the harmless error doctrine when applied to closing argument. Inflammatory appeals to passion, misstatements of the evidence, and other foul blows by prosecutors can profoundly affect the jury because they carry the imprimatur of government approval.[62] Given the peculiarities of the harmless error doctrine, however, those errors are discounted on appeal. Their impact is not calculated in isolation but in relation to the evidence as a whole. This strikes me as a fool's errand.[63] How can a court properly assess in hindsight whether the evidence in a particular case was overwhelming? The New York appellate court that reviewed Jeffrey Deskovic's case in 1994 refused to overturn his conviction in spite of a series of purported errors. It unanimously concluded that the evidence against him was "overwhelming."[64] History has proven that characterization of the Deskovic prosecution frighteningly wrong.

More to the point, how can an appellate court insert itself into the jury box and evaluate the harm caused by prosecutorial misconduct during closing argument, the heated culmination of any trial? The harmless error rule places appellate judges in the untenable position of combing through the black–and-white words of the trial transcript to make their own judgment about the effect of colorful summation missteps on the jury. The emotional impact of prosecutorial overreaching during closing argument is tough to gauge at the moment it happens, let alone on appeal when judges are removed in time and place from the event.

The bottom line is that appellate courts should consider abandoning harmless error analysis in the summation context.[65] To achieve this, courts or legislatures could craft a narrow exception to harmless error for summation misconduct. Making the threat of reversal real, more than anything else, might inhibit some trial prosecutors from doling out foul blows during closing argument. A reversal ordering a new trial erases a "win," reopens the wounds of victims, and adds to the office's workload. Retrials are burdensome for prosecutors. Memories fade, evidence vanishes, and defendants hone defenses. This proposal would decrease the rate of prosecutorial misconduct during closing arguments and protect innocent defendants in cases where the evidence may appear overwhelming in hindsight.

But my suggestion could also backfire. Troubled about granting new trials to guilty defendants, appellate judges who are unable to apply harm analysis to summation errors could simply become tightfisted in characterizing conduct as an error. Instead of the harmless error doctrine keeping convictions in place, a stricter vision of what comprises *error* at all would reach the same result. There are political obstacles, too, especially if this reform were pursued through legislative channels. Prosecutors and crime victims' groups would come out in droves to lobby against any proposal to make summation errors exempt from harm analysis, and they would likely find receptive audiences in state legislatures across the country.

Perhaps a compromise proposal is in order: sparing only egregious errors during closing argument from harm analysis.[66] This might appease judges unsettled by the thought of giving the guilty new trials because of borderline prosecutorial misconduct. Although defining and cataloguing egregious summation errors would not be a walk in the park for the appellate bench, it seems more pleasant an exercise than applying harmless error review to each and every summation mistake. Even more, it could arrive at the optimal balance between deterring prosecutorial misconduct and burdening the court system with new trials.

The key question is whether exempting summation from harmless error review in any way is worth the price. Even if only egregious errors were exempt from harm analysis, many guilty defendants would still receive new trials; a percentage of them would be acquitted on retrial or not face a new trial at all. Some might find this unfair. I do not. Slowing the flood of summation errors by prosecutors requires bold remedies, the construction of doctrinal levees of atypical sturdiness. If that means some guilty defendants benefit from an exception to harmless error, so be it. In the long run it will protect us all—from prosecutors who overreach, from wrongful convictions, and from the deterioration of the rule of law caused by government contempt for fair play.

Shaming by Naming

One reform far less drastic than ditching harmless error review would be to identify individual prosecutors in cases where summation misconduct occurred. This might affect prosecutors who are motivated primarily by the status of their reputations in the legal community. Not every prosecutor anticipates a long-term career in a district attorney's office.[67] Many hope to migrate into a criminal defense firm or a plum post on the judicial bench, dreams that could be waylaid by public awareness of unethical behavior. By denouncing prosecutors who engage in summation misconduct, appellate courts can dissuade those violators from re-offending and colleagues from going down that ill-fated road. Not incidentally, naming errant prosecutors in appellate decisions might provoke some disciplinary agencies to launch inquiries into the misconduct.[68]

Getting appellate courts to do this is no easy feat. Not only do many judges happen to be former prosecutors, but lawyers also generally shudder at the idea of raking fellow attorneys over the coals. I doubt judges will suddenly call out misbehaving prosecutors in their opinions without any incentive or legislative requirement to do so. In light of this reality, Professor Adam Gershowitz suggests forming "Prosecutorial Misconduct Projects" in which law students would scour appellate opinions where judges found prosecutorial misconduct but refrained from naming the offender.[69] The students would then locate the trial transcripts from those cases to pinpoint the prosecutors involved; if the trial transcripts proved beyond their reach, the students could submit open records requests to gather the information. The students would periodically publish a list of wrongdoers with recidivists highlighted.[70]

Like investigative journalists, students in these clinics could increase the flow of public information about summation misconduct. This greater information flow could drive individual prosecutors to think twice before leveling foul blows during closing argument. Whether students are up to this is unclear. Even if they are not, these projects are worth a try because the parties in the best position to perform this task—judges—appear unwilling to take it on.

Ethics Reform

The remedies mentioned above might prevent many prosecutors from overreaching during closing argument. But some prosecutors seem blind to the threat of reversal or public shame. For those outliers, disciplinary action may be the only way to halt their pattern of improper closings.

Think about the career of former Oklahoma prosecutor Robert "Cowboy Bob" Macy. Macy served as chief district attorney for more than twenty years in a part of the state that included Oklahoma City. His office amassed a record number of capital murder convictions during his reign; he personally served as lead prosecutor in fifty-four of them. Early in Macy's tenure, the Oklahoma Court of Criminal Appeals cited him repeatedly for misconduct during summation. Macy often ended his signature "fire and brimstone" closing arguments by collapsing into tears in front of the jury box. In reaction to those occasions where the appellate court found his theatrics to be reversible error, Macy battled back by waging campaigns to unseat appellate judges whose appointments were subject to retention elections. Even after several scandals erupted in Oklahoma City—including the DNA exoneration of one of the men Macy had put on death row—Macy emerged largely unscathed. He rode off into the sunset of early retirement.[71]

Severe discipline, like suspension or disbarment, might be the best bet to keep some overzealous prosecutors in line. To make serious sanctions viable, however, legal ethics must first provide better guidance to disciplinary agencies. The ABA's Task Force to Revise the Standards for Criminal Justice has set out to do this. I am involved with evaluating potential changes to the ABA Standards on closing argument.[72] The revisions making the rounds ask more of prosecutors than the existing guidelines. Instead of the general warnings contained in the present version,[73] the proposed revisions demand that "the prosecutor should not imply special or secret knowledge of the truth or witness credibility, or argue in terms of the prosecutor's personal opinion."[74] The revisions also clarify that "the prosecutor should make only those arguments that are consistent with the jury's duty to decide the case on the evidence, and should not seek to divert the jury from that duty by *ad hominem* disparagement or appeals to improper bias or extreme emotion."[75] This would ban emotional outbursts like Cowboy Bob Macy's fits of tears in far more certain terms than the language of the comparable provision in the current Standards.[76] Additionally, the proposed revisions give precise direction on the tactics that prosecutors may deploy during rebuttal, advice that has been missing from previous iterations.[77] I hope the final amendments to the ABA Standards retain the sharp edge needed to cut down on misconduct.

Changing the Sequence of Closing Arguments

The presumption of innocence is a venerable feature of our criminal justice landscape. It explains why criminal defendants receive the bulk of advantages at trial—why the prosecution bears the burden of proof, the defendant has the right to remain silent, and jurors must unanimously find the defendant guilty. Why, then, does the prosecution get to go both first *and* last during summation in many jurisdictions? Even if the fact that prosecutors must prove the defendant guilty beyond a reasonable doubt warrants placing them first in the sequence of summations to frame the debate, what about the justification for giving them the last word, too?[78]

The main reason for giving rebuttal to prosecutors again relates to the burden of proof. Since prosecutors must shoulder this burden, so the argument goes, they should be able to resurrect their position where the defense presents novel or unfounded arguments. True, but does this structure best suit the presumption of innocence? Professor John Mitchell thinks it does not: "this chance for the last words, words to which the defense attorney can not respond, would thus seem to have the capacity of altering juror opinions between a verdict of guilty and not guilty, in at least some cases."[79] According to Mitchell, "permitting a citizen's fate to possibly be determined by the order of arguments is not a risk our legal system should willingly take, particularly not with its unwavering, though at times more or less diluted, ideological commitment to the protection of the innocent."[80] Mitchell recommends ending with the defense summation. Two arguments, prosecution followed by defense.[81] This is a provocative recipe for closing arguments. At least it is food for thought.

As an alternative to Mitchell's proposal, the summation sequence in many states could remain intact with only a slight tweak. Instead of barring the prosecution from rebuttal, the defense could have the right to ask permission to respond to that argument—to "rebut the rebuttal"—when the defense thinks the prosecutor has gone overboard. The ABA's Task Force to Revise the Standards for Criminal Justice has endorsed this compromise.[82]

A broad range of prosecutorial behavior at trial can lead to the conviction of the innocent. The manner in which prosecutors prepare and examine witnesses can offer jurors a distorted image of the case. A prosecutor's decision to introduce dubious forensic evidence at trial can unduly influence the fact finder given the mystique associated with science. And the use of certain techniques during summation by prosecutors—appeals to emotion, witness vouching, and misstatements of the record—can sway an uncertain jury toward conviction.

Yet a guilty verdict is not the end of the road for the innocent. The postconviction process provides an opportunity for the criminal justice system to correct its errors and for prosecutors to look anew at old cases. Despite this opportunity, prosecutors who encounter post-conviction claims of innocence do not always respond in a fashion that fulfills the minister-of-justice ideal.

PART III

The Fallacy of Finality

Prosecutors and Post-Conviction Claims of Innocence

Commonwealth of Pennsylvania v. Bruce Donald Godschalk

On the night of July 13, 1986, an intruder slipped into a townhouse in an apartment complex outside Philadelphia and raped the occupant. Less than two months later, a man gained entry to an apartment in the very same complex and raped another woman. The modus operandi appeared similar in the two crimes, as did the victims' descriptions of the perpetrator: a 5-foot, 10-inch white male with a medium build. Medical examinations of each victim revealed the presence of semen. DNA technology had not yet made inroads into the criminal justice system, which meant that investigators subjected the semen only to serology tests. The blood type of the second victim's assailant could not be determined, but the crime lab concluded that the first victim's attacker had Type B blood.

Proceeding under the assumption that the same perpetrator had committed both assaults, the police prepared a composite sketch based on the victims' recollections. A woman in the community alerted the police several months later that the sketch resembled her brother, Bruce Godschalk.[1] The police put a picture of Godschalk in a photo array in January 1987. Having previously observed two photo arrays, the second victim looked at this new set of pictures and identified Godschalk as her attacker. The first victim was unable to identify anyone. The police decided to question Godschalk in light of the second victim's identification (and the fact that Godschalk's physical attributes matched the initial descriptions). Godschalk confessed to the crime at the end of the interrogation. According to the police, his statement contained facts that had not been disseminated to the public and that only the rapist would know.[2]

Montgomery County prosecutors presented a strong case at trial. In addition to the second victim's eyewitness identification testimony, the confession, and the factual similarities of the assaults, the state introduced two other key items of evidence. An informant testified that Godschalk had confessed to the rapes while they were incarcerated together in the local jail.[3] And the pièce de résistance came in the form of forensic evidence—the first victim's assailant had Type B blood and so did Godschalk.[4]

Godschalk faced an uphill climb at trial. He had previously recanted his confession, and he took the stand to explain himself. He claimed that the detectives had duped him into admitting the crime, supplying him with specifics of the assaults before turning on the tape recorder and documenting just the last few minutes of the session. The defense also argued that Godschalk had alibis at the times of the incidents. These efforts did not impress the jury, which convicted Godschalk of both crimes in 1987.[5]

Godschalk lost the appeal of his convictions and began a frustrating trek through the post-conviction process. In 1995 he filed a petition under a Pennsylvania statute that gave convicted defendants a limited right to DNA testing of previously untested evidence. Pennsylvania state courts denied the petition on the basis that the prosecution's case at trial was overwhelming. Godschalk then turned to the Innocence Project.[6]

The Innocence Project focused on gaining access to the biological evidence from the crime scenes.[7] Stymied by the Pennsylvania state courts, lawyers affiliated with the Innocence Project shifted their attention to the federal system. They filed a civil rights action in 2000 under a theory that denying access to the biological evidence violated Godschalk's constitutional right to due process, never mind that this theory had not made much headway with federal judges. The legal team's hubris paid off. A federal trial court in Pennsylvania ruled that the duty to disclose potentially exculpatory evidence under *Brady v. Maryland*[8] extended to the post-conviction phase and ordered the state to comply with the Innocence Project's request for the remaining semen samples.[9]

Compliance with the federal court's order was not high on the prosecutors' agenda. Although they agreed to relinquish the evidence, prosecutors balked at actually establishing a testing protocol and delivering the evidence. This compelled the Innocence Project to institute another federal action, this time filing a motion for summary judgment on the merits of Godschalk's innocence claim because of the prosecutors' failure to fulfill the dictates of the court order. In response, the prosecutors admitted that they had sent the evidence to a lab for testing without the Innocence Project's knowledge. Worse yet, the prosecutors reported that the evidence had been *entirely consumed* in this testing process without yielding any results.[10]

Bent, but not broken, the Innocence Project challenged the prosecution's claim that it had sent all the relevant biological evidence for testing. The dispute centered on a semen-stained carpet sample from the first victim's apartment that prosecutors had not submitted for testing. The district attorney's office contended that the carpet was insignificant to the case. The Innocence Project took issue with this characterization, because the state had used the carpet sample to tie Godschalk to the first victim who, after all, had been unable to identify him. It also appeared as if some biological evidence from the second crime scene remained. At last, under judicial supervision, the parties divvied up the leftover biological evidence for testing at laboratories of their choice. The results were startling. Each laboratory confirmed that a single male had perpetrated the crimes but that Bruce Godschalk was *not* that man.[11]

Prosecutors reacted with disbelief. Faced with the reality that its own lab tests had excluded Godschalk as the source of the semen, the Montgomery County District Attorney's Office insisted nonetheless that he was guilty and that the tests were flawed. The prosecution refused to discharge him from prison at first. Finally, Godschalk walked out of prison a free man on Valentine's Day in 2002. He had lived behind bars for fifteen years—seven of them spent wrangling for access to the biological evidence from his case. During Godschalk's incarceration, his sister, mother, and father all died.[12]

The Pennsylvania prosecutors' approach to Godschalk's post-conviction innocence claim greatly prolonged his agony. Godschalk might have spent roughly half as much time in prison had prosecutors agreed to submit the biological evidence to DNA testing in 1995 and not forced the defense to exhaust virtually every avenue in state and federal court to get it. The Godschalk experience reflects an alarming pattern of prosecutors responding defensively when confronted with post-conviction innocence claims. The next three chapters explore this phenomenon and prescribe a series of remedies to counter it.

Prosecutorial Resistance to Post-Conviction Claims of Innocence

Assume that twelve jurors decamp for the deliberation room in the Smith drunk-driving case. They return a short while later with a guilty verdict on the charges of manslaughter and DWI. The judge sentences Smith to twelve years' imprisonment. Smith is transferred from the county lockup to a state correctional facility in a far-flung corner of the state.

His appeal from his conviction is denied, as is a federal habeas corpus petition that another inmate—a prolific "jailhouse lawyer"—files on Smith's behalf in exchange for part of his commissary account. Smith grows despondent. One day, out of the blue, his cellmate tells him about a new clinic at a nearby law school where students and faculty work together to investigate post-conviction claims of innocence. Smith writes to the budding innocence project describing his predicament. The letter gathers dust before a student screens the case and decides it is worthy of a second look. She pitches the case to the rest of the class; her colleagues vote to conduct an investigation. Game on.

A team of two students begins by pursuing the "paper trail," collecting and reading every document associated with the case. As part of this process, the students figure out which items they still need to locate through government open records act requests. Once they are acquainted with the case, the students hit the streets on the "people trail" to interview key witnesses.[1] In Smith's case that means chatting with the neighbor, Wiley, and the eyewitness, Johnson.

They head to Wiley's building. Much to their surprise, Wiley has moved into Smith's more palatial apartment. Wiley opens the door a crack, but slams it shut upon learning the reason for the students' visit. The students come back the next day—and the following day and the one after that until, worn down by the tenacity of these students, Wiley relents. Over the course of the morning he admits he has something to tell them. He has never liked Smith, what with his binge drinking and boisterous singing, and has always coveted Smith's apartment. Though he is unsure whether Smith was home throughout the evening of the accident, he is certain about this: earlier that day he saw a local thug named Allen steal Smith's car. According to Wiley, Allen looks a lot like Smith. The students ask Wiley to sign an affidavit repeating this information. He shakes his head, slamming the door in their faces for good measure. They return several times, only to have their overtures denied. One of the students writes a memorandum about the encounter with Wiley and places it in the file.

Ecstatic about the newfound information, the students do a computer search to determine Allen's whereabouts. They learn that he is incarcerated for an unrelated, but intriguing, felony: grand theft of an automobile. Allen refuses to meet with them or even reply to their letters. The students track down Allen's arrest photo and compile a crude array containing pictures of Allen and Smith as well as those of four law school alumni who appear to be around the same age and race. Next stop: Johnson's home.

Johnson lives in a hospice specializing in elder care. In her feeble state, she initially fails to recall the drunk-driving accident. But then, in a burst of clarity, she claims to remember it. When shown the photo array, she points to Allen's picture and says "That's him." The students ask her to sign an affidavit to that effect, which she does in the presence of a notary public.

The students are at a crossroads. They could go down the perilous path of post-conviction litigation by filing a petition in state court based on newly discovered evidence of innocence. Alternatively, they could see if prosecutors are willing to take the high road and reinvestigate the case themselves or, better yet, submit a joint petition requesting an evidentiary hearing. This is not a clear-cut claim of innocence. Wiley has declined to sign an affidavit; Johnson does not possess her full faculties. The students and their supervisor choose to set up a meeting with the prosecutors' office. How should the prosecution respond?

Prosecutors committed to the minister-of-justice ideal *should* respond favorably—not by capitulating and asking the court to release Smith at once but by expressing openness to the possibility that Smith is innocent, maybe by offering to reinvestigate the case, maybe by joining a motion for a hearing. Although only judges normally have the legal authority to order an inmate's release, a prosecutor's openness to an innocence claim is vital to ensuring a full-fledged airing in court because of long-standing judicial and legislative concerns about reexamining old cases.[2]

Procedural Hurdles in Litigating Innocence Claims

Newspaper headlines notwithstanding, the vast majority of post-conviction innocence claims do not rely on DNA testing. Biological evidence exists in only a small percentage of criminal cases.[3] Most prisoners therefore must resort to more subjective, non-DNA evidence to prove their innocence. That evidence often consists of statements by new witnesses, confessions by the actual perpetrator, or recantations by trial participants. For defendants, compiling this evidence is burdensome. Convincing courts to take it seriously is just as taxing. After the conviction of a criminal defendant, it becomes increasingly difficult for the defense to get courts to examine the accuracy of that outcome without the prosecution's help.[4] Here are the customary procedures that state prisoners use after trial to prove their innocence:

- Defendants may file a motion for a new trial in the immediate aftermath of a conviction. Although these motions typically allow for the presentation of new evidence, they have stringent time restrictions. Chances are remote that a defendant can cobble together enough newly discovered evidence to prove his innocence before the clock runs out on a new trial motion.[5]
- Defendants may (and invariably do) appeal their conviction in a procedure called the "direct appeal," but the issues that courts review at this stage are limited. For the most part, appellate courts only consider issues and evidence previously presented to the trial judge, not anything new, during the direct appeal.[6]
- Limitations on direct appeals and new trial motions put many defendants at the mercy of state post-conviction procedures, such as writs of habeas corpus or their statutory analogues. These are not direct attacks on the judgment but rather indirect or "collateral" challenges where petitioners are entitled to introduce issues and evidence never heard before. These remedies vary depending on the jurisdiction. Even though every state permits the presentation of newly discovered evidence through some sort of collateral procedure, legislators and judges are notoriously skeptical of these claims. The post-conviction process reflects this skepticism through rigid statutes of limitations, onerous burdens of proof for defendants, and deferential standards of review for judicial decisions denying petitions.[7] In Texas, for example, defendants must prove that the newly discovered evidence "unquestionably" establishes innocence.[8]

- When defendants with innocence claims fail to obtain recourse from state courts, they can seek habeas corpus relief from the federal system. The U.S. Supreme Court has held, however, that a claim of factual innocence based on newly discovered evidence by itself is generally an insufficient ground for federal habeas corpus relief.[9]
- Assuming that legal action in state and federal courts proves futile, innocent prisoners may pursue other routes to freedom through the parole or clemency process. Yet the executive agencies entrusted with those decisions are not in the business of reexamining facts; they are concerned, instead, with whether inmates will re-offend. Parole boards tend to hold inmate assertions of innocence *against* them in the decision-making calculus, viewing these claims as evidence of psychological denial that does not bode well for obeying the law out on the streets.[10] With some exceptions, officials responsible for clemency decisions also keep their distance from the murky zone of guilt and innocence. Clemency boards and governors prefer to pardon inmates who have been model prisoners or whose personal circumstances otherwise warrant this act of grace.[11]

All told, the post-conviction road to freedom is strewn with procedural potholes. A crucial factor in a defendant's ability to make any progress with a post-conviction innocence claim is the nature of the prosecution's reaction. Prosecutorial resistance to an innocence claim can serve the death knell to a case or at least make the process infinitely more painful for the defendant.[12]

What prosecutors should do—be receptive to the possibility of a wrongful conviction—is different from what they often do. To be fair, many prosecutors respond admirably to post-conviction innocence claims. Some even take proactive steps to rectify wrongful convictions in their jurisdictions.[13] But prosecutors do not always adhere to the minister-of-justice ethos in the post-conviction arena when faced with evidence of innocence; on the contrary, many prosecutors fight these claims tooth-and-nail.[14] In post-conviction cases involving *Brady* violations, for instance, prosecutors occasionally try to stop the broadcasting of these claims in open court. One popular tactic is to argue that defendants failed to develop or "exhaust" their *Brady* claims in the lower courts when the reason for that failure stemmed from the state's refusal to disclose the exculpatory information at the outset.[15] Another common situation is where prosecutors, coping with a potential wrongful conviction, hatch revised theories of the case that bear slight resemblance to the stance at trial to justify the continued incarceration of a defendant.[16] Why do some prosecutors respond this way?

Post-Conviction Innocence Claims and the American Prosecutor

No doubt many factors lead some prosecutors to react with cynicism, even irrationality, to post-conviction pleas of innocence. Let's now turn to the main explanations: (1) cognitive biases; (2) resource constraints; (3) concerns for finality; (4) political realities; and (5) the lack of firm ethical obligations.[17]

Cognitive Bias

As a threshold matter, prosecutors face a needle-in-a-haystack dilemma. The deluge of post-conviction petitions filed by inmates each year contains only a few meritorious claims. This imbalance between the frivolous and the legitimate makes it easy for prosecutors to feel contempt for innocence claims overall. It also creates a disincentive to review each claim thoroughly.[18] Having nurtured reputations as strong crime fighters, many prosecutors wish to avoid being "taken for a ride" or "played for a fool."[19] This wariness often translates into distrust of any inmate's cry of innocence. The last thing prosecutors want is to encourage prisoners to bury them with marginal innocence claims.[20]

The literature on cognitive bias offers additional insights into prosecutorial resistance to innocence claims. The confirmation bias refers to people's tendency to seek out and value information that confirms, rather than rejects, their initial hypotheses.[21] This bias thrives in the post-conviction context. An external actor, usually a jury, has validated the prosecutor's initial theory of the case through a guilty verdict. That theory is further validated when a court upholds the conviction on direct appeal. At this point a branch of the confirmation bias known as the status quo bias takes root. Once a decision has earned corroboration from external actors, it requires a significant amount of contrary data to push the original stakeholders in that decision (prosecutors, victims, and trial judges) away from that reference point. As new information surfaces over time, these stakeholders tend to selectively process it by overvaluing data supportive of the status quo and discounting findings that defy it.[22] In short, the presumption of guilt becomes "stickier" for prosecutors after conviction.[23]

The status quo bias affects many prosecutors who handle post-conviction innocence claims. In most states these claims are assigned to the prosecutors' office in the city or county where the conviction was obtained. Information about how these offices administer the review of post-conviction innocence claims is hard to come by. It appears that many smaller offices assign these petitions to the lawyer who handled the trial: the person who has the greatest familiarity with the case and is in the best position to get up to speed. Some larger offices allocate innocence petitions to the original trial attorney as well, but many assign them to other lawyers on staff. Where post-conviction petitions are assigned to the very prosecutor who tried the case, the influence of the status quo bias is pronounced. People are especially reluctant to second-guess their *own* choices.[24]

The status quo bias persists even when innocence claims are dished out to prosecutors who had nothing to do with the case at trial. Studies show that people within the same organization tend to respect the decisions of their colleagues because of the power of "conformity effects," a wish to act in line with a peer.[25] Conformity effects are enhanced where that peer had access to greater information at the time of the preceding decision, as is the norm when a post-conviction litigator reviews the work of a trial attorney who interacted with witnesses and the police closer in time to the incident. That trial lawyer had a hands-on experience with the case far removed from the post-conviction litigator's detached perspective years down the line. The pressure to conform can prompt post-conviction litigators to defer to their predecessors or view the new evidence with a jaundiced eye.[26]

One's natural aversion to cognitive dissonance—the uncomfortable realization that one's conduct does not reflect one's noble self-image—also comes into play. Convicting an innocent person clashes with an ethical prosecutor's belief that charges should only be filed against the guilty and that his office would never do otherwise. To avoid cognitive dissonance, prosecutors may cling to the original theory of guilt in order to harmonize their beliefs with their actions. One reason, then, why some prosecutors seem indifferent to wrongful convictions is not heartlessness; they just cannot bring themselves to confront the possibility that they or their office played a role in convicting an innocent defendant. The cognitive stress is too much to bear.[27]

A post-conviction prosecutor may face professional consequences should she go against the grain and show receptivity to an innocence claim. A well-known New York case illustrates this problem. Two prisoners convicted of murder presented newly discovered evidence that cast doubt about their involvement in the shooting of a bouncer at the Palladium nightclub in Manhattan in 1990. An informant had acknowledged that he and a fellow gang member, not the two men convicted of the crime, had slain the bouncer. The New York County District Attorney's Office assigned the post-conviction matter to veteran prosecutor Daniel Bibb. Bibb and two detectives crisscrossed the country, ferreting out new witnesses and conducting more than fifty interviews. Bibb became convinced that the inmates were innocent. His bosses disagreed; they ordered him to articulate the office's position at an evidentiary hearing.[28]

This put Bibb in a conundrum. What he probably should have done was ask to be reassigned. Instead, he participated in the hearing and surreptitiously helped the defense, even going so far as to locate the defense witnesses. Toward the end of the hearing, Bibb persuaded his supervisors to drop the charges against one of the men, Olmedo Hidalgo. But higher-ups continued to dispute the innocence of the other inmate, David Lemus. A state court judge ultimately found in favor of Lemus, granting him a new trial in 2005. That retrial culminated in an acquittal in 2007. Hidalgo and Lemus proceeded to sue New York City for wrongful imprisonment and negotiated settlements in excess of $1 million apiece.[29]

Later, in explaining his behavior, Bibb claimed he had a duty to do justice and that he feared his replacement would have pursued the case more vigorously. Whatever the merits of Bibb's conduct, to perform as a less-than-zealous advocate and subvert the wishes of his office was highly controversial. A disciplinary complaint was filed against him. Even though nothing came of the complaint, the entire incident led Bibb to quit. It was the end of nearly a quarter-century-long stint with the prosecutors' office in Manhattan, the only job he had known since graduating law school.[30]

Resource Constraints

Along with cognitive biases, resource limitations may cause some prosecutors to discount the significance of post-conviction innocence claims. Prosecutors' offices, like all government agencies, have finite resources and are accountable for their expenditures. Trial prosecutors carry large caseloads. This burden would grow if offices were to apportion lawyers toward post-conviction innocence claims and steer them away from their main work: the trial and direct appellate docket. Demanding that prosecutors do more work in post-conviction matters might push many of these financially strapped organizations beyond the breaking point.[31]

Prosecutors might also have concerns about the impact of exonerations on their future budgets. More than half the states have enacted legislation to provide financial compensation for those who have been wrongfully convicted.[32] Although these statutes do not specify that funds used for compensation should come from prosecutors' own coffers, state payouts to released prisoners might have an indirect effect on sums allocated to prosecutors partially reliant on state funding. In a nutshell, worries about current resources and future funding streams discourage prosecutors from helping inmates prove their innocence.[33]

Finality

The criminal justice system has a strong interest in the finality of its decisions. Cases must become final for judges, lawyers, victims, and witnesses to attain psychological closure. Finality is also important for defendants to have a shot at rehabilitation, which arguably does not take place so long as their cases remain open and reversals of their convictions possible. Worst of all, the system could collapse without a point of finality, overwhelmed by a merciless spate of collateral petitions.[34]

Encouraging prosecutors to adopt a more open stance in reevaluating trial results violates the very principle of finality. Prosecutors may fear that opening a closed case will cause the public to doubt the accuracy of their work throughout the jurisdiction, and create pressure to reinvestigate other hard-earned convictions. It may seem prudent to keep the lid shut on that prosecutorial Pandora's Box.[35]

Political Factors

Political considerations affect many prosecutors' decisions about how to proceed with post-conviction cases. Forty-seven states elect their local chief prosecutors.[36] Even where head prosecutors are appointed, as in the federal system, the process is fraught with political overtones. As noted in chapter 4, candidates for chief prosecutor often trumpet their conviction rates and track records in high-profile cases.[37] One consequence of this approach is that prosecutors angling to retain their jobs (or move on to higher office) must keep politics in mind when responding later on to innocence claims. Conceding a past mistake could dull a chief prosecutor's tough-on-crime shine, and perhaps even call into question his fitness for the post. How many *other* innocent folks has this person put away? Is he capable of getting the bad guys?[38]

But the potential political damage of exhibiting openness to an innocence claim goes beyond generating doubts about the prosecutor's competence. A wrongful conviction usually transforms a closed case into an open one. That means one more unsolved crime on the books, a development that occurs in front of a nosy public given the media frenzy associated with these cases.[39] And what if an inmate the prosecutor helps free later goes out and commits a crime? A chief prosecutor, or any elected official, puts political capital on the line whenever he publicly sides with a defendant.

Take the Steven Avery case from Wisconsin. Avery spent eighteen years in prison for sexual assault and attempted murder before he was exonerated in 2003 based on DNA tests. That exoneration provided the impetus for a state legislator, Mark Gundrum, to form a commission called the Avery Task Force to consider a slate of innocence-related reforms. Weeks after the legislature passed the Avery Task Force bill in 2005, Avery was charged with raping and killing a woman; DNA evidence linked him to the subsequent crime. Gundrum rushed to rename the legislation the Criminal Justice Reform Package.[40] Although Gundrum's political career apparently did not suffer as a result of his tie with Avery—he was elected a state court judge in 2010[41]—the incident may give some prosecutors pause before openly assisting a prisoner with his innocence claim.

Indeed, it is politically expedient for many prosecutors to hold fast in response to post-conviction innocence claims. Letting a petition hobble through the post-conviction process reinforces a prosecutor's tough-on-crime image. Any political fallout from a subsequent reversal of the conviction can be ascribed to the system as a whole, not the individual prosecutor or his office. In non-DNA cases where the evidence is subjective, the judge becomes the one vilified as soft on crime. And in reversals based on DNA testing conducted pursuant to a court order, prosecutors can argue that the system worked, that justice was served in the end.[42]

Prosecutors all too often agree to cooperate with the defense, and bypass the adversary process, only when it is politically advantageous. These cases typically fall into one of several categories:

- Post-conviction DNA testing specifically implicated another culprit and prosecutors have no other choice but to appear receptive.
- The conviction occurred on a previous chief prosecutor's watch and the successor is happy to highlight the faults of his rival.
- The wrongfully convicted inmate was simultaneously serving a prison sentence for an unrelated crime, and the exoneration would have no effect on public safety.[43]

Post-Conviction Prosecutorial Ethics

The ethical rules that apply to prosecutors' decisions in the post-conviction setting are even more abstract than those in the pretrial and trial stages.[44] The vagueness of these rules reflects the unusual foundation upon which innocence claims rest. Many of the ethical prohibitions in the pretrial and trial contexts—the obligation to disclose *Brady* material and so forth—are based on concerns for fairness and due process to criminal defendants. Post-conviction claims of innocence do not necessarily invoke process-oriented values; the crux of an innocence claim lies not in whether the trial was fair but whether it was accurate. Most ethical rules for prosecutors therefore fail to mold themselves easily to the odd shape of innocence claims after trial. The lack of ethical obligations for prosecutors in the innocence sphere is also attributable to the basic fact that legislators and professional code drafters have historically ignored post-conviction issues. For example, a well-regarded fount of prosecutorial ethics—the American Bar Association's Standards for Criminal Justice—covers prosecutorial behavior at each phase of the pretrial and trial process through sentencing but then abruptly ceases.[45]

Allow me to reiterate that not every post-conviction prosecutor responds defensively to innocence claims. Symbols of hope exist: prosecutors who have risen above the fray and candidly owned up to past gaffes. Still, the truth is that many prosecutors recoil at even the hint that they or their colleagues convicted an innocent person—unless there are countervailing political benefits. The practical and political realities need to change if the minister-of-justice ideal is to achieve even a modest foothold in the post-conviction turf.

Countering Prosecutors' Opposition to Post-Conviction Innocence Claims
Putting Finality in Its Proper Place

Finality is a treasured value in the criminal justice system. So, too, is the adage that only the guilty should endure the consequences of a criminal conviction. These principles collide in the post-conviction context when an inmate raises a claim of innocence. In reconciling them, finality should give way when the prisoner's claim appears to have merit. What good is finality if the final result is the incarceration of the innocent? The true perpetrator remains unpunished; the victim has not achieved genuine closure; and the state continues to pay large sums to imprison the wrong person. A 2011 study of 85 exonerations in Illinois reported that those cases had cost state taxpayers $214 million after calculating the expenses of incarcerating the wrong people, compensating them, and picking up the tab for litigation fees. While the innocent were imprisoned in Illinois, the actual perpetrators in those cases committed at least 94 additional felonies, including 14 murders.[46]

In light of the societal and financial costs of wrongful convictions, prosecutors should conduct close reviews of potentially meritorious innocence claims and act appropriately when a review substantiates the allegation. Appropriate responses include joining a prisoner's request for an evidentiary hearing on the new evidence or even urging the judge to vacate the conviction.

What changes to the criminal justice system might stimulate prosecutors to let their concerns with finality recede in the face of powerful innocence claims? For one thing, courts could clarify that prosecutors' legal duty to act as ministers of justice persists beyond sentencing day. Strands of judicial doctrine suggest that prosecutors should take post-conviction claims of innocence seriously. Language from case law intimates that a prosecutor's disclosure obligations under *Brady v. Maryland* continue into the post-conviction sphere: that a prosecutor should disclose information acquired after the conviction that undermines confidence in the integrity of the verdict.[47] Yet the post-conviction scope of the duty to disclose exculpatory evidence is far from clear.[48] In fact, the U.S. Supreme Court's recent jurisprudence in this area has taken pains to avoid recognizing a constitutional right to *Brady* material after conviction.[49] Judges should send a much clearer message that the prosecutor's duty to protect the innocent is alive and well during the post-conviction phase.

Next, educating prosecutors about wrongful convictions would aid in overcoming the obsession with finality. Incoming prosecutors may attend educational programs about their ethical duties, but these issues are not always emphasized as they progress through the office. Discussions about wrongful convictions, their causes, and post-conviction ethical issues deserve emphasis.[50]

Done right, training about post-conviction topics must be supplemented with incentives for prosecutors to heed the lessons drawn from that training. Prosecutors have few incentives to remain open to the possibility that some innocence claims are valid. Openness leads to more work in the future and more criticism of their work from the past. Rewarding prosecutors for reacting favorably to viable innocence claims might go far in encouraging model behavior. The district attorney's office in Santa Clara County, California, has made strides in this regard. Employees who uncover innocent defendants in Santa Clara earn prizes and public recognition. It is amazing what a nifty plaque can do to motivate people who work in demanding jobs with relatively low, and often lockstep, salaries.[51]

Stronger signals from the courts about the ongoing duty to do justice, along with education and rewards for displaying openness to innocence claims, would soften the death grip that far too many prosecutors have on the principle of finality. But it is naïve to view these steps as a complete answer to the deeply ingrained impediments to prosecutors doing justice after conviction. The rest of this chapter focuses on potential antidotes to three major sources of intransigence to post-conviction innocence claims: the flimsy ethical obligations imposed on prosecutors after conviction, the ills of cognitive bias, and the peculiar dynamics of prosecutorial politics.

Reforming Post-Conviction Ethical Rules

It is hardly surprising that prosecutors have behaved inconsistently in responding to post-conviction innocence claims given the lack of rules in this area to provide an ethical roadmap. There is cause for optimism, though. Innocence issues have captured the attention of ethicists in recent years, and this has generated frank discussion about revising the ethical rules for post-conviction prosecutors.

The American Bar Association amended Rule 3.8 of the Model Rules of Professional Conduct in 2008 to clarify that in some circumstances prosecutors should play an active role in enabling the release of innocent prisoners. Rule 3.8(g) now provides that when "a prosecutor knows of new, credible, and material evidence creating a reasonable likelihood that a convicted defendant did not commit an offense of which the defendant was convicted," that attorney must act by "promptly disclosing that evidence to an appropriate court or authority."[52] If the original conviction occurred within the prosecutor's jurisdiction, he has an added responsibility to "undertake further investigation, or make reasonable efforts to cause an investigation, to determine whether the defendant was convicted of an offense that the defendant did not commit."[53] Where that evidence rises to the level of "clear and convincing" evidence of innocence, prosecutors under Rule 3.8(h) must do more: "the prosecutor shall seek to remedy the conviction."[54]

At the risk of bursting the bubble of enthusiasm spawned by these changes, I must note that Rule 3.8(g)–(h) has no binding effect.[55] It is a model rule that just five states adopted within three years of its enactment.[56] Although other states are considering adopting it, I am not sanguine about the rule's prospects for passage across the country.[57] Opponents have criticized revised Rule 3.8, arguing that it would burden law enforcement, drain prosecutorial time and resources better allocated to other matters, result in freedom for the guilty, and compromise finality.[58] Even if amended Rule 3.8 gains widespread acceptance, it may remain too nebulous to limit prosecutorial discretion in practice.[59]

Regardless of Rule 3.8's lack of teeth and limited implementation so far, it shows a shift in thinking about prosecutorial ethics. For the first time in history, hordes of scholars, judges, and lawyers are aware that innocent defendants fall through the cracks of due process and wind up imprisoned. A by-product of this awareness is a growing appreciation that prosecutors are uniquely positioned to correct these errors.[60]

The chief question, then, becomes the following: Without guidance from the canons of ethics, how should post-conviction prosecutors actually proceed in putting the minister-of-justice concept into practice? Situations involving *Brady* material in the post-conviction arena yield rather easy fixes, as Rule 3.8's new requirements make plain. Where prosecutors know of credible exculpatory evidence, they should provide notice and sometimes do much more. But these rules are a floor, not a ceiling. They leave vast discretion to prosecutors in responding to many innocence claims.[61] What about instances other than a prosecutor's knowledge of an inmate's probable innocence or the surfacing of *Brady* material after conviction? Might not the lessons of the innocence movement suggest that prosecutors should be proactive—not just reactive—in grappling with the inevitable existence of wrongful convictions in their jurisdictions?[62] In my view, the answer is a loud and unequivocal yes. That is why I consider my next proposal essential.

Taking a Fresh Look at Innocence: The Case for Prosecutorial Innocence Units

A recurring theme throughout this book is the idea that prosecutors should form review structures to examine major decisions. Structural distance between the original decision maker and the reviewer allows for a new look at an old choice—or at least permits the possibility of such a look. A review apparatus forces the decision maker to communicate the reasons behind his choice, a process that by itself brings flaws in the underlying hypothesis to the forefront.[63]

My main recommendation in this chapter is that prosecutors establish divisions to investigate post-conviction innocence claims. This proposal has special currency because prosecutors are well situated to rectify wrongful convictions. They are better positioned, in fact, than any other stakeholder in the criminal justice system.

Inmates who want to investigate and litigate post-conviction claims of innocence ordinarily depend on the help of the Innocence Project in New York City or one of the other, smaller innocence projects nationwide. Many projects are affiliated with law schools that offer clinics where students conduct the investigative work under the supervision of law faculty. Others are freestanding nonprofit organizations or operate in conjunction with journalism schools. Some represent prisoners in particular jurisdictions or impose substantive restrictions on the cases they pursue. Nevertheless, they share features beyond a passion for justice. They offer their services for free—and they struggle to make ends meet.[64]

Post-conviction innocence work takes time and money. Most innocence projects use a laborious case screening process to isolate the few meritorious cases from the heaps of requests directed their way. Costs soar as a case marches from investigation to litigation. The very survival of an innocence project may depend on luck, on the goodwill of a smattering of donors and law school deans.[65]

Even without funding worries, innocence projects face a more formidable problem. Nonprofits unconnected with law enforcement are poorly positioned to investigate innocence claims. Law students, as sincere and energetic as they might be, lack the experience in field investigations so often needed to verify an innocence claim. Projects can conscript private investigators and lawyers to do their heavy lifting *pro bono*, but it would be silly to rely on such generosity in the long-term.[66]

Unlike innocence projects, prosecutors' offices are nicely situated to investigate post-conviction innocence claims for two main reasons. First, prosecutors have access to case files in their jurisdictions. This is a significant advantage in analyzing, say, an innocence claim revolving around an assertion that the main prosecution witness lied and it turns out that the witness has testified in other matters in the county. Second, prosecutors can tap into a ready, able, and conceivably willing group of veteran investigators—the police—who have a strong information network and their own file cabinets jam-packed with cases.[67]

Other benefits of prosecutorial innocence units emerge upon reflection. Prosecutors in these units would soon become specialists in post-conviction innocence claims, making them far more efficient evaluators of a claim's strength than generalist criminal lawyers from other divisions. Moreover, organizational separation between the trial bureau and the attorneys in charge of reviewing post-conviction petitions could blunt the effect of the status quo bias. Consolidating responsibility for post-conviction innocence claims might also cultivate strong relationships between individual attorneys in the unit and lawyers aligned with innocence projects. Stronger relationships could produce greater cooperation in submitting innocence claims to the courts. This, in turn, could breed greater openness on the part of judges in reviewing those claims in which the defense and the prosecution put forth a united front.[68]

Before being branded a pie-in-the-sky thinker, let me return to earth for a moment and sift through the arguments against prosecutorial innocence units. The power of conformity effects would linger, as prosecutors within the unit might hesitate to second-guess the trial decisions of a co-equal in the office. Lawyers might loathe assignments to the innocence unit, seeing the group as similar to a police Internal Affairs Bureau entrusted with the task of ratting out their colleagues. Attorneys in an innocence unit could have a hard time in wresting information from scornful peers or fear reprisals that could banish them to the professional hinterlands. Political considerations also cut against creating these entities. Prosecutors might worry about voters viewing an innocence unit as a chink in prosecutors' tough-on-crime armor and hold it against them come Election Day. And, without a doubt, resource constraints may make this entire enterprise impractical, particularly in smaller offices.[69]

On balance, though, the combination of the prosecutor's special duty to serve as a minister of justice, the lessons taught by this era of DNA exonerations, the difficulties that nonprofit innocence projects encounter, and the reality that prosecutors are in the best position to evaluate innocence claims after trial all support the idea of internal innocence units. The growth of these units would lead to more fruitful investigations, more exonerations, and more consistent treatment of inmate petitions within each jurisdiction.[70] These units would also boost the legitimacy of the criminal justice system by giving the public reason to believe in the accuracy of trials and prosecutors' dedication to justice.[71]

In an ideal world, a prosecutorial innocence unit would investigate claims brought to its attention by prisoners as well as cases identified as questionable by the unit itself. Prosecutors who behave proactively by sleuthing out possible wrongful convictions advance justice on many levels. They can free the innocent, catch the guilty, and provide closure to the victim. Fair-minded prosecutors who neglect to take initiative, who only operate reactively by responding to defense requests for aid, deserve praise, too. But they might not get all the results they want.

Consider the following case from Michigan. In April 1994 a man barged into a house in Clinton Township, startling a woman from her sleep. The intruder, whose face was covered by a stocking, ordered her to lie face down while he handcuffed and blindfolded her. With a sharp instrument at her throat, he raped and sodomized her multiple times in different parts of the house. The victim described the perpetrator as a white male in his twenties between 6 feet and 6 feet, 2 inches in height and weighing between 200 and 225 pounds, and she helped the police develop a composite sketch. The crime scene also yielded valuable evidence, as investigators retrieved semen samples that serology tests later found to be consistent with Type A blood.[72]

Flash forward to July 1994. Ken Wyniemko sat in the county jail on unrelated misdemeanor charges. The police told him he resembled the composite sketch from the Clinton rape and put him in a lineup. The victim identified the forty-three-year-old Wyniemko as the man who raped her. At trial, the identification evidence proved integral in linking Wyniemko to the crime. Although tests showed that he had Type O blood, the police reasoned that the semen must have come from the victim's husband, a person with Type A blood. The jury apparently agreed, finding Wyniemko guilty of fifteen counts of criminal sexual conduct as well as robbery and breaking and entering.[73] At sentencing, Wyniemko proclaimed that "putting me away is not going to take a criminal off the street. I swear to God, it's not me."[74]

Years later Wyniemko asked for assistance from the innocence project at the Thomas M. Cooley School of Law in Lansing, Michigan. The Cooley legal team eagerly signed on and pushed for DNA tests on the remaining biological evidence from the crime scene. Carl Marlinga, the chief prosecutor in the county that included Clinton Township, complied with this request. In 2003 state crime lab tests determined that the semen was a mixed sample belonging to the victim's husband and an unknown male profile; forensic scientists excluded Wyniemko as a possible source. The authorities released Wyniemko from prison that June.[75]

In a sense, the Wyniemko case shows the post-conviction process at its best. Inmate contacts innocence project; lawyers seek DNA testing of existing crime scene evidence; open-minded prosecutor consents; test results from the state crime lab vindicate the wrongfully convicted; and an innocent man goes free. It gets even better. Since the exoneration, Marlinga has become committed to innocence issues in Michigan.[76]

Here's the kicker. Wyniemko's 2003 exoneration occurred three years after the statute of limitations had run out on charging someone else with the crime. Not until 2008 did the police determine the identity of the unknown male profile from the Clinton crime scene: Craig Gonser, a serial sex offender 6 inches taller and 100 pounds heavier than Wyniemko. Gonser had been in his mid-twenties and on probation for sex crimes at the time of the 1994 tragedy in Clinton.[77] Although it is unclear whether Gonser could have been connected to the Clinton crimes before the statute of limitations passed, this much is clear—the failure of prosecutors' offices to initiate review of questionable convictions can keep the innocent in prison and the guilty from ever being held accountable. Had there been an internal innocence unit in place that took this type of initiative, Gonser might have been identified within the statute of limitations and several of his later victims spared the agony of his abuse.

A Blueprint for Action: The Conviction Integrity Unit in Dallas

So, what should an innocence unit look like? A handful of prosecutors' offices already have divisions that focus on post-conviction DNA testing. Many of these units are reactive in orientation; they field requests from inmates and then assess the merits. Others operate more proactively by instituting voluntary reviews of cases where biological evidence could be available for DNA testing. These examples show that the DNA era has enriched how some prosecutors conceive of their duty to serve justice. That said, these programs fall short of embodying the minister-of-justice ideal, because their missions target only the small fraction of criminal cases in which biological evidence exists for DNA testing.[78]

The Conviction Integrity Unit in the Dallas County District Attorney's Office may provide the best contemporary model for structuring an internal innocence unit. Newly elected chief prosecutor Craig Watkins formed the unit in July 2007, shortly after the exoneration of James Curtis Giles.[79] Watkins assigned a senior deputy chief to supervise a well-stocked team consisting of an assistant prosecutor, investigator, and legal assistant. The team took on the review of more than four hundred DNA cases in conjunction with the Innocence Project of Texas. The Conviction Integrity Unit also agreed to evaluate all cases (DNA and non-DNA) where evidence identifies different perpetrators.[80]

In terms of its methodology, the staff at the Conviction Integrity Unit examines all relevant convictions case by case with "a critical eye." If a claim meets a certain baseline of eligibility, the unit tries to determine guilt or innocence without deference to the jury decision or considerations of finality. Roughly 25 percent of the requests to the unit have nothing to do with factual innocence and can be quickly dismissed. Many others go by the wayside after a cursory phone call or follow-up interview. If the remaining inquiries point to potential innocence, the unit investigates further. When additional investigation signals a reasonable possibility of innocence, the unit fully reviews the case. If the fruits of that review still indicate a reasonable possibility of innocence, the unit supports setting the conviction aside. On those occasions where the investigation does not produce such evidence, the unit leaves it to the defense to seek post-conviction relief and prove that the new evidence points "unquestionably" to innocence, as required by Texas law.[81] This approach is sound. One cannot expect prosecutors to support an inmate's release whenever the new evidence raises only a reasonable doubt about guilt without necessarily pointing to innocence. If that were the case, criminal defendants might game the system by withholding certain pieces of evidence at trial and reserving them for a post-conviction petition.[82]

Watkins seems proud of the Conviction Integrity Unit, which his website plugs as "the first of its kind in the United States."[83] His pride is justified. Watkins's team has spearheaded the exoneration of at least eight prisoners and accommodated DNA testing requests for twenty inmates whose overtures had been rebuffed by previous prosecutors.[84] The publicity surrounding these exonerations has not caused the citizens of Dallas to think that the office is soft on crime. Watkins's first assistant reports that, if anything, jurors trust the district attorney *more* based on the notion that "'if you guys say he did it, he did it.'"[85]

The response to the Conviction Integrity Unit within the Dallas County prosecutors' office has been more mixed. Some employees view the Conviction Integrity Unit as a type of Internal Affairs Bureau and treat it with commensurate scorn. Even then, this attitude is waning and the unit's internal status has little impact beyond social ostracism of its staff.[86] What matters is that the unit is an accepted and respected office fixture.

A combination of factors, some of them distinctive to Dallas, converged to make Watkins's unit prosper. Watkins's personal beliefs and his visceral rejection of the conviction psychology are major reasons. Dallas's atrocious history of wrongful convictions also created a fertile political environment where someone like Watkins could be elected and his idea for a post-conviction unit could bloom.[87] Post-conviction DNA testing produced more than twenty exonerations in Dallas from 2001 to 2011, a number surpassing that of any other county in the nation and most other states.[88] Watkins persuaded county commissioners early on to fund the unit by earmarking more than $300,000 in 2007. He secured another sizable grant in 2008. Devising a novel idea is one thing; developing one that can attract financial backing is something else.[89]

Watkins's brief tenure in office means that the "integrity" of most of the convictions his unit is examining occurred during his predecessors' terms in office. This is significant, because discovery of error casts a pall on his political rivals and accrues to his benefit. It will be interesting to see if the Conviction Integrity Unit stands the test of time: whether it survives in the event that Watkins retains his job in future elections and post-conviction claims of innocence relating to trials prosecuted under his auspices trickle in.[90] When Watkins was first up for reelection in November 2010 he defeated his challenger by only a few thousand votes.[91]

Notwithstanding its idiosyncrasies, the Craig Watkins experiment represents a shining beacon to guide other chief prosecutors.[92] Some leading law enforcement officials have already seen the light, including prosecutors in two of the country's largest cities. Patricia Lykos, who took over as Houston's chief prosecutor in January 2009, established a post-conviction review unit within her first one hundred days in office "to thoroughly and aggressively investigate credible claims of innocence."[93] She assigned two assistant district attorneys and an investigator to do nothing but scour through potential cases of actual innocence. The squad's work has led to the release of three wrongfully convicted men.[94] Miles away from Texas, New York County District Attorney Cyrus Vance, a newcomer to the post long held by Robert Morgenthau, announced the launch of a Conviction Integrity Program in 2010 to monitor cases that generate red flags and to manage reinvestigations. Led by a veteran assistant district attorney, the program includes a panel of ten top prosecutors to evaluate cases and office practices more generally, and an additional group of outside experts to counsel on policy matters.[95]

States could supplement county and city prosecutorial innocence units by forming review bodies that cover the whole jurisdiction. State attorney general offices, for example, could oversee the post-conviction review process. This would promote consistency in the treatment of innocence claims throughout any particular state, and possibly counteract the effects of cognitive biases in local units. Similarly, states could appoint a special prosecutor or establish an independent, bipartisan "innocence commission" with subpoena powers as a vehicle to investigate innocence claims.[96]

One state has adopted this type of commission. The North Carolina Innocence Inquiry Commission, which was approved in the summer of 2006, has authority to investigate claims of innocence based on new evidence unavailable at the time of trial. If a majority of the committee (composed of, among others, a judge, prosecutor, and defense lawyer) considers a case credible, the state's chief justice must appoint three judges to assess it. The case is reversed

only upon a unanimous finding of "clear and convincing evidence" of innocence by the three-judge panel. The Commission's efforts produced its first
exoneration in 2010. North Carolina's initiative is patterned after the United
Kingdom's Criminal Cases Review Commission, a body that has facilitated
the exoneration of numerous inmates since its formation in 1995. I welcome
the establishment of more innocence commissions like North Carolina's to
serve, in part, as complements to prosecutorial innocence units.[97]

Changing Politics as Usual

Politics and prosecutors go hand in hand, which is not altogether bad. We
want prosecutors who respond to the wishes of the electorate, who crack
down on narcotics traffic in communities overrun by drugs, who use sophisticated measures to counter prostitution where the sex trade is rampant.[98]
But there is a downside to the vision of prosecutors as political animals; they
can quickly morph into beasts. In the words of former federal prosecutor
Thomas DiBiagio: "Prosecutors are not part of a non-partisan priesthood
purified of all base motives. Many are political actors who are more attentive
to their own interests than those of the institutions they serve."[99]

Divorcing prosecutors from political interests in the post-conviction setting is a daunting task. Revisit the Hidalgo and Lemus murder case for a
moment. The *New York Times* insinuated that politics factored into District
Attorney Robert Morgenthau's refusal to take Daniel Bibb's advice to drop
charges even as compelling evidence of innocence mounted. Morgenthau
faced a difficult reelection campaign that year, and the opposition had criticized his handling of the case. This may have contributed to Morgenthau's
choice to stick to his guns, a decision that proved costly to the reputation of
his office.[100]

If it is unrealistic to indoctrinate prosecutors fully into the priesthood of
non-partisanship, perhaps we should at least ask them to act as ministers of
justice in the post-conviction realm. A major obstacle, despite the experience
in Dallas, is the fear that the public will construe prosecutorial openness
to innocence claims as being soft on crime and remember those events in
future political campaigns. The electorate is accustomed to tough-on-crime
language from law enforcement officials. Showing openness to an inmate's
possible innocence does not fit squarely into that rhetorical box; it is too
nuanced for packaging into a thirty-second sound-bite.[101]

One way to transform the political incentives for prosecutors in the post-
conviction setting involves using community outreach to provide the public

with greater information about prosecutorial decision making.[102] Even the savviest citizens struggle to evaluate candidates for chief prosecutor, because many of the candidates' activities occur in secret. Political scientists call this a citizen oversight problem.[103] So let's improve the capacity of voters to monitor prosecutorial candidates by giving them access to more information.[104] Getting citizens to seek out this newly accessible information may prove difficult, but at least it would be available and some citizens would refer to it. A better-informed electorate will recognize that wrongful convictions waste money and keep the real perpetrators in their neighborhoods. Aware that the public has some background in the complexities of post-conviction innocence issues, prosecutors might retreat from their tough-on-crime platform and take steps to look into these allegations when warranted.[105]

Jurisdictions could also modify the rules that apply to prosecutors' political campaigns. Although prosecutors are forbidden to let political calculations dictate the initial decision to charge or seek a type of punishment in a particular case, comment on past conquests is fair game. Prosecutors on the campaign trail play this card to the hilt.[106] This produces a dilemma when a prisoner later claims innocence in a case upon which the chief prosecutor previously campaigned. Even the most noble of prosecutors might feel conflicted in responding to such claims. There is a rather simple solution: states could ban prosecutors from ever participating in the post-conviction proceedings or retrial of a defendant whose case they relied on during a political campaign.[107]

Structural changes to the electoral process could also lower the political incentive for prosecutors to resist post-conviction claims of innocence. Here are a few thoughts.

Term Limits

Stiff term limits on a district attorney's tenure in office could defuse the conviction psychology and prevent chief prosecutors from becoming personally attached to cases that date back many years. Term limits might also stir some talented lawyers to seek office, candidates who would otherwise back off from a longtime incumbent.[108] Data compiled by Professor Ronald Wright show that incumbents who sought reelection as chief prosecutor between 1996 and 2006 won 95 percent of the time. More astonishing, incumbents during that period ran unopposed in *85 percent* of the general elections they entered.[109] Statistics suggest that the absence of contested elections skews prosecutorial decision making.[110] Challengers who are knowledgeable about an incumbent's performance can act as auditors by publicly advertising the chief prosecutor's performance inside and outside the courtroom.[111]

I concede that term limits have disadvantages. For one, they could deter a number of able attorneys from ever vying for the position. For another, term limits do not differentiate between the good and the bad. Many successful chief prosecutors would face mandatory ouster at the end of their terms, including those who had established solid working relationships with judges and members of the defense bar.[112]

The Timing of Prosecutorial Elections

Citizens typically vote for their chief prosecutors on the same day that other elections are held, with the effect that more celebrated gubernatorial or other statewide contests overshadow the prosecutorial races. Holding prosecutorial elections on a separate date could encourage the public to examine the candidates' policies and practices more carefully and foster greater accountability to the electorate.

One drawback is that turnout would decline without glamorous races to lure people to the voting booth. But what is worse—widespread participation by voters uninformed about the candidates for chief prosecutor who cast their ballots based on name recognition and party affiliation or input from the well-informed few who care about criminal justice policy?[113]

Forsaking the Elective Model

A far more radical proposal—abandoning the norm of electing prosecutors and embracing an appointment model—has its virtues. One step removed from the direct political process, appointees might find it easier to fend off public pressures and protect the interests of the minority from the whims of the majority. A 2009 study found that appointed prosecutors have lower conviction rates than their elected counterparts, a result the authors attributed to appointees being "less worried about poorly informed public opinion."[114] The American reliance on elected prosecutors is an aberration worldwide. The office of prosecutor in most countries is a civil service post.[115]

Certainly the elective model has its benefits. The paradigm of the elected prosecutor in the United States emerged during the populist era of the 1820s as a way to ensure that "the People" have a say in law enforcement.[116] This right to make one's voice heard is important. As noted above, law enforcement priorities should reflect the needs of the public.[117] Democratic elections, in theory, build an overlap between prosecutorial goals and community concerns by demanding that candidates for chief prosecutor listen to their constituents.

Appointing chief prosecutors is also unlikely to end the impact of partisan politics on applicants for these jobs. To earn and then retain their appointed offices after presidential changes, U.S. Attorneys must navigate the precarious shoals of politics.[118] And the political concerns of appointed prosecutors may revolve around pleasing party leaders, not the electorate as a whole. For instance, some New York attorneys believe that prosecutors in neighboring New Jersey, who are appointed, are far less inclined to file corruption charges against state officials than are their colleagues to the north.[119]

The Public Prosecutor

Suspend your disbelief for a moment. Envision the U.S. criminal justice system departing from the public prosecutor model by outsourcing prosecutorial functions to private attorneys through contracts. In Great Britain, a nation applauded for its lack of rabid partisanship between prosecuting lawyers and defense attorneys, there was no institutional public prosecutor until 1985. Even today, some prosecutorial chores in that country are performed by private lawyers hired to represent the Crown on a piecemeal basis.[120]

Although this reform has its fair share of flaws—preserving quality control and consistency come to mind—it should not be dismissed out of hand for the United States. Privatizing the occupation would introduce lawyers who do not have an entrenched interest in obtaining and maintaining convictions into the prosecutorial profession. In the absence of any institutional stake in upholding trial convictions, and with work experience on the other side of the fence as a criminal defense attorney, prosecuting lawyers under this regime might show greater receptivity to post-conviction innocence claims. Exposing attorneys to both prosecution and defense work could, at the very least, sensitize them to the quandaries facing innocent inmates.[121]

Prosecutors confronted with post-conviction innocence claims should be open to the possibility that some portion of those cases have merit. To do otherwise is to reject the minister-of-justice ideal and to play a role in perpetuating an unknown and unknowable number of miscarriages of justice that fail to result in reversal through the adversary process. The manner in which prosecutors respond to inmate requests for DNA testing of biological evidence is particularly consequential. DNA tests have the capacity to prove innocence (or confirm guilt) to a degree of accuracy never imagined throughout much of human history. If prosecutors care about accuracy, they should comply with requests for post-conviction DNA testing in all cases where the requests are not frivolous.

A Closer Look

Prosecutors and Post-Conviction DNA Testing

Suppose Smith's innocence claim pointing the finger at Allen in the drunk-driving case enters the post-conviction process. Skeptical about the alleged new evidence from Johnson and Wiley, prosecutors vigorously oppose the defense motion for an evidentiary hearing. The judge sides with the state, denying the motion without so much as holding a hearing. "If these new facts are truly credible," the judge writes, "then why did the witnesses fail to mention them at the time of the original trial? It seems quite convenient to blame this crime now on Allen, a convicted thief who may not be able to defend himself against these old charges." A panel of judges later affirms this decision on appeal.[1]

The future looks bleak for Smith, but there is one last litigation option.[2] The fleeing driver bumped into a fire hydrant right after the accident, lacerating his leg. The cut oozed blood onto the hydrant before the perpetrator staggered off. Further assume that Johnson witnessed this sequence of events and that crime scene investigators retrieved the blood. Serology tests indicated that the sample came from someone with Type O blood, which matched Smith's blood type as well as that of a large percentage of the population. Because of miscommunication, police detectives neglected to examine Smith later that night for leg wounds. Nevertheless, this blood evidence comprised a brick in the wall of the case against Smith at trial. Removing this brick could send the whole case crashing down. To date, the biological evidence has never been subjected to DNA testing, a circumstance Smith would love to change.

Several obstacles loom. Smith has to either convince prosecutors to agree to post-conviction DNA testing or seek recourse through litigation to demand compliance from the state. Smith also has to find out whether the biological evidence from his case still exists. If Smith clears these hurdles, the subsequent DNA test might solve the mystery of who committed the crime once and for all.

Although an in-depth discussion of the scientific basis for DNA testing far exceeds the scope of this chapter (and my knowledge), indulge me for a moment in offering a brief primer. DNA is genetic material contained in chromosomes found inside the nuclei of most cells. Roughly 99.9 percent of human DNA is identical from person to person. The remaining one-tenth of 1 percent distinguishes one human from another. Scientists since the 1950s have studied that small fraction in order to understand individuals' genetic blueprints. By the early 1980s scientists had perfected a process called restriction-fragment-length-polymorphism (RFLP) testing that allowed them to detect those microscopic differences. The problem with RFLP testing was that it was a painstaking process that required large quantities of non-degraded biological material. Fortunately, in the late 1980s, scientists developed a reliable shortcut through a method known as polymerase chain reaction (PCR) that could replicate small amounts of biological material and turn them into large quantities. Testing technologies based on PCR could not only produce comparable results in hours (as opposed to the weeks involved in RFLP testing), but those results could stem from minute fragments of genetic material, even if the material was not in ideal condition.[3]

The advantages of modern DNA testing methodologies emerged in the post-conviction litigation related to Gary Dotson's rape conviction in Illinois. A woman claimed she was walking home from work in 1977 when two men forced her into the back of a car and sexually assaulted her. The victim later identified Dotson as one of her assailants. The prosecution buttressed the identification evidence with trial testimony from a forensic analyst who reported that semen from the rape kit could have come from Dotson based on serology tests and that pubic hairs removed from the victim's underwear were similar to Dotson's. Convicted of aggravated kidnapping and rape in 1979, Dotson received a sentence of twenty-five to fifty years' imprisonment.[4]

The outlook for Dotson brightened in 1985 when the victim recanted her testimony. She admitted that she had fabricated her account of rape to cover up a consensual sexual encounter with her boyfriend. A judge nevertheless rejected Dotson's petition for a new trial because he found the original trial testimony more credible than the recantation. In 1988 Dotson's new attorney had DNA tests conducted on the biological evidence from the case. A sample was sent to England for RFLP analysis, but the evidence was badly degraded and yielded only inconclusive results. Another sample was dispatched to a lab in California. The application of PCR to that sample generated a sufficient quantity of material for DNA tests—and the results of those tests had significance. The semen on the victim's underwear could *not* have come from Dotson and may have originated from the victim's boyfriend instead. An Illinois court overturned Dotson's conviction in August 1989, the first known post-conviction exoneration of an innocent prisoner based on DNA testing in the United States.[5]

DNA technology has improved in the decades following Dotson's exoneration. The evolution of short tandem repeat (STR) markers has allowed for new testing methods that fuse many of the benefits of PCR analysis (the ability to produce results from minuscule samples) and RFLP (precision).[6] Scientists can now identify perpetrators who left biological evidence at the crime scene based on smaller specimens and with a larger degree of accuracy. The costs of DNA tests are also falling. What used to cost thousands of dollars per test now costs as little as a few hundred dollars.[7]

Law enforcement quickly recognized the potential of DNA to solve crimes. The Federal Bureau of Investigation and many states established databases for the entry and storage of DNA profiles.[8] Running the genetic profile of an unidentified perpetrator through these databases occasionally produces a match. Along with solving crimes at the front end of the investigative process, DNA has the capacity to rectify error at the back end: to confirm whether a prisoner's claim of innocence holds water and even spot the true culprit. Empirical studies of exonerations show that post-conviction DNA testing often answers the question of "whodunit." Professor Brandon Garrett analyzed the first two hundred DNA exonerations in the United States and found that in forty-nine of those cases the same DNA evidence that freed the innocent prisoner served to inculpate the actual perpetrator after putting the profile through a database.[9] DNA's incomparable accuracy, then, can both vindicate the innocent and condemn the guilty. But just getting to that stage—submitting biological samples to labs for modern DNA testing—is a challenge in itself.

Barriers to Post-Conviction DNA Testing

Seeking Cooperation from Prosecutors

Prisoners hoping to subject biological evidence from their cases to post-conviction DNA testing usually seek the consent of prosecutors before resorting to litigation. Getting the prosecution onboard eliminates the middle man, the courts, and can expedite the process considerably. A significant number of prosecutors do eagerly climb aboard. Some even act affirmatively to ferret out wrongful convictions in their jurisdictions. In addition to Craig Watkins in Dallas,[10] prominent ministers of justice in the DNA context include Woody Clarke in San Diego and Susan Gaertner in St. Paul, each of whom championed the formation of internal post-conviction units to reassess convictions where DNA testing of biological evidence could prove innocence.[11]

Despite these efforts, prosecutorial resistance surfaces in many cases involving requests for post-conviction DNA testing. Wary prosecutors give various explanations for rejecting inmate overtures: strained finances, the importance of finality, and the fear of being swamped with frivolous requests.[12] According to Garrett's study, prosecutors originally refused to cooperate with DNA testing requests in roughly half the first two hundred cases that led to exonerations.[13] Much of this resistance eased over time. Nearly 60 percent of the first two hundred DNA exonerations eventually involved consent from law enforcement or prosecutors; law enforcement initiated the tests in twenty-two cases.[14] Yet prosecutors far too often reacted defensively in the cases studied by Garrett, taking stands that prolonged the incarceration of the innocent.[15] Bruce Godschalk's experience in Pennsylvania is just one among many examples of this trend—and prosecutorial opposition served only to delay, not prevent, his release.[16] Defensive reactions by prosecutors to post-conviction innocence claims have presumably kept an indeterminate number of innocent prisoners behind bars. Equally troubling, holdups in post-conviction DNA testing can cause the statute of limitations to pass and rule out prosecuting the actual perpetrator, as occurred in the Wyniemko case discussed in chapter 7.[17]

Asking for Judicial Intervention

One reason why obtaining consent for post-conviction DNA testing from prosecutors beforehand is so valuable is that innocent defendants do not always get justice through the courts.[18] Although every state except Massachusetts and Oklahoma has a law entitling defendants to apply for post-conviction DNA testing,[19] those procedures are full of obstacles that litigants might stumble over. Common barriers include:

- Denying access to defendants who pled guilty
- Restricting eligibility only to defendants convicted of serious felonies
- Demanding that petitioners under these statutes prove an unbroken "chain of custody" over the biological evidence since it was retrieved from the crime scene

- Erecting rigid time limits on the application process
- Prohibiting defendants from appealing denials of requests for testing.[20]

These are not trivial hurdles. Courts *rejected* petitions for post-conviction testing in sixteen of the first two hundred cases where defendants were ultimately proven innocent through DNA.[21]

Considering that two states lack statutes in this area, and that the procedures in the remaining forty-eight have problems, several scholars have argued for a federal constitutional right to post-conviction DNA testing where innocence could be proven.[22] These calls have largely gone unheeded. The U.S. Supreme Court refused to recognize an unqualified, freestanding constitutional right to post-conviction DNA testing when confronted with the question in 2009.[23] In that case, the Court considered whether William Osborne had a constitutional right to obtain DNA testing of biological evidence related to his 1994 conviction for the kidnapping and sexual assault of a prostitute in Anchorage. State prosecutors from Alaska—which had not yet enacted a post-conviction DNA testing law—had denied Osborne's pleas to turn over the evidence. In treating Osborne's request as frivolous, prosecutors explained that he had confessed to the crime and that a rudimentary DNA test prior to trial placed him within the pool of men who could have committed the crime.[24] But advanced DNA tests available in 2009 could definitively prove Osborne's guilt or innocence, putting to rest any nagging suspicions about his involvement.[25] In validating the prosecutors' decision to withhold the evidence, Chief Justice John Roberts wrote in the Court's majority opinion that "to suddenly constitutionalize this area would short-circuit what looks to be a prompt and considered legislative response."[26] Alaska's legislative response to this case was indeed prompt and (one hopes) considered; the state enacted a post-conviction DNA testing law in 2010.[27]

Locating the Biological Evidence

Finding the biological evidence from the crime scene may be even more challenging for an inmate than persuading a prosecutor to agree to post-conviction DNA testing. Physical evidence in a criminal case can take many forms, including biological specimens suitable for DNA tests (semen, hair samples, saliva) as well as other items (boot prints, bullet fragments, clothing). The manner in which jurisdictions preserve this evidence after trial takes almost as many forms.[28]

Evidence preservation in many states depends on local custom. Cities and counties often designate custodians to preserve evidence and develop procedures for destroying it in old cases, which may be crucial to alleviate overcrowding. In some places court clerks bear the brunt of responsibility for storing evidence until a judge authorizes its destruction. Elsewhere evidence is maintained by the police department or at a crime lab for a set period. Biological evidence in several jurisdictions is destroyed shortly after trial. Whatever the specific policies, the existence of preservation procedures in a particular locality does not mean that practices comply with those rules. Deficient cataloguing and tracking systems can make it difficult for custodians to locate evidence.[29]

Some states have sought to rein in the discretion of local authorities by standardizing retention policies. Approximately half the states have preservation laws that require the storage of biological evidence for a specific amount of time or even indefinitely. But most statutes have strings attached that curtail their effectiveness, for example, restrictions mandating evidence preservation only for particular types of crimes, cases starting after the date of the law's passage, or instances where a request for testing has been made. Many of these statutes also lack proper means of enforcement by failing to specify how and when to sanction officials for improper disposal of evidence.[30] One consequence of these defects is that prisoners struggle to find the evidence from their cases. Statistics compiled in 2008 suggest that more than one-third of the Innocence Project's requests for biological evidence in cases with potentially viable innocence claims do not result in usable DNA.[31]

Consider Robin Lovitt's case. Lovitt was convicted of capital murder in 2000 for killing and robbing a pool hall employee in Arlington, Virginia. The key piece of evidence consisted of the murder weapon, a pair of blood-stained scissors. When Lovitt appealed his conviction, he learned that a court clerk had discarded the scissors contrary to Virginia's evidence preservation law. At the time of Lovitt's trial, DNA testing could only link the blood on the weapon to the victim. Innovations in DNA technology in the ensuing years had developed the capacity to prove much more about the blood evidence. Lovitt was cheated of the chance to test the evidence—and courts the chance to confirm guilt or prove innocence—by virtue of a lone court clerk's disregard of state law. Slated for execution, Lovitt received a last-minute reprieve when Governor Mark Warner commuted his sentence to life in prison.[32] Still, a cloud lurks over Lovitt's head—one that could have either vanished or settled in for the long haul had the scissors been available for DNA testing.

The Supreme Court has neglected to fill the gaping holes in state evidence preservation policies. The Court has held that the intentional destruction of evidence by the government in criminal cases may violate due process but has put up nearly impregnable barriers to proving such a violation. Only the purposeful destruction of evidence that the government *knows* is exculpatory infringes upon due process. Not so with respect to potentially exculpatory evidence. Defendants in those cases must show that the destruction occurred in bad faith and that the items' exculpatory value was apparent before the evidence was destroyed.[33] This creates a Catch-22 in DNA cases. Without testing the now destroyed biological evidence, how can a defendant prove that the exculpatory value was apparent at the outset? Even if a defendant satisfies that element, he must grapple with the problem of bad faith. The cases in which courts have found the bad faith test satisfied are few and far between.[34]

Inspiring Evolution in Prosecutors' Attitudes about the DNA Revolution

Prosecutors should respond more openly to inmate requests for post-conviction DNA testing.[35] Accommodating these requests clashes with the principle of finality, but the outcome can provide more than adequate compensation: an unmatched level of certainty about guilt or innocence. This certainty can benefit victims in achieving psychological closure in their cases, a goal often touted in support of finality. Although DNA tests are not free, many prisoners are willing to foot the bill and some statutes require that they do so in particular circumstances.[36] The expense of a DNA test also pales in comparison with the sums needed to imprison a single person for a year (more than $20,000).[37] Even assuming that the costs associated with post-conviction DNA testing are noteworthy, inmate requests are bound to dwindle in the years ahead as *pretrial* testing weeds out an ever greater number of innocent suspects before trial.[38]

How might prosecutors become inspired to show greater openness to post-conviction DNA testing at this unique moment in history? The remedies advanced in chapter 7 could help. Educating prosecutors about wrongful convictions would offset the influence of the status quo bias and other psychological impediments. Installing an incentive structure to motivate prosecutors to take innocence claims seriously would provide a fine complement to training and education. And the meatiest of my proposals—beefing up legal and ethical rules to counteract prosecutorial resistance,[39] encouraging prosecutors to offer these claims a fresh look through internal innocence units, and refashioning prosecutorial politics—might give prosecutors the fortitude to change their ways. In light of the idiosyncrasies of post-conviction DNA testing, I feel compelled to put forward two additional ideas.

Honing Post-Conviction DNA Testing Legislation

It is unlikely that the U.S. Supreme Court will recognize a freestanding constitutional right to post-conviction DNA testing any time soon. This leaves the ball in the legislative court. The fact that forty-eight states have post-conviction DNA testing laws is commendable, a tribute to how swiftly legislators have responded to the onslaught of exonerations over the past twenty years. Many of these laws walk a fine line between enabling defendants to pursue testing in legitimate cases and discouraging frivolous submissions.

One way that states try to reach this equilibrium is by requiring petitioners to show that the DNA testing, if it were to exclude the defendant as the source of the evidence, would cast fundamental doubt on the verdict.[40] Another feature designed to lessen the chance that guilty inmates will take a flyer—in the hope that the evidence has been degraded or that the testing might generate flawed results—is the presence of a cost-shifting stipulation that forces petitioners to pay the expenses of any tests that corroborate the defendant's guilt.[41] But that is not all. Utah, for instance, requires that any defendant seeking post-conviction DNA testing waive the statute of limitations for any felony offense that person has committed that is identified through DNA database comparison.[42] Utah law also tells judges to notify the state Board of Pardons and Parole about any adverse results from a defendant's post-conviction testing.[43]

Despite attempts to balance the scales of justice, many post-conviction DNA testing laws have features that tip against innocent prisoners. Specifically, these laws often bar access to defendants who pled guilty. This may appear wise at first blush. If a defendant pled guilty, then the evidence in his case was not completely contested through the litigation process. It may now seem unfair to give the defendant a shot at a process he previously rejected. However, as discussed in chapter 3, plea bargaining practices are configured so that innocent prisoners face huge pressures to plead guilty in order to dodge the trial tax.[44] Some innocent defendants who are risk-averse surrender to these pressures—and for rational reasons. To avoid penalizing innocent prisoners for succumbing to the temptation to plead guilty, the happenstance that a prisoner's conviction came from a guilty plea should not prevent him from invoking post-conviction DNA testing procedures.[45]

Other potential improvements in this area include expanding the class of prisoners eligible to apply for post-conviction DNA testing beyond those convicted of serious crimes, lengthening time limits for applications, and allowing appellate review of denied requests. Another vital change would be to abandon the requirement that defendants prove an unbroken chain of custody over biological evidence that they may not even know exists, much less control.[46] Notably, Congress passed the Justice for All Act in 2004 to give states financial incentives to enact post-conviction DNA testing statutes that offer broad protection to defendants and omit time limits.[47]

Greater access to post-conviction DNA testing would do more than just help prisoners during litigation. It might nudge prosecutors to think twice about snubbing an inmate who asks for testing before seeking relief in court. The higher the chance defendants will eventually obtain court-ordered DNA testing, the lower the advantage prosecutors may perceive in fighting inmate requests. Professor Bennett Gershman offers an intriguing suggestion to further push prosecutors to err on the side of consent. He proposes statutory amendments that would grant DNA testing whenever a prosecutor is unwilling to consider a legitimate defense request.[48] Gershman's proposal is attractive, despite inevitable difficulties with proving that an individual prosecutor neglected to consider an application for DNA testing in good faith.

The Role of Prosecutors in Preserving Evidence after Trial

Few innocent prisoners will ever benefit from post-conviction DNA testing laws, even improved ones, without rules ensuring that biological material is available for testing. One can only imagine how many of the cases in which the Innocence Project fails to locate biological evidence involve wrongful convictions. Without a doubt, the flood of DNA exonerations in Dallas relates partly to the county's policy of saving biological evidence indefinitely in storage lockers at the Southwestern Institute of Forensic Sciences. This practice differs from those in many other places in Texas.[49]

Encouraging states to adopt strong retention policies for biological evidence would promote the ends of justice without breaking the bank. Biological evidence is recovered primarily in rape and sexual assault cases. Those incidents account for less than 1 percent of reported crimes. Not only is biological evidence seldom found in criminal cases, but it also consumes small amounts of storage space. When biological evidence is found on a large piece of evidence (say, a blood stain on a couch) the government need not warehouse that bulky item forever. Law enforcement only has to take a sample (a mere swatch of upholstery) for DNA testing. Also, contrary to popular perception, costly refrigeration and temperature-controlled facilities are not necessary to preserve biological evidence. DNA testing can yield accurate results on biological material that is kept in a dry, dark, and air-conditioned area.[50] State legislatures unmoved by these arguments can take solace in Congress's allocation of federal funds to states that enact comprehensive evidence preservation statutes.[51]

Assuming that evidence retention statutes are essential, what should these laws look like? The Innocence Project recommends that evidence preservation statutes provide for the maintenance of biological evidence in *all* criminal cases, not just those commencing after a particular date or falling within a distinct category of crime. This obligation should only cease after the defendant is freed from any form of state-ordered supervision (prison, probation, parole, or registration as a sex offender).[52] Furthermore, the duty to preserve evidence ought to encompass only evidence that the government found during its initial investigation. None of the proposed evidence retention statutes anticipates asking the government to collect new evidence.[53]

To promote compliance, preservation statutes must have sections that describe in detail when and how to sanction officials who improperly maintain evidence. Scholars are split on what constitutes the most effective sanction. Some endorse criminal penalties for the wrongdoer. Others deem those sanctions redundant of state laws that criminalize evidence tampering and unlikely to deter custodians keen on ignoring preservation requirements.[54]

While agnostic about criminal penalties, I am a true believer about another aspect of this debate—the need for remedies benefiting the party most directly injured by the disappearance of evidence. But for Governor Warner's act of grace in commuting his sentence, Robin Lovitt might have been executed in spite of the court clerk's flouting of evidence preservation rules. Virginia's retention law specified that violations should *not* result in post-conviction relief to the injured defendant.[55] This is tragic. A defendant who cannot pursue post-conviction DNA testing because of a custodian's failure to maintain biological evidence deserves a sentence reduction, a new trial, or (in extreme situations) a reversal.[56] As harsh as these remedies might sound, they are needed to push officials to preserve evidence and to compensate defendants when officials do not.

A reasonable question at this point is whether prosecutors should play a part in evidence preservation at all. Why not leave this to the police or the courts? Their duties already involve evidence maintenance to an extent, and they probably have some facilities available for storage. But those circumstances do not let prosecutors off the hook. Prosecutors serve a different post-conviction function from the police and the courts by virtue of their minister-of-justice role. As advocates, prosecutors are well aware of any post-conviction filings in a case; as servants of justice, they should make sure these filings are treated as fairly as possible.

Prosecutors consequently have a stake in the preservation of evidence. Preservation affects the course of post-conviction litigation related to DNA testing. And the outcome of that litigation *matters*—to the district attorney's office as a whole, to victims, and to public perceptions of the competence of their elected crime fighters. Prosecutors are also the actors most likely to be influenced by the threat of sanctions for failing to abide by preservation requirements. Prosecutors care about the prospect of a post-conviction reversal, less so the police, and even less so the judiciary. To that end, evidence preservation statutes should mandate some element of prosecutorial oversight regardless of how custodial responsibilities are formally divided between the police, the courts, and the prosecution.[57]

Even if a prisoner locates biological evidence, obtains state-of-the-art DNA testing, and receives favorable results, his freedom is not guaranteed. Prosecutors may challenge the legal significance of those scientific results: behavior that may postpone, possibly even foil, an innocent prisoner's release.

In Denial

*Prosecutors' Refusal to Accept Proof of
an Inmate's Innocence*

Imagine that Smith convinces a judge to order post-conviction DNA testing in his drunk-driving case. The prosecution submits the blood sample taken from the fire hydrant to the state crime lab for DNA tests. The parties wait for the results. At last they arrive—excluding both Smith *and* Allen as the source of the blood. The blood contains the DNA profile of an unknown male. Prosecutors run the profile through every available state and federal DNA database but come up empty.

Smith and the defense team breathe a sigh of relief. The prosecution's case at trial had relied on evidence that Johnson saw the perpetrator cut his leg on the hydrant and that serology tests determined the blood found on the hydrant was Type O, matching the blood type of Smith. Now that more sophisticated tests prove that Smith was not the source of the blood, the defense expects prosecutors to support reversal of the conviction. Is this expectation reasonable?

Many prosecutors would interpret the DNA results to exonerate Smith,[1] but others might cling to their theory of guilt and revise the formulation of that theory to fit the newfound information. Post-conviction prosecutors could argue that the blood sample did not come from the perpetrator and that it derived instead from some previous, unknown incident. To back this up, prosecutors could throw the crime scene investigators under the bus by suggesting that they overlooked Smith's blood elsewhere on the hydrant. Or prosecutors could say that Johnson was mistaken about this (and just this) detail. Revisionist history of this sort occurs even in the context of exculpatory DNA evidence. Prosecutors typically accept the reliability of the results but may disagree with the defense about the legal significance.[2]

Denial in Action

Many prosecutors respond favorably to exculpatory DNA results and act with haste to accelerate an inmate's exoneration. Two days after Frank Sedita, the chief prosecutor in Erie County in upstate New York, learned about the results of Douglas Pacyon's post-conviction DNA test, Sedita filed an affidavit with the court to dismiss the case. Sedita told Pacyon: "You're owed an apology, and we apologize to you." Pacyon was exonerated in June 2010 after having spent nearly seven years in prison and then twenty years on parole for a rape he did not commit.[3]

Sedita's cohorts across the country do not always react as graciously when faced with powerful new evidence of innocence. Prosecutors have used a range of arguments to explain away exculpatory DNA results: minimizing the importance of the findings, devising new scenarios of guilt, even condemning the actions of the victim.[4] A post-conviction case from my early years on the University of Utah law faculty shows this phenomenon in action.

Prosecutors convicted Bruce Goodman of killing Sherry Ann Fales Williams, a twenty-one-year-old woman whose corpse was found on the morning of November 30, 1984, near Interstate 15 north of Beaver, Utah. Naked below the waist, Williams had lacerations across her body as well as signs of head trauma. Crime scene investigators collected a partially smoked cigarette from the snow close to the body. Serology tests confirmed the presence of saliva on the cigarette from a Type A secretor. An autopsy further revealed that Williams had engaged in sexual intercourse with a Type A secretor at some point during the previous twenty-four to thirty-six hours. A Type A secretor is a person with A blood who secretes A antigens into bodily fluids; expert testimony at Goodman's trial suggested that 32 percent of the population falls into this category. At the time of the murder more accurate methods of testing biological evidence, including DNA testing, had not yet been refined.[5]

Goodman, an A secretor, emerged as the prime suspect. He had become intimate with Williams after they met in October 1984, and by all accounts they left Las Vegas together in a truck on November 19. At trial, Goodman insisted he had abandoned the vehicle later on the 19th at a truck stop and left for California without Williams. She supposedly wanted to reconcile with her estranged husband. Two defense witnesses corroborated Goodman's claim that he was in California when Williams died.[6]

The prosecution had a different take on the case. Utah prosecutors introduced evidence indicating that Goodman had continued to accompany Williams after November 19. The key witness was a woman who worked at a casino in Mesquite, Nevada. She placed a man who fit Goodman's description arguing with Williams at the casino between 2:00 a.m. and 4:00 a.m. on November 30. Mesquite lies off Interstate 15 between Las Vegas and the Utah border.[7]

In 1986 a Utah judge found Goodman guilty of murder after a bench trial. The Utah Supreme Court acknowledged on appeal that "without question this was a close case" but affirmed Goodman's murder conviction. Justice Daniel Stewart wrote a spirited dissent. In his view, the absence of *any* evidence connecting Goodman to Williams between the early morning sighting at a crowded Mesquite casino and the discovery of the body five hours later in rural Utah placed the soundness of the case in doubt.[8]

Many years later, Goodman enlisted the help of the Rocky Mountain Innocence Center (RMIC), an organization in Salt Lake City that investigates and litigates post-conviction claims of innocence by prisoners in Nevada, Utah, and Wyoming. Goodman was among the very first inmates to contact the fledgling group. RMIC obtained the leftover biological evidence from the state crime lab. Subsequent DNA tests proved that neither the specimen salvaged from the cigarette nor the sample contained in the rape kit belonged to Goodman. The DNA evidence showed that two other, unidentified people had deposited the fluids.[9]

These results shocked the post-conviction prosecutors. The government's stance all along had been that Goodman had killed Williams by himself. These new findings shattered that hypothesis. Yet the prosecutors did not conclude that Goodman was innocent. Instead, a novel prosecution theory arose to rationalize the status quo: that Goodman was one of several perpetrators who participated in the Williams murder that morning and that the absence of his biological evidence did not prove his innocence. This about-face occurred after relying for nearly twenty years on the argument that Goodman and the murderer were A secretors. It also meant that the state was not going to facilitate Goodman's release.[10] What was RMIC's next move?

I participated in RMIC's strategy discussions in 2004 as a member of its board of directors. We knew we could file a motion under Utah's Post-Conviction DNA Testing Statute asking the court to reverse Goodman's conviction based on the DNA results. Under this remedy, a judge may dismiss the charges if the defendant proves his actual innocence by clear and convincing evidence; a dismissal pursuant to this law would bar the prosecution from ever trying Goodman again for the Williams murder. Alternatively, we considered proceeding under the state habeas corpus remedy, which permits courts to overturn convictions when presented with newly discovered evidence that undermines confidence in the verdict. But the habeas corpus procedure had some downsides. For one thing, it did not allow for a definitive ruling on the grounds of innocence; for another, it left open the possibility that prosecutors could retry the defendant.[11]

Prosecutors in the Goodman case refused to consent to a hearing under the DNA statute and vowed to challenge any filing under that act. Recognizing that Goodman's freedom was its top objective, RMIC agreed to file a state habeas corpus petition. In return, the state promised not to contest the habeas petition or seek a retrial. In November 2004 Goodman left prison a free man, yet he was not altogether absolved of the crime through an official declaration of innocence.[12]

The Innocence Project in New York City lists Goodman as one of the innocent inmates exonerated through post-conviction DNA testing.[13] Some observers might dispute this characterization. It is conceivable that Goodman acted with two or more unknown assailants in murdering Williams, as the post-conviction prosecutors claimed, but no evidence supports that narrative.[14] What is clear is that an asterisk remains next to Goodman's name courtesy of the prosecutors' baffling reluctance to consider the possibility of a mistake.

The refusal of prosecutors to accept a prisoner's innocence, even after the discovery of DNA evidence pointing to that conclusion, may also hinder that person's efforts to gain compensation. The wrongfully convicted have struggled to win damages through traditional civil lawsuits because of procedural hurdles and doctrines that grant government officials immunity.[15] To remedy this problem, twenty-seven states have passed legislation targeted at wrongful conviction compensation.[16] Some compensation laws require an official declaration of innocence as a prerequisite to monetary relief.[17] Prosecutorial opposition to labeling an inmate "innocent" diminishes the chance that a clemency board or court will ever reach such a finding. And without that finding, the prisoner's pursuit of compensation is bound to end in disappointment. Goodman, who walked out of Utah state prison without enough money to pay for underwear, has not received a dime to compensate him for his suffering.

Prosecutors may even seek to retry a defendant after he is released on grounds consistent with innocence. This happened to Kennedy Brewer. On May 3, 1992, three-year-old Christine Jackson was abducted from her home in Noxubee County, Mississippi. Two days later she was found dead in a creek five hundred yards from her home, and there was evidence she had been raped. Kennedy Brewer, the boyfriend of Christine's mother, surfaced as the main suspect. He had been home that evening babysitting Christine. There was also no sign of forced entry, although a broken window near the toddler's room could have provided access to an intruder. The state's theory was that Brewer had raped and murdered Christine in the Jackson home, and then hauled her to the creek to cover up the crime. A semen sample taken from Christine was deemed inadequate for DNA testing. The police arrested Brewer shortly after the discovery of Christine's body.[18]

Brewer remained in jail until the case went to trial in March 1995. The state's case against Brewer was circumstantial except for one piece of forensic evidence—the medical examiner who had conducted the autopsy found several blemishes that he thought were likely bite marks. Enter Dr. Michael West, a bite mark analyst who had already received the ignominious distinction of being the first member ever suspended by the field's professional association, the American Board of Forensic Odontology. Noxubee County prosecutors put West on the stand anyway, and the trial judge let his testimony into evidence. West told the jury that nineteen marks on Christine's skin "indeed and without a doubt" came from Brewer's teeth. West went on to claim that Brewer's top two front teeth alone had created these indentations. The defense countered with its own expert who testified that the marks were not the product of human teeth at all but of insect bites that accumulated as the body floated in a creek for days. The defense expert also pointed out that creating bite marks from one's two front teeth—without the use of bottom teeth—is an implausible physical feat. Somehow the jury believed West (or at least felt moved by the circumstantial evidence) and convicted Brewer of capital murder and sexual battery.[19]

Brewer's case languished until advanced DNA tests conducted on the semen sample in 2001 excluded him as the rapist. Those tests revealed the genetic profile of an unknown male. The prosecution compared the results to those obtained from DNA tests performed on several of Brewer's friends and relatives. All of them were cleared as suspects; nothing suggests the prosecution took further steps to reinvestigate the crime. In 2002 a state court vacated Brewer's conviction. Prison officials transferred him from death row to pretrial detention to await decision on whether he would be retried.[20]

Word soon came that Noxubee County prosecutors planned to re-file capital murder charges against Brewer. He sat in lockup for five more years. Because of conflicts of interest, the chief prosecutor from another county took over the Brewer case in 2007. That prosecutor decided against charging the case as a capital crime and did not oppose bail. Even though a judge released Brewer on bail in August 2007, the specter of a new murder trial still hung over him.[21]

The Innocence Project begged the Mississippi Attorney General's Office to reexamine the case. DNA testing during the ensuing investigation produced a match of the unknown profile of Christine's rapist to Justin Albert Johnson, a local man who had been one of the original suspects. Johnson later confessed and swore that he had acted alone. In February 2008 prosecutors dropped charges against Brewer—nearly sixteen years after the crime had occurred, thirteen years after his trial, and seven years after DNA testing first excluded him as a source of the semen.[22]

Reasons for Continued Intransigence by Prosecutors

Why do some prosecutors react so obstinately when faced with scientific evidence that signals a prisoner's innocence? To be sure, the institutional, political, and psychological factors discussed in chapter 7 continue to affect prosecutors after the emergence of DNA test results. Prosecutors want to preserve individual and office-wide conviction rates; elected district attorneys detest the thought of nasty headlines; and cognitive biases stop prosecutors from interpreting the newfound information with equanimity. The absence of firm legal and ethical rules in the post-conviction setting also contributes to how prosecutors respond to proof of innocence.[23]

Other factors come into play, including the psychological concept of "denial." Like the aversion to cognitive dissonance,[24] denial acts as a defense mechanism to avoid, even justify, one's dishonorable behavior. The scholarly literature on denial suggests that it is "a deeper, more emotional" experience than most cognitive biases and that it often crops up in reaction to trauma.[25] Prosecutors confronted with the prospect of a wrongful conviction may erect any number of cognitive barriers to discount that possibility. But once DNA tests come back that are favorable to the defendant, and possibility becomes reality, then discounting is no longer an option. Only denial or acceptance remains. And many prosecutors succumb to denial so as to avoid "facing the unfaceable."[26] They do so not by denying the facts outright but by interpreting those facts in a bizarre way.[27] Denial may lead prosecutors to behave in a churlish fashion, even after an official declaration of innocence, by refusing to apologize or engaging in petty behavior that strains the bounds of logic.[28]

Finally, some prosecutors may believe in theories of criminal punishment that would support the continued incarceration of an inmate despite powerful DNA evidence of innocence. Many innocent prisoners have prior criminal records. Indeed, that is how most of their photos appear in mug books for witnesses to misidentify—from prior arrests. Post-conviction prosecutors may dwell on these backgrounds and infer that, even if the prisoner is innocent of the crime for which he is currently locked up, he did other bad things for which he never paid the price. In other words, he is not "innocent" in a karmic sense.[29] The presence of a rap sheet may also convince prosecutors that the inmate poses a risk of causing *future* harm. Keeping him in confinement, then, at least incapacitates him from committing new crimes against the public.[30]

Prosecutors in Denial: Potential Responses

Defense lawyers and innocence projects could pursue litigation to stop prosecutors from tailoring their original theories of the case to fit compelling new evidence of innocence. Some creative litigators have sought to do this through the doctrine of "judicial estoppel." This doctrine bars a party from prevailing in one phase of a proceeding based on one argument and then advancing a contradictory argument in another phase. The rationale is that allowing parties to advance inconsistent positions in the same case could bring the entire system into disrepute and undermine confidence in the litigation process. Yet judicial estoppel is largely a creature of civil case law. When it does appear in criminal cases, it is almost always used *against* defendants to ban them from asserting a position on appeal that differs from the one employed at trial.[31] Judicial estoppel nevertheless holds promise for inmates faced with prosecutors who construct novel theories to square exculpatory evidence with their vision of guilt. Innocence advocates are currently presenting estoppel-type arguments in courts across the country.[32]

Together with litigation, defendants might consider filing ethics complaints against post-conviction prosecutors whose revised theories of guilt depart significantly from those presented at trial. These complaints would stand a much better chance of resulting in discipline if rules were passed to forbid prosecutors from developing new or inconsistent theories of a case to substantiate their belief in a prisoner's guilt. Even without a specific ethical rule, the thrust of these complaints could be that revisionist accounts of a case violate the minister-of-justice principle. As merely a cursory reading of this book reveals, however, disciplinary agencies seldom sanction prosecutors for violating the amorphous duty to do justice.

Using outside pressure through litigation and ethics complaints is just one way of triggering change. Another potential catalyst involves nurturing change from within by exposing prosecutors to the problem of wrongful convictions and cognitive biases over time. Most prosecutors presumably want to manifest the minister-of-justice ideal at all stages of a criminal case. A major aim of this book is to help meet that goal through a series of modest legal, ethical, and institutional reforms. And if my reforms prove ineffective, there is always the option of starting from scratch. Some scholars, in fact, believe that the best hope for American justice lies in dismantling the adversary system altogether.

Conclusion

American prosecutors have tough jobs. They are asked to serve as zealous crime fighters for the state while acting as compassionate public officials concerned with the rights of criminal defendants. Juggling these responsibilities causes some prosecutors to participate in the conviction of the innocent.

I have tried to tackle this problem head-on. The bulk of my proposed reforms embrace a "gradualist"[1] or evolutionary approach to the prosecutorial function. I do not favor razing the institution of the American prosecutor and installing an entirely new structure in its stead; I prefer renovation to demolition. Lift the legal bar that prosecutors must meet in order to justify major decisions. Hone the rules of ethics and motivate disciplinary agencies to enforce them. Design internal review committees to improve decision making and counter cognitive bias. My approach is informed by ideology and reality, a belief that a more finely tuned adversary system can best protect the innocent and that forsaking this system is politically impossible in the United States.

Some scholars believe that gradualism does not go far enough: that the only way to safeguard the innocent and stop prosecutorial misadventures is to overhaul the American criminal justice system. As DNA exonerations have continued to make news, it has become popular within the legal academy to assign blame to American institutions and look abroad for guidance. Professors Erik Luna and Marianne Wade, for instance, recently published an excellent survey of prosecutorial practices across Europe and suggested that the American criminal justice system could benefit from "selective transplants" from overseas.[2]

This look outward has generated reform proposals that would revolutionize criminal justice in the United States. I have scattered some of these revolutionary ideas throughout the book.[3] What I have not yet discussed are proposals aimed at changing the very *role* played by prosecutors in investigating and litigating criminal cases. Let's take a brief look at those recommendations.

May the Revolution Begin?

Several American scholars who have studied criminal justice systems in continental Europe have come away from that enterprise with a high regard for the inquisitorial model in France, where magistrate judges, not prosecutors, dominate the investigative and adjudicative processes. Various judicial officers take part in French criminal cases. The *procureur*, who is both a public prosecutor and a member of the judiciary, reviews the evidence and determines whether to charge the accused with a crime. The *procureur* resembles the American prosecutor in some respects but with a fundamental distinction; he is a judicial officer required to act neutrally in directing the police and inspecting the evidence. No advocacy obligation exists as a counterweight to the *procureur*'s nonpartisan function.[4] In some cases, the *procureur* will turn over the inquiry to the *juge d'instruction*, a judicial official authorized to supervise criminal investigations.[5] The *juge d'instruction* is deeply integrated into the pretrial investigation of a potential criminal case, bearing responsibility for evaluating all relevant information and questioning the accused.[6] Then a trial judge enters the picture. That judge presides over the trial, assesses the evidence presented by a trial prosecutor and defense lawyer, and takes a much more interventionist approach than is common in the United States. The presiding judge in France tends to call and examine witnesses on his own initiative.[7] Unlike in the United States, few French criminal cases are resolved through negotiated settlements.[8]

Fans of the French system often suggest that the United States should borrow from it. Decades ago Professor Lloyd Weinreb proposed an innovative, French-influenced system where magistrate judges would handle the investigation in lieu of the police, followed by a trial where a presiding judge would present the evidence and even serve on the jury.[9] Professor George Thomas recently put forward "a much more modest revolution."[10] He recommended that, as in France, American judges should actively review cases as "screening magistrates" at the front end of the investigative process.[11] Thomas also advised a rigorous pretrial review through a process comparable to that of France, where judges dismiss a large number of cases because of insufficient evidence.[12] Among his other fascinating ideas, Thomas envisions a more vigilant American trial judge who, if not quite as interventionist as the French archetype, instructs juries more thoroughly, allows in evidence supporting the innocence of the accused more readily, and gives witnesses more leeway to tell their accounts.[13]

Although some reforms drawn from the French experience may have merit, I am less enthusiastic than many other observers are. A thread connecting these proposals, whether explicit or implicit, is profound faith in judges—the notion that judges could do a better job than American prosecutors in remaining objective and advancing justice. Perhaps that is partially true. But I fear that over time interventionist judges will suffer from many of the cognitive biases (tunnel vision, the aversion to cognitive dissonance, and so forth) that plague American prosecutors at the moment. Also, I am not sure that the United States has the political will to deviate from the adversary system. Nor am I sure that we *need* substantial deviation. What we need are reforms that add heft to the ethereal minister-of justice principle. Justice Oliver Wendell Holmes once proclaimed: "I hate justice, which means that I know if a man begins to talk about that, for one reason or another he is shirking thinking in legal terms."[14] Thinking about justice should be synonymous with thinking in legal terms. To achieve an overlap between justice and legal terms, I believe evolution—not revolution—is the way to go.

The Evolutionary Approach, Once Again

Some evolutionary steps must come from the top. Courts and legislatures should change the laws surrounding charging decisions, demand open file discovery, modify the trial tax, forbid wink-and-nod cooperation agreements, take crime labs out from under the law enforcement umbrella, and otherwise implement the slew of legal reforms advocated throughout this book. States should fortify these changes by adopting precise ethical rules and standards, and by motivating disciplinary agencies to enforce these new provisions.

But many reforms must come from the bottom up. Keep in mind the practices of the most thoughtful present-day prosecutors. Like the Nassau County prosecutors' office in New York, prosecutors should have single-eyewitness review committees prior to charging. Like the Los Angeles District Attorney's office, they should have a *Brady* Compliance Division and a committee to vet jailhouse informant testimony. Like prosecutors in Santa Clara, California, they should reward attorneys who uncover innocent defendants. And like county prosecutors' offices in Dallas, Houston, and Manhattan, they should have post-conviction units committed to investigating claims of innocence. As these real-world examples illustrate, prosecutors do have a choice. They need not let their work be controlled by cognitive bias and perverse institutional and political pressures. If they have the willpower, the capacity to think creatively, and solid ethical compasses, they can stamp out the prosecution complex.[15]

In the end, maintaining an ethical culture within prosecutors' offices is the key to enhancing the likelihood that justice will prevail. I have devoted much of this book to asking others to change their ways. It is only fair for me to look in the mirror and figure out what I can do to help as a law professor.

The culture of legal institutions, including prosecutorial agencies, has its genesis in law school education. Law professors should reconsider the structure of the curriculum and the manner in which students are trained. Instead of emphasizing the black letter of legal doctrine and the techniques of advocacy above all, a premium should be placed on ethics and the importance of empathizing with clients as well as adversaries.[16] In 1940 U.S. Attorney General Robert H. Jackson observed that "sensitiveness to fair play and sportsmanship is perhaps the best protection against abuse of power."[17] Jackson went on to caution that "the citizen's safety lies in the prosecutor who tempers zeal with human kindness, who seeks truth and not victims, who serves the law and not factional purposes, and who approaches his task with humility."[18]

Promoting these characteristics in prosecutors will breathe life into the minister-of-justice principle and, most of all, reduce wrongful convictions. Wrongful convictions tear at the tattered fabric of public confidence in the rule of law and the people chosen to enforce it. Without major repair efforts, the damage may soon be too great to restore faith in the idea of justice.

Notes

INTRODUCTION

1. For a current listing of DNA exonerations in the United States, see the Innocence Project home page (available at http://www.innocenceproject.org). See also Samuel R. Gross et al., "Exonerations in the United States, 1989 through 2003," 95 *J. Crim. L. & Criminology* 523, 524 (2005). For a discussion of the empirical studies related to this topic, see Daniel S. Medwed, "Innocentrism," 2008 *U. Ill. L. Rev.* 1549, 1553 nn. 15–16 (2008).

2. See Medwed, *Innocentrism*, at 1570–71.

3. Samuel R. Gross, "Souter Passant, Scalia Rampant: Combat in the *Marsh*," 105 *Mich. L. Rev. First Impressions* 67, 69 (2006).

4. See, e.g., Kathleen M. Ridolfi & Maurice Possley, *Preventable Error: A Report on Prosecutorial Misconduct in California 1997–2009*, Oct. 2010 (available at http://law.scu.edu/ncip/file/ProsecutorialMisconduct_BookEntire_online%20version.pdf).

5. Much of this introduction derives from two law review articles that I have published: Daniel S. Medwed, "The Prosecutor as Minister of Justice: Preaching to the Unconverted from the Post-Conviction Pulpit," 84 *Wash. L. Rev.* 35 (2009); and Daniel S. Medwed, "The Zeal Deal: Prosecutorial Resistance to Post-Conviction Claims of Innocence," 84 *B.U. L. Rev.* 125 (2004). See also *Brady v. Maryland*, 373 U.S. 83 (1963); Model Rules of Prof'l Conduct R. 3.8 cmt 1 (2008).

6. See Peter A. Joy & Kevin C. McMunigal, *Do No Wrong: Ethics for Prosecutors and Defenders* (Chicago: ABA, 2009), 14–17.

7. See, e.g., Michael Cassidy, "Character and Context: What Virtue Theory Can Teach Us about a Prosecutor's Ethical Duty to 'Seek Justice,'" 82 *Notre Dame L. Rev.* 635, 637–38 (2005); Fred C. Zacharias, "Structuring the Ethics of Prosecutorial Trial Practice: Can Prosecutors Do Justice?" 44 *Vand. L. Rev.* 45, 46 (1991).

8. See Ellen Yaroshefsky, "Wrongful Convictions: It is Time to Take Prosecution Discipline Seriously," 8 *D.C. L. Rev.* 275, 294 (2004); Fred C. Zacharias, "The Professional Discipline of Prosecutors," 79 *N.C. L. Rev.* 721 (2001).

9. See Medwed, *Preaching*, at 36.

10. See Kenneth J. Melilli, "Prosecutorial Discretion in an Adversary System," 1992 *BYU L. Rev.* 669, 698 (1992).

11. See Innocence Project, "Understand the Causes: Government Misconduct" (available at http://www.innocenceproject.org/understand/Government-Misconduct.php). See also Medwed, *Preaching*; Medwed, *Zeal Deal*. I am not the first person to use the term "prosecution complex." See, e.g., George F. Cole & Christopher E. Smith, *The American System of Criminal Justice* 322 (11th ed. 2007).

12. See Medwed, *Innocentrism*, at 1553 nn. 15–16. A 1 percent error rate would produce roughly ninety thousand wrongful convictions each year in nontraffic offense cases. See George C. Thomas III, "When Lawyers Fail Innocent Defendants: Exorcising the Ghosts That Haunt the Criminal Justice Systems," 2008 *Utah L. Rev.* 25, 25–26 (2008).

13. This adage is generally attributed to either William Blackstone or Matthew Hale. See, e.g., Harold J. Berman & Charles J. Reid, Jr., "The Transformation of English Legal Science: From Hale to Blackstone," 45 *Emory L. J.* 437, 482 (1996).

14. See Medwed, *Innocentrism*, at 1565.

15. See Keith A. Findley & Michael S. Scott, "The Multiple Dimensions of Tunnel Vision in Criminal Cases," 2006 *Wis. L. Rev.* 291 (2006).

16. See, e.g., George T. Felkenes, "The Prosecutor: A Look at Reality," 7 *Sw. U. L. Rev.* 98, 99 (1975).

17. See, e.g., Medwed, *Preaching*, at 48–49. See also Aviva Orenstein, "Facing the Unfaceable: Dealing with Prosecutorial Denial in Postconviction Cases of Actual Innocence," 48 *San Diego L. Rev.* 401, 413–16 (2011).

18. See, e.g., Angela J. Davis, "Prosecution and Race: The Power and Privilege of Discretion," 67 *Fordham L. Rev.* 13 (1998); Angela J. Davis, "Racial Fairness in the Criminal Justice System: The Role of the Prosecutor," 39 *Colum. Hum. Rts. L. Rev.* 202 (2007).

19. As Professor Alafair Burke points out, the wrongful conviction literature has endorsed for far too long a "language of fault" when talking about prosecutors. See Alafair S. Burke, "Talking about Prosecutors," 31 *Cardozo L. Rev.* 2119, 2119–22 (2010). One of my goals here is to go beyond fault-based rhetoric and pursue a constructive dialogue. See also Ellen Yaroshefsky, "Foreword: New Perspectives on *Brady* and Other Disclosure Obligations: What Really Works?" 31 *Cardozo L. Rev.* 1943, 1945–46 (2010).

20. See Steven W. Perry, "Prosecutors in State Courts, 2005," *Bureau of Just. Statistics Bulletin,* July 2006, 1–2 (available at http://www.bjs.ojp.usdoj.gov/content/pub/pdf/psc05.pdf).

PART I. FAIR PLAY?

1. The facts in this prelude to part 1 derive from the Innocence Project's 2007 Application for a Writ of Habeas Corpus on Behalf of James Curtis Giles, the State's Response, and Dallas County Criminal District Court Judge Robert Francis's Decision (documents on file with author) [hereinafter "2007 Habeas Corpus Materials"]. See also Michael Hall, "The Exonerated," *Texas Monthly,* Nov. 2008; Steve McGonigle, "Rape Victim Is for Exoneration," *Dallas Morning News,* Apr. 6, 2007; Steve McGonigle, "Judge Backs Exoneration of Man Convicted of Rape," *Dallas Morning News,* Apr. 9, 2007; Innocence Project, "Profile of James Curtis Giles" (available at http://www.innocenceproject.org/Content/James_Curtis_Giles.php) [hereinafter "Media Accounts"].

2. See 2007 Habeas Corpus Materials at GIL-001709. See also Media Accounts.

3. 2007 Habeas Corpus Materials at GIL-001709. Both the victim's husband and another man who evidently observed part of the assault, refused to testify, citing their privilege against self-incrimination. See 2007 Habeas Corpus Materials at GIL-001710.

4. See 2007 Habeas Corpus Materials at GIL-001710.

5. See 2007 Habeas Corpus Materials; Media Accounts.

6. *Id.*

7. *Id.*

8. Brady v. Maryland, 373 U.S. 83, 87 (1963).

9. See Bennett L. Gershman, *Prosecutorial Misconduct,* 2d ed. (St. Paul, MN: Thomson-West, 2007), 231–34; Kyles v. Whitley, 514 U.S. 419 (1995).

10. See 2007 Habeas Corpus Materials; Media Accounts.

11. *Id.*

12. Moore relayed this story to the victim and her husband and his friend Jeff Shea. After informing Moore that he wanted to collect the $1,000 reward for providing information about an unsolved crime, Shea called Crime Stoppers and passed along the name "James Giles" in connection with the North Dallas incident. See 2007 Habeas Corpus Materials at GIL-001707-08.

13. See 2007 Habeas Corpus Materials; Media Accounts.

14. See the Innocence Project home page (available at http://www.innocenceproject.org/about/).

15. As of July 11, 2011, the Innocence Project had either directly represented defendants or consulted on 154 DNA exonerations. See e-mail from Emily West to Daniel S. Medwed and accompanying attachment, July 11, 2011 (copy on file with author).

16. See Daniel S. Medwed, "The Prosecutor as Minister of Justice? Preaching to the Unconverted from the Post-Conviction Pulpit," 84 *Wash. L. Rev.* 37, 58–60 (2009). See also Daniel S. Medwed, "Actual Innocents: Considerations in Selecting Cases for a New Innocence Project," 81 *Neb. L. Rev.* 1097 (2003). Centurion Ministries, founded in 1983, was the first organization in the United States devoted to investigating and litigating claims of actual innocence by prisoners. See Centurion Ministries, "About Us" (available at http://www.centurionministries.org/aboutus.html).

17. See 2007 Habeas Corpus Materials; Media Accounts.

18. *Id.*

19. *Id.*

20. *Id.*

21. Specifically, while responding to the Innocence Project's initial request for DNA testing in 2003, a prosecutor in the appellate division of the Dallas County District Attorney's Office found Stanley Bryant's statements in Giles's trial file and other materials related to the Indianapolis interrogation in Bryant's own trial files; she turned those documents over to the defense. See 2007 Habeas Corpus Materials at GIL-001855-56.

22. See Medwed, *Preaching,* at 64–66.

23. Hall, *The Exonerated.*

24. John Council, "Witnesses to the Prosecution: Current and Former ADAs Who Helped Convict Exonerated Men Reflect," *Texas Lawyer,* June 9, 2008.

25. See Steve McGonigle & Jennifer Emily, "Dallas Inmate Set to Be Freed after Buried Evidence Found," *Dallas Morning News,* Oct. 8, 2009.

26. Prosecutorial behavior during other parts of the pretrial process may also tilt the scales of justice unfairly toward conviction. See Angela J. Davis, "The American Prosecutor: Independence, Power, and the Threat of Tyranny," 86 *Iowa L. Rev.* 393, 422–29 (2001) (discussing abuse of the grand jury process); Laurie L. Levenson, "Prosecutorial Sound Bites: When Do They Cross the Line?" 44 *Ga. L. Rev.* 1021 (2010) (discussing improper pretrial publicity).

1. Model Rules of Prof'l Conduct R. 3.8 (a) (2008). Portions of this chapter stem from Daniel S. Medwed, "Emotionally Charged: The Prosecutorial Charging Decision and the Innocence Revolution," 31 *Cardozo L. Rev.* 2187 (2010).

2. A mere 50 percent chance of guilt may be enough to justify a charging decision. See Fred C. Zacharias & Bruce A. Green, "The Duty to Avoid Wrongful Convictions: A Thought Experiment in the Regulation of Prosecutors," 89 *B.U. L. Rev.* 1, 9 (2009). Others have suggested that the probable cause standard is (and should be) even lower than that, at least in the search and seizure context. See Joseph D. Grano, "Probable Cause and Common Sense: A Reply to the Critics of *Illinois v. Gates*," 17 *U. Mich. J. L. Reform* 465, 488–501 (1984). The Supreme Court has indicated that probable cause to justify an arrest by the police occurs when facts and circumstances exist "to warrant a prudent man in believing that the [suspect] had committed or was committing an offense." Beck v. Ohio, 379 U.S. 89, 91 (1964); Gerstein v. Pugh, 420 U.S. 103, 111 (1975).

3. See, e.g., R. Michael Cassidy, *Prosecutorial Ethics* (St. Paul, MN: Thomson-West, 2005), 15.

4. Cross-racial identifications—those involving a witness identifying a suspect of a different race—are notoriously unreliable. See, e.g., John P. Rutledge, "They All Look Alike: The Inaccuracy of Cross-Racial Identifications," 28 *Am. J. Crim. L.* 207 (2001).

5. See Bennett L. Gershman, *Prosecutorial Misconduct*, 2d ed. (St. Paul, MN: Thomson-West, 2007), 155–56; Leslie C. Griffin, "The Prudent Prosecutor," 14 *Geo. J. Legal Ethics* 259, 263–66 (2001).

6. See Bennett L. Gershman, "A Moral Standard for the Prosecutor's Exercise of the Charging Discretion," 20 *Fordham Urb. L. J.* 513, 513 (1993).

7. See Angela J. Davis, *Arbitrary Justice: The Power of the American Prosecutor* (New York: Oxford University Press, 2007), 23; Amie N. Ely, Note, "Prosecutorial Discretion as Ethical Necessity: The Ashcroft Memorandum's Curtailment of the Prosecutor's Duty to 'Seek Justice,'" 90 *Cornell L. Rev.* 237, 242–48 (2004).

8. See Cassidy, *Prosecutorial Ethics*, at 18–19. Similar to overcharging to gain leverage in plea negotiations, prosecutors sometimes threaten to charge potential witnesses in a case unless they agree to "cooperate" and testify against that person. Angela J. Davis, "The American Prosecutor: Independence, Power, and the Threat of Tyranny," 86 *Iowa L. Rev.* 393, 433–34 (2001).

9. Studies of the federal system reveal a declination rate of roughly 25 percent. See Michael Edmund O'Neill, "Understanding Federal Prosecutorial Declinations: An Empirical Analysis of Predictive Factors," 41 *Am. Crim. L. Rev.* 1439, 1444 (2004). An analysis of charging in New York City suggests declinations occur in about one-third of all felony cases. See Josh Bowers, "Punishing the Innocent," 156 *U. Pa. L. Rev.* 1117, 1129 (2008).

10. See Patrick J. Fitzgerald, "Thoughts on the Ethical Culture of a Prosecutor's Office," 84 *Wash. L. Rev.* 11, 12 (2009).

11. See Davis, *Arbitrary Justice*, at 33–34; Erik Luna & Marianne Wade, "Prosecutors as Judges," 67 *Wash. & Lee L. Rev.* 1413, 1419–20 (2010); Kenneth J. Melilli, "Prosecutorial Discretion in an Adversary System," 1992 *BYU L. Rev.* 669, 683, 687 (1992). Very few prosecutorial offices appear to have written standards or manuals to guide prosecutors in rendering discretionary decisions. See Peter A. Joy, "The Relationship between Prosecu-

torial Misconduct and Wrongful Convictions: Shaping Remedies for a Broken System," 2006 *Wis. L. Rev.* 399, 420–22 (2006).

12. See Cassidy, *Prosecutorial Ethics*, at 23–24. Prosecutors may not arbitrarily select a defendant for prosecution without violating equal protection principles. Similarly, defendants have constitutional protections against prosecutors who possess a "vindictive" personal motive for charging them. See Gershman, *Prosecutorial Misconduct*, at 164–206.

13. See United States v. Armstrong, 517 U.S. 456, 465 (1996); Gershman, *Prosecutorial Misconduct*, at 156.

14. See Robert L. Misner, "Recasting Prosecutorial Discretion," 86 *J. Crim. L. & Criminology* 717, 743 (1996).

15. In his well-known book on prosecutorial discretion, Professor Kenneth Culp Davis criticized the lack of transparency surrounding prosecutorial decision making—and the decision whether to charge in particular—and estimated "that more than nine-tenths of local prosecutors' decisions are supervised or reviewed by no one." Kenneth Culp Davis, *Discretionary Justice: A Preliminary Inquiry* (Baton Rouge: Louisiana State University Press, 1969), 188–89, 207–8.

16. See Davis, *Arbitrary Justice*, at 24. A federal criminal defendant has a constitutional right to an indictment for all "capital, or otherwise infamous crimes." U.S. Const., amend. V. The U.S. Supreme Court, however, has not required convening grand juries at the state level and more than half the states have selected other methods. See Cassidy, *Prosecutorial Ethics*, at 26.

17. See, e.g., Gershman, *Moral Standard*, at 520; Andrew D. Leipold, "Why Grand Juries Do Not (and Cannot) Protect the Accused," 80 *Cornell L. Rev.* 260 (1995).

18. See Cassidy, *Prosecutorial Ethics*, at 26–29; Davis, *Arbitrary Justice*, at 24.

19. See United States v. Armstrong, 517 U.S. 456, 464 (1996).

20. The description of the Duke Lacrosse Rape Case comes from Robert P. Mosteller, "The Duke Lacrosse Case, Innocence, and False Identifications: A Fundamental Failure to 'Do Justice,'" 76 *Fordham L. Rev.* 1337, 1342–46 (2007).

21. *Id.*

22. *Id.*

23. *Id.*

24. Nifong was subsequently sanctioned for his improper pretrial publicity. *Id.* at 1348–50.

25. For a description of the evidence implicating the three defendants, see *Id.* at 1373.

26. *Id.* at 1372–73.

27. *Id.* at 1348–64. See also Zacharias & Green, *Duty to Avoid*, at 12.

28. Rev. R. Prof'l Conduct, N.C. State Bar R. 3.8(a) (2007). See also Mosteller, *Duke Lacrosse Case*, at 1367.

29. *Id.* at 1368.

30. *Id.* at 1373–74.

31. *Id.* at 1372. See also *Id.* at 1376 ("That Nifong knew no probable cause existed in this case is not clearly established. However, that he had abundant notice of the problematic nature of the case is undeniable").

32. *Id.* at 1366. See also Melilli, *Prosecutorial Discretion*, at 672.

33. Professor Kenneth Melilli views the probable cause standard as "little more than heightened suspicion and it is not even remotely sufficient to screen out individuals who

are factually not guilty." Melilli, *Prosecutorial Discretion*, at 680-81. See also Bruce A. Green, "Prosecutorial Ethics as Usual," 2003 *U. Ill. L. Rev.* 1573, 1584 n. 53 (2003); Griffin, *Prudent Prosecutor*, at 268-70. Professor Alafair Burke, however, has recently argued that ethical prosecutors can be agnostic about a defendant's factual guilt. See Alafair S. Burke, "Prosecutorial Agnosticism," 8 *Ohio St. J. Crim. L.* 79 (2010).

34. See Mosteller, *Duke Lacrosse Case*, at 1368. See also Angela J. Davis, "The Legal Profession's Failure to Discipline Unethical Prosecutors," 36 *Hofstra L. Rev.* 275, 284–85 (2007); Melilli, *Prosecutorial Discretion*, at 681–82, 701.

35. Gershman, *Moral Standard*, at 522. Professor Bruce Green advocates an intermediate standard in which "charges should not be brought unless the prosecutor reasonably believes that the accused is guilty of the crimes charged." Green, *Prosecutorial Ethics*, at 1589.

36. Gershman, *Moral Standard*, at 524.

37. Bennett L. Gershman, "The Prosecutor's Duty to Truth," 14 *Geo. J. Legal Ethics* 309, 338 (2001).

38. See Mosteller, *Duke Lacrosse Case*, at 1367–68.

39. See, e.g., Melilli, *Prosecutorial Discretion,* at 691–93; H. Richard Uviller, "The Virtuous Prosecutor in Quest of an Ethical Standard: Guidance from the ABA," 71 *Mich. L. Rev.* 1145, 1159, 1168 (1973).

40. Juries are unreliable evaluators of guilt or innocence, as shown by the hundreds of documented wrongful convictions from jury trials, and the deliberation room is just as often a forum for prejudice as it is a sanctuary of dispassionate debate. See, e.g., Melilli, *Prosecutorial Discretion*, at 700. Acquittal rates have fallen to unprecedented lows. Russell D. Covey, "Fixed Justice: Reforming Plea Bargaining with Plea-Based Ceilings," 82 *Tul. L. Rev.* 1237, 1238–39 (2008).

41. See, generally, Lawton P. Cummings, "Can an Ethical Person Be an Ethical Prosecutor? A Social Cognitive Approach to Systemic Reform," 31 *Cardozo L. Rev.* 2139 (2010).

42. See, e.g., Melilli, *Prosecutorial Discretion*, at 700.

43. Professor Bennett Gershman claims that prosecutors too often place responsibility for close questions on the jury and that a prosecutor instead should serve as "a gatekeeper of justice" considering the risk of jury error. See Gershman, *Moral Standard*, at 521. See also Abbe Smith, "Can You Be a Good Person and a Good Prosecutor?" 14 *Geo. J. Legal Ethics* 355, 387 (2001).

44. See Mosteller, *Duke Lacrosse Case*, at 1367 n.140.

45. Some jurisdictions use the phrase "or it is obvious" in exchange for "or reasonably should know." *Id.*

46. The extent to which prosecutors undertake an independent review of the evidence assembled by the police before filing charges varies significantly. See Mary Prosser, "Reforming Criminal Discovery: Why Old Objections Must Yield to New Realities," 2006 *Wis. L. Rev.* 541, 550–51 (2006). Several scholars propose creating an investigative obligation for prosecutors prior to charging. See Mosteller, *Duke Lacrosse Case*, at 1369–70 nn.148–50.

47. *Id.* at 1370–71.

48. Professor Robert Mosteller suggests confining this duty to "high-profile" or "problematic" matters like the Duke Lacrosse case. *Id.* at 1370–79. Mosteller's plan is laudable but would also face difficulties, specifically in terms of how to determine whether a particular case fits into this category. More worrisome is the prospect that defendants in

certain high-profile cases—perhaps those involving wealthy or notorious parties—would receive more protection than others. See also Judith L. Maute, "'In Pursuit of Justice' in High Profile Criminal Matters," 70 *Fordham L. Rev.* 1745, 1747–50 (2002).

49. Several scholars have argued that prosecutors, like all humans, are not entirely rational actors but rather suffer from "bounded rationality." See, e.g., Alafair S. Burke, "Improving Prosecutorial Decision Making: Some Lessons of Cognitive Science," 47 *Wm. & Mary L. Rev.* 1587, 1590–91 (2006). As Professor Alafair Burke notes, "the potential for cognitive bias to creep into prosecutorial decision making starts from the earliest case-screening stages, when prosecutors must determine whether sufficient evidence exists to proceed with a prosecution." *Id.* at 1603. See also Barbara O'Brien, "A Recipe for Bias: An Empirical Look at the Interplay between Institutional Incentives and Bounded Rationality in Prosecutorial Decision Making," 74 *Mo. L. Rev.* 999 (2009).

50. See Keith A. Findley & Michael S. Scott, "The Multiple Dimensions of Tunnel Vision in Criminal Cases," 2006 *Wis. L. Rev.* 291 (2006); Dianne L. Martin, "Lessons about Justice from the 'Laboratory' of Wrongful Convictions: Tunnel Vision, the Construction of Guilt, and Informer Evidence," 70 *UMKC L. Rev.* 847 (2002).

51. See Findley & Scott, *Multiple Dimensions*, at 308. See also Alafair S. Burke, "Neutralizing Cognitive Bias," 2 *N.Y.U. J.L. & Liberty* 512, 517 (2007). The tendency of people to balk at changing an existing viewpoint and, instead, to interpret new evidence in a manner supportive of the preexisting theory has also been called "cognitive conservatism." See Scott E. Sundby, "Fallen Superheroes and Constitutional Mirages: The Tale of *Brady v. Maryland*," 33 *McGeorge L. Rev.* 643, 655 (2002).

52. Findley & Scott, *Multiple Dimensions*, at 307. See also Burke, *Improving Prosecutorial Decision Making*, at 1594–96.

53. See Burke, *Improving Prosecutorial Decision Making*, at 1596–99, 1604; Findley & Scott, *Multiple Dimensions*, at 309.

54. Burke, *Improving Prosecutorial Decision Making*, at 1599–1601; Burke, *Neutralizing Cognitive Bias*, at 518–19; Findley & Scott, *Multiple Dimensions*, at 314. Other cognitive biases also intersect with the confirmation bias to produce tunnel vision. See Burke, *Improving Prosecutorial Decision Making*, at 1601–2; Findley & Scott, *Multiple Dimensions*, at 318–20. Belief perseverance is related to the idea of "defensive bolstering," that is, "when people must justify a decision to which they have already committed," they often "hold fast to that position even in the face of contrary evidence." O'Brien, *Recipe for Bias*, at 1004.

55. See Findley & Scott, *Multiple Dimensions*, at 323–26.

56. *Id.* at 295.

57. *Id.* at 327–31.

58. Randolph N. Jonakait, "The Ethical Prosecutor's Misconduct," 23 *Crim. L. Bull.* 550, 553 (1987).

59. See Findley & Scott, *Multiple Dimensions*, at 329–30. Another problem with the "picture" in the police reports is that these reports often rely on boilerplate language. See Erwin Chemerinsky, "The Role of Prosecutors in Dealing with Police Abuse: The Lessons of Los Angeles," 8 *Va. J. Soc. Pol'y & L.* 305, 316 (2001).

60. See Daniel Richman, "Prosecutors and Their Agents, Agents and Their Prosecutors," 103 *Colum. L. Rev.* 749, 786–92 (2003). See also Davis, *Arbitrary Justice*, at 23; Melilli, *Prosecutorial Discretion*, at 676, 689.

61. See, e.g., Susan Bandes, "Loyalty to One's Convictions: The Prosecutor and Tunnel Vision," 49 *How. L. J.* 475, 482 (2006). Professor Daniel Richman notes that federal law enforcement agencies may not necessarily abhor decisions to decline to prosecute a referred case and may even view declinations positively as a way to "pass the responsibility" for a failure to pursue certain matters. Richman, *Prosecutors and Their Agents*, at 763–64.

62. See, e.g., Chemerinsky, *Role of Prosecutors*, at 305; Laurie L. Levenson, "The Future of State and Federal Civil Rights Prosecutions: The Lessons of the Rodney King Trial," 41 *UCLA L. Rev.* 509, 536–37 (1994). See also Davis, *Arbitrary Justice*, at 39–41; Daniel S. Medwed, "The Zeal Deal: Prosecutorial Resistance to Post-Conviction Claims of Innocence," 84 *B.U. L. Rev.* 125, 145 (2004).

63. See, e.g., Bandes, *Loyalty*, at 486; Medwed, *Zeal Deal*, at 145–46; Melilli, *Prosecutorial Discretion*, at 689.

64. See Medwed, *Zeal Deal*, at 146. See also Burke, *Neutralizing Cognitive Bias*, at 519; Stanley Z. Fisher, "In Search of the Virtuous Prosecutor: A Conceptual Framework," 15 *Am. J. Crim. L.* 197, 208 (1988); Melilli, *Prosecutorial Discretion*, at 689.

65. See Melilli, *Prosecutorial Discretion*, at 688; O'Brien, *Recipe for Bias*, at 1013.

66. See Prosser, *Reforming Criminal Discovery*, at 550–53.

67. See, e.g., Russell D. Covey, "Signaling and Plea Bargaining's Innocence Problem," 66 *Wash. & Lee L. Rev.* 73, 92 (2009).

68. See Burke, *Improving Prosecutorial Decision Making*, at 1605–9.

69. *Id.* at 1614–15.

70. Some offices already do so. See *Id.* at 1615; Findley & Scott, *Multiple Dimensions*, at 387–88.

71. See, generally, Burke, *Improving Prosecutorial Decision Making*, at 1616–18; Ellen S. Podgor, "The Ethics and Professionalism of Prosecutors in Discretionary Decisions," 68 *Fordham L. Rev.* 1511, 1531–34 (2000).

71. See Burke, *Neutralizing Cognitive Bias*, at 522–23. Nevertheless, many educational programs are deficient in offering training about charging in particular. See Melilli, *Prosecutorial Discretion*, at 686–87.

73. See Burke, *Improving Prosecutorial Decision Making*, at 1618–20; Burke, *Neutralizing Cognitive Bias*, at 523–25; Findley & Scott, *Multiple Dimensions*, at 370–71.

74. See Fred C. Zacharias, "The Professional Discipline of Prosecutors," 79 *N.C. L. Rev.* 721, 762–63 (2001). For example, the office manual for U.S. Attorneys prescribes that "merely because [the probable cause standard] can be met in a given case does not automatically warrant prosecution; further investigation may be warranted, and the prosecutor should still take into account all relevant considerations." U.S. Attorneys' Manual Sec. 9-27.200(B). (U.S. Dep't of Justice 1997) (available at http://www.justice.gov/usao/eousa/foia_reading_room/usam/title9/27mcrm.htm#9-27.200). See also Stephanos Bibas, "Prosecutorial Regulation versus Prosecutorial Accountability," 157 *U. Pa. L. Rev.* 959, 1003 (2009) (describing how the New Jersey Attorney General drafted statewide guidelines to govern charging enhanced drug penalties).

75. See *Russell D. Hauge, Kitsap County Prosecuting Attorney, Mission Statement and Standards and Guidelines* (2007) (available at http://www.kitsapgov.com/pros/Standards-Guidelines2007.pdf), at 6.

76. *Id.*

77. The New Orleans District Attorney's Office during Harry Connick's reign claimed to scrutinize cases prior to charging and only pursue matters in which experienced supervisors believed they had an excellent chance of prevailing at trial. See Darryl K. Brown, "The Decline of Defense Counsel and the Rise of Accuracy in Criminal Adjudication," 93 *Cal. L. Rev.* 1585, 1619–20 (2005); Ronald Wright & Marc Miller, "The Screening/Bargaining Tradeoff," 55 *Stan. L. Rev.* 29, 60–84 (2002). In some cases seasoned prosecutors may do better than their junior colleagues in making charging decisions. See, e.g., Rachel E. Barkow, "Institutional Design and the Policing of Prosecutors: Lessons from Administrative Law," 61 *Stan. L. Rev.* 869, 903 (2009). For a discussion of the benefits of a horizontal office structure (with different units handling different functions of a case) versus a vertical one (where a single lawyer handles a case from soup to nuts), see "New Perspectives on *Brady* and Other Disclosure Obligations: Report of the Working Groups on Best Practices," 31 *Cardozo L. Rev.* 1961, 2003–2004 (2010).

78. Erik Eckholm, "'Smart on Crime Mantra' of Philadelphia Prosecutor," *New York Times*, June 19, 2010.

79. One study suggested that prosecutors exhibiting a strong focus on securing convictions had roughly twice as much work experience as those attorneys concerned mainly with obtaining justice. See George T. Felkenes, "The Prosecutor: A Look at Reality," 7 *Sw. U. L. Rev.* 98, 111–12 (1975).

80. As Professor Bennett Gershman notes, prosecutorial offices may formulate guidelines, but these guidelines are often too general and "an institutional reluctance to unduly restrict their own discretion makes it even more unlikely that prosecutors would promulgate overly specific guidelines." Gershman, *Moral Standard*, at 519–20. See also Melilli, *Prosecutorial Discretion*, at 683; Misner, *Recasting*, at 744.

81. Findley & Scott, *Multiple Dimensions*, at 388–89; Griffin, *Prudent Prosecutor*, at 262; Ellen Yaroshefsky, "Wrongful Convictions: It is Time to Take Prosecution Discipline Seriously," 8 *D.C. L. Rev.* 275, 280–82 (2004).

82. See Bibas, *Prosecutorial Regulation*, at 1006.

83. See Burke, *Improving Prosecutorial Decision Making*, at 1621.

84. See O'Brien, *Recipe for Bias*, at 1018–19. Professor Barbara O'Brien emphasizes that, in order for this review to be effective, prosecutors must "know that they will be judged primarily for the process of their decision making, as opposed to the outcome." *Id.* at 1047.

85. Some U.S. Attorneys' Offices require assistant prosecutors to receive approval from supervisors or committees before proceeding with particular types of cases. See Findley & Scott, *Multiple Dimensions*, at 388; Fitzgerald, *Ethical Culture*, at 25.

86. See Burke, *Improving Prosecutorial Decision Making*, at 1620; Findley & Scott, *Multiple Dimensions*, at 388–89. Professor Susan Bandes advises that "review mechanisms should exist at every level of decision-making" but warns that "review may become simply a way of reinforcing group norms." Bandes, *Loyalty*, at 493. To avoid this trap, Bandes insists that there must be transparency through adequate record keeping and discovery, and that "the process needs to be explicitly structured to perform a critical role" with a "naysaying function." *Id.* at 493–94.

87. See Burke, *Improving Prosecutorial Decision Making*, at 1621–24; Burke, *Neutralizing Cognitive Bias*, at 527.

88. See Bandes, *Loyalty*, at 493–94; Findley & Scott, *Multiple Dimensions*, at 391.

89. See O'Brien, *Recipe for Bias*, at 1045–46.

90. See Barkow, *Institutional Design*, at 898–99.

91. See Burke, *Improving Prosecutorial Decision Making*, at 1623; Burke, *Neutralizing Cognitive Bias*, at 527.

92. Professor Rachel Barkow notes that "a panel of adjudicative decision makers is preferred" to counter individual biases, but she suggests that it might not be practical in many offices. Barkow, *Institutional Design*, at 904.

93. See Brown, *Decline of Defense Counsel*, at 1620; Melilli, *Prosecutorial Discretion*, at 683.

94. See, e.g., Burke, *Neutralizing Cognitive Bias*, at 526.

95. See Barry C. Scheck et al., *Actual Innocence: When Justice Goes Wrong and How to Make It Right* (New York: Signet, 2001). Many current charging review committees and scholarly calls for their enactment focus on complex cases. See, e.g., Fitzgerald, *Ethical Culture*, at 25; Griffin, *Prudent Prosecutor*, at 293.

96. See Innocence Project, *250 Exonerated: Too Many Wrongly Convicted* (2010) (available at http://www.innocenceproject.org/docs/InnocenceProject_250.pdf). See also Samuel R. Gross et al., "Exonerations in the United States, 1989 through 2003," 95 *J. Crim. L. & Criminology* 523, 524, 544–46 (2005).

97. See, e.g., Daniel S. Medwed, "Anatomy of a Wrongful Conviction: Theoretical Implications and Practical Solutions," 51 *Vill. L. Rev.* 337, 358–64 (2006).

98. See Innocence Project, *250 Exonerated*, at 30 (mentioning that 21% of the exonerations in this study involved the use of hair microscopy at trial).

99. For instance, in a simulated robbery trial, a jury found the defendant guilty 18 percent of the time when the prosecution's case had no eyewitness. Elizabeth F. Loftus, *Eyewitness Testimony* (Cambridge, MA: Harvard University Press, 1979), 9–10. The addition of a single eyewitness raised the conviction rate to 72 percent. *Id.*

100. See Robin Topping, "Panel Puts Justice before Prosecution," *Newsday*, Jan. 8, 2003, at A21.

101. See, e.g., Griffin, *Prudent Prosecutor*, at 282–83.

102. See Imbler v. Pachtman, 424 U.S. 409, 430–31 (1976).

103. See Adam M. Gershowitz, "Prosecutorial Shaming: Naming Attorneys to Reduce Prosecutorial Misconduct," 42 *U.C. Davis L. Rev.* 1059, 1067–69 (2009); Medwed, *Zeal Deal*, at 172–73. As Professor Leslie Griffin has noted, even when prosecutorial error is detected and reviewed on appeal, harmless error analysis means that courts focus on the error's effect on the defendant, not the intent of the prosecutor. Griffin, *Prudent Prosecutor*, at 282–83.

104. See Yaroshefsky, *Wrongful Convictions*, at 289; Zacharias, *Professional Discipline*, at 762–63. Professor Janet Hoeffel makes the interesting point that many scholars in favor of self-regulation themselves spent time as federal prosecutors, "an elite group with enormous prestige" that benefited from ample training and supervision. See, e.g., Janet C. Hoeffel, "Prosecutorial Discretion at the Core: The Good Prosecutor Meets *Brady*," 109 *Penn. St. L. Rev.* 1133, 1138 (2005). Federal prosecutors may file criminal charges against prosecutors who willfully violate the constitutional rights of a defendant, but those actions are extremely rare. See Rachel E. Barkow, "Organizational Guidelines for the Prosecutor's Office," 31 *Cardozo L. Rev.* 2089, 2094 (2010).

105. See, generally, Bibas, *Prosecutorial Regulation*; Stephanos Bibas, "Rewarding Prosecutors for Performance," 6 *Ohio St. J. Crim. L.* 441 (2009); Marc L. Miller & Ronald F. Wright, "The Black Box," 94 *Iowa L. Rev.* 125, 129 (2008).

106. See Yaroshefsky, *Wrongful Convictions*, at 280–82, 289–91. See also Joy, *Prosecutorial Misconduct and Wrongful Convictions*, at 427 (urging prosecutors' offices to develop an internal system of "graduated discipline"). For a discussion of the ethics officer's role in the Kings County (Brooklyn, NY) prosecutors' office, see Cummings, *Ethical Person*, at 2158.

107. See Imbler v. Pachtman, 424 U.S. 409, 429 (1976). Much of the following discussion derives from Daniel S. Medwed, *"Brady's* Bunch of Flaws,"67 *Wash. & Lee L. Rev.* 1533, 1547-50 (2010).

108. See, e.g., Attorney Registration and Disciplinary Commission of the Supreme Court of the State of Illinois, "Mission Statement" (available at https://www.iardc.org/mission_statement.asp).

109. See Medwed, *Zeal Deal*, at 173.

110. Zacharias, *Professional Discipline*, at 744–45. Professor Fred Zacharias observes that "the body of cases is not entirely negligible," especially given its confinement to matters of public record. *Id.* at 743–45.

111. See Bennett L. Gershman, "The New Prosecutors," 53 *U. Pitt. L. Rev.* 393, 445 (1992); Yaroshefsky, *Wrongful Convictions*, at 277, 282–83; Zacharias, *Professional Discipline*, at 754-55.

112. See Kathleen M. Ridolfi & Maurice Possley, *Preventable Error: A Report on Prosecutorial Misconduct in California 1997-2009*, Oct. 2010, 3 (available at http://law.scu.edu/ncip/file/ProsecutorialMisconduct_BookEntire_online%20version.pdf).

113. See Zacharias, *Professional Discipline*, at 749–50, 758.

114. See Gershman, *New Prosecutors*, at 445. Criminal defendants are motivated to file formal complaints but often lack the resources to pursue claims with the tenacity required to substantiate them. See Zacharias, *Professional Discipline*, at 749–50. Criminal defense lawyers who file complaints against prosecutors risk alienating common adversaries whom they will encounter in the future and upon whom they rely for favorable plea bargains and scheduling accommodations. *Id.* at 749–50. Judges also appear reluctant to alert bar authorities to prosecutorial misconduct. See Barkow, *Organizational Guidelines*, at 2096. See also Yaroshefsky, *Wrongful Convictions*, at 295–96 (discussing other explanations for the reluctance of disciplinary agencies to sanction prosecutors, including resource limitations and little expertise in criminal justice ethics).

115. See Davis, *Legal Profession's Failure*, at 282–91.

116. See Gershman, *New Prosecutors*, at 445; Zacharias, *Professional Discipline*, at 725–27. Disciplinary agencies may also be leery of identifying cases of misconduct and interfering with what they perceive to be a judicial role. See Bibas, *Prosecutorial Regulation*, at 977–78; Zacharias, *Professional Discipline*, at 754.

117. See Gershman, *New Prosecutors*, at 445; Yaroshefsky, *Wrongful Convictions*, at 292; Zacharias, *Professional Discipline*, at 761. As Professor Stephanos Bibas notes, it may also be that "bar authorities have bigger fish to fry, such as blatant financial pilfering by civil lawyers." Bibas, *Prosecutorial Regulation*, at 977.

118. See, e.g., Zacharias & Green, *Duty to Avoid*, at 27.

119. Zacharias, *Professional Discipline*, at 774.

120. See, e.g., *Id.* at 736.

121. See Davis, *American Prosecutor*, at 463–64. See also Yaroshefsky, *Wrongful Convictions*, at 297–99.

122. See Davis, *American Prosecutor*, at 463–64.

123. *Id.* See also Scott J. Krischke, Note, "Absent Accountability: How Prosecutorial Impunity Hinders the Fair Administration of Justice in America," 19 *J.L. & Pol'y* 395, 428–32 (2010).

124. See Zacharias, *Professional Discipline*, at 771–72.

125. See, e.g., Andrew D. Leipold, "How the Pretrial Process Contributes to Wrongful Convictions," 42 *Am. Crim. L. Rev.* 1123, 1160 (2005).

CHAPTER 2. IN THE INTEREST OF FULL DISCLOSURE

1. See, generally, Mary Prosser, "Reforming Criminal Discovery: Why Old Objections Must Yield to New Realities," 2006 *Wis. L. Rev.* 541, 561, 573–94 (2006). Much of this chapter derives from Daniel S. Medwed, "Brady's Bunch of Flaws," 67 *Wash. & Lee L. Rev.* 1533 (2010).

2. Brady v. Maryland, 373 U.S. 83, 87 (1963).

3. *Id.*

4. See R. Michael Cassidy, *Prosecutorial Ethics* (St. Paul, MN: Thomson-West, 2005), 72–73; Angela J. Davis, "The American Prosecutor: Independence, Power, and the Threat of Tyranny," 86 *Iowa L. Rev.* 393, 431 (2001).

5. Giglio v. United States, 405 U.S. 150, 154–55 (1972); United States v. Bagley, 473 U.S. 667, 676 (1985). See also Cassidy, *Prosecutorial Ethics*, at 69; R. Michael Cassidy, "'Soft Words of Hope': *Giglio,* Accomplice Witnesses, and the Problem of Implied Inducements," 98 *Nw. U. L. Rev.* 1129, 1131 (2004).

6. United States v. Agurs, 427 U.S. 97, 110–11 (1976).

7. See Cassidy, *Prosecutorial Ethics*, at 71–72.

8. See Kyles v. Whitley, 514 U.S. 419, 437–38 (1995). See also Cassidy, *Prosecutorial Ethics*, at 74; Angela J. Davis, "The Legal Profession's Failure to Discipline Unethical Prosecutors," 36 *Hofstra L. Rev.* 275, 287 n. 59 (2007); Bennett L. Gershman, *Prosecutorial Misconduct,* 2d ed. (St. Paul, MN: Thomson-West, 2007), 231–34.

9. See Bruce A. Green, "Beyond Training Prosecutors about Their Disclosure Obligations: Can Prosecutors' Offices Learn from Their Lawyers' Mistakes," 31 *Cardozo L. Rev.* 2161, 2165 (2010).

10. Model Rules of Prof'l Conduct R. 3.8(d) (2008).

11. See Cassidy, *Prosecutorial Ethics*, at 70–71; Kyles v. Whitley 514 U.S. 419, 437 (1995).

12. See, e.g., Steven M. Dettelbach, "Commentary: *Brady* from the Prosecutor's Perspective," 57 *Case W. Res. L. Rev.* 615, 615–16 (2007); John G. Douglass, "Fatal Attraction? The Uneasy Courtship of *Brady* and Plea Bargaining," 50 *Emory L.J.* 437, 457–60 (2001).

13. See prelude to Part 1; Ellen Yaroshefsky, "Wrongful Convictions: It Is Time to Take Prosecution Discipline Seriously," 8 *D.C. L. Rev.* 275, 278, 285 (2004).

14. See, e.g., Hugo Adam Bedau & Michael L. Radelet, "Miscarriages of Justice in Potentially Capital Cases," 40 *Stan. L. Rev.* 21, 23–24, 57 (1987) (citing data that 10% of 350 wrongful convictions studied involved the suppression of evidence by prosecutors).

15. See Davis, *American Prosecutor*, at 431.

16. Prosecutors are not required to disclose all information that might be helpful to the defense, just favorable evidence. Such determinations may be difficult to make in certain cases. See Gershman, *Prosecutorial Misconduct*, at 225–27.

17. United States v. Bagley, 473 U.S. 667, 682 (1985). See also Strickler v. Greene, 527 U.S. 263, 281–82 (1999).

18. Kyles v. Whitley, 514 U.S. 419, 434 (1995).

19. See Cassidy, *Prosecutorial Ethics*, at 74; Gershman, *Prosecutorial Misconduct*, at 221–22, 224–25. Materiality is evaluated based on the undisclosed evidence in its entirety. Gershman, *Prosecutorial Misconduct*, at 221 n. 7. Some items of evidence are so fundamental that withholding them is reversible error regardless of the strength of the prosecution case. The Supreme Court has indicated that a police report showing that fingerprints on the murder weapon exculpate the accused must be disclosed as a matter of "elemental fairness." United States v. Agurs, 427 U.S. 97, 110 (1976). Similarly, if one of two key prosecution eyewitnesses were to inform the police that the defendant was not the perpetrator, the prosecution's later failure to turn over that statement would mandate reversal. *Id.* at 112 n. 21.

20. See Davis, *American Prosecutor*, at 432.

21. See Bennett L. Gershman, "Litigating *Brady v. Maryland*: Games Prosecutors Play," 57 *Case W. Res. L. Rev.* 531, 537 (2007).

22. See Alafair S. Burke, "Improving Prosecutorial Decision Making: Some Lessons of Cognitive Science," 47 *Wm. & Mary L. Rev.* 1587, 1610 (2006). See also *Id.* at 1593–1601; Alafair Burke, "Commentary: *Brady*'s Brainteaser: The Accidental Prosecutor and Cognitive Bias," 57 *Case W. Res. L. Rev.* 575, 576 (2007).

23. Burke, *Improving Prosecutorial Decision Making*, at 1611. See also Alafair S. Burke, "Revisiting Prosecutorial Disclosure," 84 *Ind. L.J.* 481, 495 (2009). As Justice Thurgood Marshall noted, "given this unharmonious role, it is not surprising that these advocates oftentimes overlook or downplay potentially favorable evidence, often in cases in which there is no doubt that the failure to disclose was a result of absolute good faith." United States v. Bagley, 473 U.S. 667, 697 (1985) (Marshall, J., dissenting).

24. Burke, *Improving Prosecutorial Decision Making*, at 1611–12; Burke, *Revisiting*, at 495.

25. This is what Professor Maria Hartwig calls "asymmetrical skepticism: You are more skeptical of the evidence that is counter to your beliefs than the evidence that fits your beliefs." See "Voices from the Field: An Inter-Professional Approach to Managing Critical Information," 31 *Cardozo L. Rev.* 2037, 2062 (2010).

26. Burke, *Revisiting*, at 495–96.

27. Mark Twain, "What Is Man?" in *What Is Man? And Other Essays* (New York: Harper & Brothers, 1917), 1, 17. For an interesting discussion of this issue, see Lawton P. Cummings, "Can an Ethical Person Be an Ethical Prosecutor? A Social Cognitive Approach to Systemic Reform," 31 *Cardozo L. Rev.* 2139, 2142–43 (2010).

28. See Davis, *American Prosecutor,* at 431–32; Bill Moushey, "Win at All Costs: Out of Control," *Pittsburgh Post-Gazette*, Nov. 22, 1998, at A-1. Another study found a reversal rate of less than 12 percent of all cases involving *Brady* allegations decided in 2004. See Burke, *Revisiting*, at 490 n.54.

29. See Alafair S. Burke, "Talking about Prosecutors," 31 *Cardozo L. Rev.* 2119, 2129 (2010).

30. See Gershman, *Litigating Brady*, at 538–42, 548–64; Scott E. Sundby, "Fallen Superheroes and Constitutional Mirages: The Tale of Brady v. Maryland," 33 *McGeorge L. Rev.* 643, 645 (2002).

31. See Burke, *Revisiting*, at 488–93.

32. See Bennett L. Gershman, "Reflections on *Brady v. Maryland*," 47 *S. Tex. L. Rev.* 685, 723 (2006). In some jurisdictions the canons of ethics even ask supervisory lawyers to monitor subordinates in prosecutors' offices to ensure compliance with disclosure rules. See Standing Comm. on Ethics and Prof'l Responsibility, Am. Bar Ass'n, Formal Opinion 09-454, *Prosecutor's Duty to Disclose Evidence and Information Favorable to the Defense* 8 (2009) [hereinafter *ABA Op. 09-454*]. This is not to say that ethical rules in the discovery area are perfect. The rules could be far more explicit in requiring individual prosecutors to undertake a diligent search for *Brady* material in law enforcement's possession. Niki Kuckes, "The State of Rule 3.8: Prosecutorial Ethics Reform since Ethics 2000," 22 *Geo. J. Legal Ethics* 427, 453–54 (2009). In an effort to beef up its ethical rules in this area, North Carolina now requires that prosecutors make a "reasonably diligent inquiry" to locate potentially exculpatory evidence. See Kuckes, *State of Rule 3.8*, at 454 n. 133. Massachusetts has taken a novel approach to the prosecutor's ethical duty in investigating crime, adopting a rule that a prosecutor should not "intentionally avoid pursuit of evidence because the prosecutor believes it will damage the prosecution's case or aid the accused." Mass. Rules of Prof'l Conduct R. 3.8(j) (2010). See also Kuckes, *State of Rule 3.8*, at 452–53.

33. See Richard A. Rosen, "Disciplinary Sanctions against Prosecutors for *Brady* Violations: A Paper Tiger," 65 *N.C. L. Rev.* 693, 696–97, 730–31 (1987).

34. Joseph R. Weeks, "No Wrong without a Remedy: The Effective Enforcement of the Duty of Prosecutors to Disclose Exculpatory Evidence," 22 *Okla. City U. L. Rev.* 833 (1997).

35. See, e.g., Yaroshefsky, *Wrongful Convictions*, at 276, 278, 285.

36. See Mark Curriden, "Harmless Error? A New Study Claims Prosecutorial Misconduct Is Rampant in California," *ABA Journal* 18–19 (Dec. 2010); Kathleen M. Ridolfi & Maurice Possley, *Preventable Error: A Report on Prosecutorial Misconduct in California 1997–2009*, Oct. 2010, 4–5 (available at http://law.scu.edu/ncip/file/ProsecutorialMisconduct_BookEntire_online%20version.pdf). Two of the other tapes demonstrated how Cline coached the victim's four-year-old daughter prior to her testimony and urged her not to let the defense change her mind about who "put fire on her mommy." Curriden, *Harmless Error*, at 19. In his defense, Cline claims that he did not know about the existence of the tapes involving the star witness and that he did turn over the tapes of the sessions with the victim's daughter. *Id.*

37. See Curriden, *Harmless Error*, at 18–19; Ridolfi & Possley, *Preventable Error*, at 4–5.

38. *Id.*

39. See Tulare County District Attorney, "Welcome to the Office of the Tulare County District Attorney" (available at http://www.da-tulareco.org/).

40. See Burke, *Revisiting*, at 491 nn. 58–59. In 2011 the U.S. Supreme Court examined the topic of prosecutorial immunity and *Brady* violations in *Connick v. Thompson*. See Connick v. Thompson, 131 S. Ct. 1350 (2011). The Court held that a district attorney's office may not be held liable in a federal 1983 action for the failure to train its prosecutors based on a single *Brady* violation. *Id.*

41. See Adam M. Gershowitz, "Prosecutorial Shaming: Naming Attorneys to Reduce Prosecutorial Misconduct," 42 *U.C. Davis L. Rev.* 1059, 1067–69 (2009).

42. See Burke, *Revisiting*, at 491; Sara Gurwitch, "When Self-Policing Does Not Work: A Proposal for Policing Prosecutors in Their Obligation to Provide Exculpatory Evidence to the Defense," 50 *Santa Clara L. Rev.* 303, 322 (2010); Janet C. Hoeffel, "Prosecutorial Discretion at the Core: The Good Prosecutor Meets *Brady*," 109 *Penn. St. L. Rev.* 1133, 1152 (2005).

43. See, generally, Stephanos Bibas, "Rewarding Prosecutors for Performance," 6 *Ohio St. J. Crim. L.* 441 (2009); Tracey L. Meares, "Rewards for Good Behavior: Influencing Prosecutorial Discretion and Conduct with Financial Incentives," 64 *Fordham L. Rev.* 851 (1995).

44. See Erwin Chemerinsky, "The Role of Prosecutors in Dealing with Police Abuse: The Lessons of Los Angeles," 8 *Va. J. Soc. Pol'y & L.* 305, 317 n. 69 (2001); Gershman, *Reflections*, at 687 n. 10. See also Prosser, *Reforming Criminal Discovery*, at 569. It seems as if many prosecutors' offices now have training programs on *Brady*. See Gail Donaghue, "Section 1983 Cases Arising from Criminal Convictions," 18 *Touro L. Rev.* 725, 731 (2002). An ethics opinion from the American Bar Association clarified that prosecutorial supervisors should ensure that "subordinate prosecutors are adequately trained" about their disclosure duties and that "internal office procedures must facilitate such compliance." See *ABA Op. 09-454* at 8. The Department of Justice (DOJ) announced discovery reforms for U.S. Attorney's Offices in 2010. This announcement occurred after several much publicized foul-ups, including the dismissal of criminal charges against Senator Ted Stevens as a result of the failure to turn over *Brady* material. These incidents cast aspersions on federal prosecutors. Among other initiatives, the DOJ appointed a national criminal discovery ombudsman to oversee internal education and vowed that discovery coordinators must provide annual training in each office. See Green, *Beyond Training*, at 2161–63.

45. See, generally, "New Perspectives on *Brady* and Other Disclosure Obligations: Report of the Working Groups on Best Practices," 31 *Cardozo L. Rev.* 1961 (2010).

46. See *Voices from the Field* at 2065.

47. See Barry Scheck, "Professional and Conviction Integrity Programs: Why We Need Them, Why They Will Work, and Models for Creating Them," 31 *Cardozo L. Rev.* 2215, 2216 (2010). See also Rachel E. Barkow, "Organizational Guidelines for the Prosecutor's Office," 31 *Cardozo L. Rev.* 2089, 2105–12 (2010); Green, *Beyond Training*, at 2171–72.

48. See Scheck, *Integrity Programs*, at 2237–38.

49. See, generally, *Id.*

50. For some interesting and creative ideas about how to prompt prosecutors' offices to adopt entity-level compliance programs, see Barkow, *Organizational Guidelines*, at 2112–18. As Professor Bruce Green points out, one challenge with disclosure review processes is how to avoid motivating prosecutors to conceal their errors. See Green, *Beyond Training*, at 2183–84.

51. See Burke, *Improving Prosecutorial Decision Making*, at 1626–31.

52. See, e.g., Patrick J. Fitzgerald, "Thoughts on the Ethical Culture of a Prosecutor's Office," 84 *Wash. L. Rev.* 11, 25 (2009).

53. See Daniel J. Capra, "Access to Exculpatory Evidence: Avoiding the *Agurs* Problems of Prosecutorial Discretion and Retrospective Review," 53 *Fordham L. Rev.* 391, 427–28 (1984). See also Darryl K. Brown, "The Decline of Defense Counsel and the Rise of Accuracy in Criminal Adjudication," 93 *Cal. L. Rev.* 1585, 1636–38 (2005).

54. See Mass. R. Crim. P. 11(a)(1) (2010).

55. As one judge put it, the materiality analysis is "speculative on so many matters that simply are unknown and unknowable before trial begins." United States v. Safavian, 233 F.R.D. 12, 16 (D.D.C. 2005).

56. See, e.g., Christopher Deal, Note, "*Brady* Materiality before Trial: The Scope of the Duty to Disclose and the Right to a Trial by Jury," 82 *N.Y.U. L. Rev.* 1780, 1790–93 (2007).

57. See, generally, People v. Fuentes, 907 N.E.2d 286 (N.Y. 2009). For alleged *Brady* errors where there was no specific request, the test remains "reasonable probability." *Id.* at 289.

58. Several scholars have criticized the U.S. Supreme Court for neglecting to require that prosecutors on appeal must prove that the withholding of favorable evidence was not material. After all, prosecutors usually bear the burden of proving that a constitutional error, once established, was not harmless. See Gershman, *Reflections*, at 713; Hoeffel, *Prosecutorial Discretion*, at 1144.

59. See State v. Laurie, 653 A.2d 549, 552 (N.H. 1995).

60. Burke, *Improving Prosecutorial Decision Making*, at 1610–12; Burke, *Revisiting*, at 495.

61. Gershman, *Reflections*, at 713.

62. See Hoeffel, *Prosecutorial Discretion*, at 1151–52; Sundby, *Fallen Superheroes*, at 661–63.

63. United States v. Bagley, 473 U.S. 667, 695–96 (1985) (Marshall, J., dissenting).

64. See Sundby, *Fallen Superheroes*, at 646–47.

65. See *ABA Op. 09-454* at 2.

66. See, e.g., Ill. Sup. Ct. R. 412(c) (2011).

67. See Burke, *Revisiting*, at 513–14.

68. *Id.* (presenting a similar example). Cf. Sundby, *Fallen Superheroes*, at 662 (suggesting that prosecutors would not struggle too much if required only to disclose evidence "reasonably favorable" to the accused).

69. See Burke, *Revisiting*, at 514 nn. 195–96; Robert P. Mosteller, "Exculpatory Evidence, Ethics, and the Road to the Disbarment of Mike Nifong: The Critical Importance of Full Open-File Discovery," 15 *Geo. Mason L. Rev.* 257, 262 (2008); Yaroshefsky, *Wrongful Convictions*, at 295.

70. See Gershman, *Reflections*, at 725–28. Professor Alafair Burke notes that changing the rules of criminal procedure or recognizing increased discovery rights under state constitutional law could expand the discovery obligation, but those reforms would "lack the sweeping impact of a change to federal constitutional doctrine." Burke, *Revisiting*, at 500. Professor Paul Giannelli, in advocating expanded discovery, has observed that he encountered few *Brady* issues as a lawyer in the military where the practice was to give the prosecution and the defense "the same case," normally "at the same time." See Paul C. Giannelli, "*Brady* and Jailhouse Snitches," 57 *Case W. Res. L. Rev.* 593, 604 (2007).

71. See, e.g., Peter J. Henning, "The Pitfalls of Dealing with Witnesses in Public Corruption Prosecutions," 23 *Geo. J. Legal Ethics* 351, 366 n.61 (2010).

72. See Brown, *Decline of Defense Counsel*, at 1622–24; Janice Morse, "Ohio's New Criminal Court Rules Kick In," *Cincinnati Enquirer*, July 1, 2010.

73. Federal prosecutor Steven Dettelbach has noted that the materiality requirement is partly a "self-defense mechanism" to protect prosecutors and rightful convictions from creative defense attorneys and "armchair quarterbacking" by judges. Dettelbach, *Prosecutor's Perspective*, at 616–17.

74. United States v. Garsson, 291 F. 646, 649 (S.D.N.Y. 1923).

75. See Burke, *Revisiting*, at 515.

76. See *Id.*; Burke, *Talking*, at 2126.

77. Brown, *Decline of Defense Counsel*, at 1622–24; Burke, *Revisiting*, at 515–16; Gershman, *Litigating Brady*, at 543–44.

78. See *Voices from the Field* at 2074–77; Ellen Yaroshefsky, "Foreword: New Perspectives on *Brady* and Other Disclosure Obligations: What Really Works?" 31 *Cardozo L. Rev.* 1943, 1951 (2010).

79. See Gershman, *Litigating Brady*, at 544. Some offices do not have a formal open file discovery policy but vest discretion in individual prosecutors to utilize this practice if they wish. This means that the availability of open file discovery is often haphazard and subject to the whims of individual prosecutors. See Peter A. Joy, "*Brady* and Jailhouse Informants: Responding to Injustice," 57 *Case W. Res. L. Rev.* 619, 641 (2007).

80. See Gershman, *Litigating Brady*, at 544–48; Gurwitch, *Self-Policing*, at 316; Prosser, *Reforming Criminal Discovery*, at 600–601.

81. See Green, *Beyond Training*, at 2178.

82. See Gershman, *Litigating Brady*, at 548.

83. *Id.* at 544.

84. *Id.* at 547–48.

85. North Carolina's alterations to its disclosure rules had emerged in response to the wrongful capital murder conviction of Alan Gell, in which prosecutors withheld evidence indicating that Gell was imprisoned at the time of the murder and could not have committed the crime. Despite the disgracefulness of this misconduct, the prosecutors involved in the Gell case scarcely received a slap on the wrist from the Disciplinary Hearing Committee of the state bar, earning only a lukewarm reprimand. The fallout from the Gell case paved the way for the state legislature to establish an open file discovery regime. See Gershman, *Litigating Brady*, at 546–47; Mosteller, *Exculpatory Evidence*, at 264–76, 288–92; Fred C. Zacharias & Bruce A. Green, "The Duty to Avoid Wrongful Convictions: A Thought Experiment in the Regulation of Prosecutors," 89 *B.U. L. Rev.* 1, 12 (2009).

86. See Gershman, *Litigating Brady*, at 546–47; Mosteller, *Exculpatory Evidence*, at 264–76, 288–92; Zacharias & Green, *Duty to Avoid*, at 12. On a positive note, North Carolina's open file discovery statute did not prove entirely impotent in the Nifong case. That statute provided the means through which the defense team was able to file motions that led to receiving the exculpatory test results and ultimately vindicating the three student-athletes. See Ellen Yaroshefsky, "Ethics and Plea Bargaining: What's Discovery Got to Do with It?" 23-FALL *ABA Crim. Just.* 28, 33 (2008).

87. See, e.g., Kyles v. Whitley, 514 U.S. 419, 437-38 (1995).

88. See Stanley Z. Fisher, "The Prosecutor's Ethical Duty to Seek Exculpatory Evidence in Police Hands: Lessons from England," 68 *Fordham L. Rev.* 1379, 1382–84 (2000).

89. *Id.* at 1385–1420.

90. *Id.* at 1423–25.

91. As Professor Stanley Fisher points out, "police reports may mislead by misstating facts, omitting facts, or a combination of both." Stanley Z. Fisher, "'Just the Facts, Ma'am': Lying and the Omission of Exculpatory Evidence in Police Reports," 28 *New Eng. L. Rev.* 1, 6 (1993). Fisher further explores how resource conservation, self-protection, and partisanship conspire to motivate police to take a "minimalist approach" to drafting reports. See *Id.* at 8–9.

92. See *Id.* at 36–38.

93. See Prosser, *Reforming Criminal Discovery*, at 607–13.

94. See *Id.* at 613.

95. See *Id.*; see also Fla. R. Crim. P. 3.220(h) (2011).

96. See Prosser, *Reforming Criminal Discovery*, at 613.

97. See, e.g., State v. Lopez, 974 So.2d 340, 349–50 (Fla. 2008).

98. See Fla. R. Crim. P. 3.220(l) (2011).

99. See Fla. R. Crim. P. 3.220(h)(7) (2011).

100. See Fla. R. Crim. P. 3.220(h)(4) (2011).

101. See Prosser, *Reforming Criminal Discovery*, at 581, 607–13; George C. Thomas III, "Two Windows into Innocence," 7 *Ohio St. J. Crim. L.* 575, 590–600 (2010). As Professor George Thomas notes, merely granting defendants the right to receive a list of prosecution witnesses, a right that does not exist in thirty states, would be a significant step in the right direction. See Thomas, *Two Windows*, at 591.

102. See Mosteller, *Exculpatory Evidence*, at 259–60.

103. See Eugene Cerruti, "Through the Looking-Glass at the *Brady* Doctrine: Some New Reflections on White Queens, Hobgoblins, and Due Process," 94 *Ky. L.J.* 211, 246-74 (2005).

104. Fitzgerald, *Ethical Culture*, at 14.

105. *Id.* at 14–16. See also Stephanos Bibas, "Prosecutorial Regulation versus Prosecutorial Accountability," 157 *U. Pa. L. Rev.* 959, 963 (2009); Fred Klein, "A View from Inside the Ropes: A Prosecutor's Viewpoint on Disclosing Exculpatory Evidence," 38 *Hofstra L. Rev.* 867, 878–79 (2010).

106. See *Voices from the Field* at 2072–73.

CHAPTER 3. PLEA BARGAINING PITFALLS

1. See, e.g., Daniel Givelber, "Punishing Protestations of Innocence: Denying Responsibility and Its Consequences," 37 *Am. Crim. L. Rev.* 1363, 1364–71 (2000); Erik Luna & Paul G. Cassell, "Mandatory Minimalism," 32 *Cardozo L. Rev.* 1, 14 (2010).

2. See Mary Prosser, "Reforming Criminal Discovery: Why Old Objections Must Yield to New Realities," 2006 *Wis. L. Rev.* 541, 554, 556 n. 41 (2006).

3. Professor Darryl Brown suggests that the requirement that judges find a factual basis to the plea provides "little judicial check on party fact determination" because judges rarely hear from witnesses to substantiate the plea and instead rely on the prosecutor's oral account of what the evidence would prove. Darryl K. Brown, "The Decline of Defense Counsel and the Rise of Accuracy in Criminal Adjudication," 93 *Cal. L. Rev.* 1585, 1610–11 (2005).

4. See Andrew D. Leipold, "How the Pretrial Process Contributes to Wrongful Convictions," 42 *Am. Crim. L. Rev.* 1123, 1153–54 (2005).

5. Albert W. Alschuler, "The Prosecutor's Role in Plea Bargaining," 36 *U. Chi. L. Rev.* 50, 50 (1968).

6. See Samuel R. Gross et al., "Exonerations in the United States, 1989 through 2003," 95 *J. Crim. L. & Criminology* 523, 536 (2005); Vanita Gupta, "Critical Race Lawyering in Tulia, Texas," 73 *Fordham L. Rev.* 2055 (2005); Kevin R. Johnson, "Taking the 'Garbage' Out in Tulia, Texas: The Taboo on Black-White Romance and Racial Profiling in the 'War on Drugs,'" 2007 *Wis. L. Rev.* 283 (2007).

7. See Peter Neufeld, "Legal and Ethical implications of Post-Conviction DNA Exonerations," 35 *New Eng. L. Rev.* 639, 639–40 (2001); Ellen Yaroshefsky, "Ethics and Plea Bargaining: What's Discovery Got to Do with It?" 23-FALL *Crim. Just.* 28, 29 (2008).

8. See Innocence Project, *250 Exonerated: Too Many Wrongly Convicted* (2010), 36–37 (available at http://www.innocenceproject.org/docs/InnocenceProject_250.pdf).

9. See Gross et al., *Exonerations*, at 524, 536. Professor Ron Wright's analysis of federal sentencing practices suggests that enormous plea discounts/trial penalties in the federal system are convincing innocent defendants to plead guilty at disturbingly high rates. See, generally, Ronald F. Wright, "Trial Distortion and the End of Innocence in Federal Criminal Justice," 154 *U. Pa. L. Rev.* 79 (2005).

10. See Josh Bowers, "Punishing the Innocent," 156 *U. Pa. L. Rev.* 1117, 1131–32 n. 62 (2008). Prosecutors may even require a waiver of the right to preserve evidence from the case as a precondition to a plea arrangement. See Yaroshefsky, *Ethics and Plea Bargaining*, at 29.

11. See Bowers, *Punishing the Innocent*, at 1152–53 n. 182. See also Wright, *Trial Distortion*, at 109.

12. The description of this case derives largely from Daniel S. Medwed, "Up the River without a Procedure: Innocent Prisoners and Newly Discovered Non-DNA Evidence in State Courts," 47 *Ariz. L. Rev.* 655, 662–64 (2005).

13. *Id.* at 662.

14. The cook denied he had received any benefit in exchange for his testimony, a claim placed in doubt by the fact that his own felony charge for weapon possession, pending at the time of the robbery, had been resolved in the interim through a plea to disorderly conduct. *Id.* at 663.

15. *Id.* at 663.

16. *Id.*

17. *Id.* at 663–64; Schulz v. Marshall, 528 F. Supp.2d 77 (E.D.N.Y. 2007).

18. See Janet C. Hoeffel, "Prosecutorial Discretion at the Core: The Good Prosecutor Meets *Brady*," 109 *Penn. St. L. Rev.* 1133, 1141–42, 1148–49 (2005); Randolph N. Jonakait, "The Ethical Prosecutor's Misconduct," 23 *Crim. L. Bull.* 550, 553–54 (1987); Abbe Smith, "Can You Be a Good Person and a Good Prosecutor?" 14 *Geo. J. Legal Ethics* 355, 391 (2001).

19. See R. Michael Cassidy, *Prosecutorial Ethics* (St. Paul, MN: Thomson-West, 2005), 81–82.

20. See Stephanos Bibas, "Plea Bargaining Outside the Shadow of Trial," 117 *Harv. L. Rev.* 2464, 2507–15 (2004); Alafair S. Burke, "Prosecutorial Passion, Cognitive Bias, and Plea Bargaining," 91 *Marq. L. Rev.* 183, 199 (2007). See also, generally, Russell Covey, "Reconsidering the Relationship between Cognitive Psychology and Plea Bargaining," 91 *Marq. L. Rev.* 213 (2007). To be fair, a prosecutor who is especially vested in a case might view a plea bargain as a *loss* and barely negotiate with a defendant prior to trial, if at all. Burke, *Prosecutorial Passion*, at 199–200. Professor Alafair Burke also suggests that prosecutors may become "anchored" to their initial plea offer and fail to deviate from it or be influenced by the amount of time and resources expended on a particular case in arriving at an appropriate plea offer. *Id.* at 201–3.

21. See Burke, *Prosecutorial Passion*, at 186–92, 196–98. Passion can lead prosecutors to selectively process information so as to overestimate the probability of a defendant's conviction and the severity of the likely sentence after trial. Having overrated their chances for success, prosecutors might offer little in the way of a "bargain" to the defense during plea discussions. *Id.*

22. See Steven W. Perry, "Prosecutors in State Courts, 2005," *Bureau of Just. Statistics Bulletin*, July 2006, 6 (available at http://www.bjs.ojp.usdoj.gov/content/pub/pdf/psco5.pdf).

23. See, e.g., Rebecca Hollander-Blumoff, "Social Psychology, Information Processing, and Plea Bargaining," 91 *Marq. L. Rev.* 163, 170–77 (2007). See also Bowers, *Punishing the Innocent*, at 1140–41.

24. See Robert E. Scott & William J. Stuntz, "A Reply: Imperfect Bargains, Imperfect Trials, and Innocent Defendants," 101 *Yale L.J.* 2011, 2012 (1992).

25. See Bibas, *Outside the Shadow*, at 2475; Burke, *Prosecutorial Passion*, at 190.

26. A prosecutor eyeing a long-term future with the district attorney's office may have a different approach to plea bargaining than one contemplating a shift to private practice that could be facilitated by currying favor with the defense bar. See, e.g., Stephen J. Schulhofer, "Plea Bargaining as Disaster," 101 *Yale L.J.* 1979, 1987–88 (1992); Fred C. Zacharias, "Justice in Plea Bargaining," 39 *Wm. & Mary L. Rev.* 1121, 1181 (1998).

27. See Bibas, *Outside the Shadow*, at 2470–76. For an argument against fixed, lockstep salaries for prosecutors, see Stephanos Bibas, "Rewarding Prosecutors for Performance," 6 *Ohio St. J. Crim. L.* 441 (2009).

28. Although there is no direct financial incentive to litigate difficult cases, many young prosecutors want to develop trial experience, in part to improve their prospects with future employers. See Steve Weinberg, "Inside an Office: An Elected Prosecutor Explains," *Harmful Error: Investigating America's Local Prosecutors*, June 26, 2003 (available at http://projects.publicintegrity.org/pm/default.aspx?act=sidebarsa&aid=28). An empirical study by Professors Richard Boylan and Cheryl Long concluded that assistant U.S. attorneys in regions of the country with high private-sector salaries are more likely to take cases to trial than federal prosecutors in places with low private wages. They offered the following explanation for these findings. In regions where government salaries are not competitive with salaries in the private sector, federal prosecutors want to gain trial experience to obtain lucrative private-sector employment down the road. See Richard T. Boylan & Cheryl X. Long, "Salaries, Plea Rates, and the Career Objectives of Federal Prosecutors," 48 *J. L. & Econ.* 627 (2005).

29. See Bibas, *Outside the Shadow*, at 2472; Schulhofer, *Plea Bargaining as Disaster*, at 1987; Zacharias, *Justice in Plea Bargaining*, at 1181–82.

30. See Chicago Appleseed Fund for Justice, *A Report on Chicago's Felony Courts* (Dec. 2007), 27 (available at http://www.chicagoappleseed.org/publications).

31. See, e.g., Bibas, *Outside the Shadow*, at 2474–75.

32. See Cassidy, *Prosecutorial Ethics*, at 83–84. For a detailed discussion of the restrictions on prosecutors inducing defendants to plead guilty, see Bennett L. Gershman, *Prosecutorial Misconduct*, 2d ed. (St. Paul, MN: Thomson-West, 2007), 288–303.

33. See, e.g., Givelber, *Punishing Protestations*, at 1366.

34. United States v. Ruiz, 536 U.S. 622, 625, 630–31 (2002).

35. *Id.* at 630.

36. See Cassidy, *Prosecutorial Ethics*, at 87. The Court did not squarely address this question because the prosecution's proposed plea agreement in *Ruiz* promised that the government would provide "information establishing the factual innocence of the defendant." United States v. Ruiz, 536 U.S. 622, 631 (2002). In the aftermath of *Ruiz*, several courts have suggested that the decision should be restricted to its narrow holding and that

exculpatory evidence should be disclosed prior to the entry of a plea. See, e.g., McCann v. Mangialardi, 337 F.3d 782, 787-88 (7th Cir. 2003); In re Miranda, 182 P.3d 513, 542–43 (Cal. 2008).

37. See Erica Hashimoto, "Toward Ethical Plea Bargaining," 30 *Cardozo L. Rev.* 949, 954 (2008); Leipold, *Pretrial Process*, at 1150.

38. See Cassidy, *Prosecutorial Ethics*, at 88–89; R. Michael Cassidy, "Some Reflections on Ethics and Plea Bargaining: An Essay in Honor of Fred Zacharias," 48 *San Diego L. Rev.* 93, 96–97 (2011). Even so, a 2009 ethics opinion suggests that the Model Rules of Professional Conduct require the disclosure of favorable evidence before a guilty plea. Standing Comm. on Ethics and Professional Responsibility, Am. Bar Ass'n, Formal Opinion 09-454, *Prosecutor's Duty to Disclose Evidence and Information Favorable to the Defense* 6 (2009) [hereinafter *ABA Op. 09-454*].

39. See Cassidy, *Prosecutorial Ethics*, at 88–89; Cassidy, *Some Reflections*, at 96–97.

40. See Cassidy, *Some Reflections*, at 96–97; Fred C. Zacharias, "The Professional Discipline of Prosecutors," 79 *N.C. L. Rev.* 721, 735 n. 55 (2001).

41. See Cassidy, *Prosecutorial Ethics*, at 88–91; chapter 1, this volume. Professor Fred Zacharias has recommended self-regulation in the plea bargaining context, urging prosecutorial offices to enact specific plea bargaining policies to guide individual prosecutors. Zacharias, *Justice in Plea Bargaining*, at 1184–88.

42. See, e.g., Givelber, *Punishing Protestations*, at 1399.

43. See Bibas, *Outside the Shadow*, at 2464–70; Robert E. Scott & William J. Stuntz, "Plea Bargaining as Contract," 101 *Yale L.J.* 1909 (1992); Zacharias, *Justice in Plea Bargaining*, at 1146–47.

44. See, e.g., Erik Luna & Marianne Wade, "Prosecutors as Judges," 67 *Wash. & Lee L. Rev.* 1413, 1423–64 (2010).

45. See, e.g., Bibas, *Outside the Shadow*, at 2493–96 (discussing the information deficit experienced by defendants in plea bargaining). Pretrial detention in minor cases where imprisonment upon conviction is unlikely may encourage defendants to push for quick plea bargains. *Id.* at 2491–93. See also Covey, *Reconsidering*, at 239–43. Professor Josh Bowers argues that plea bargaining, particularly in low-stakes cases, may be the *best* way for innocent defendants to limit wrongful punishment given the enormous process costs imposed by pretrial detention and court appearances because of pecuniary loss, inconvenience, and uncertainty. Bowers, *Punishing the Innocent*, at 1132.

46. I should note that the official ground for Schulz's writ of federal habeas corpus was ineffective assistance of trial counsel and not factual innocence per se. See Schulz v. Marshall, 528 F. Supp. 2d 77 (E.D.N.Y. 2007).

47. See, e.g., Santobello v. New York, 404 U.S. 257, 260 (1971). Cf. Albert W. Alschuler, "Implementing the Criminal Defendant's Right to Trial: Alternatives to the Plea Bargaining System," 50 *U. Chi. L. Rev.* 931 (1983). Some jurisdictions have experimented with abolition, including Alaska which banned the practice in 1975. See Gershman, *Prosecutorial Misconduct*, at 287 n. 9. Abolishing plea bargaining would also not solve the problem of wrongful convictions because innocent defendants would still face trial, an imperfect institution that would grow increasingly faulty in a system where every case went to trial. If all innocent defendants were tried, fewer of them would be convicted given the probability of at least some acquittals—but those who were wrongfully convicted would receive stiffer sentences than if they had pled out to begin with. See Russell D. Covey, "Signaling

and Plea Bargaining's Innocence Problem," 66 *Wash. & Lee L. Rev.* 73, 83–84 (2009); Scott & Stuntz, *Imperfect Bargains*, at 2013–14.

48. See, e.g., Mary Patrice Brown & Stevan E. Bunnell, "Negotiating Justice: Prosecutorial Perspectives on Federal Plea Bargaining in the District of Columbia," 43 *Am. Crim. L. Rev.* 1063, 1064–65 (2006). See also Santobello v. New York, 404 U.S. 257, 261 (1971).

49. See Givelber, *Punishing Protestations*, at 1363–71.

50. See *Id.* at 1372–76.

51. See *Id.* at 1366. Cf. Richard Birke, "Reconciling Loss Aversion and Guilty Pleas," 1999 *Utah L. Rev.* 205, 209 (1999) (attributing the high rate of guilty pleas not to the trial tax but to poor advice by defense lawyers).

52. See Givelber, *Punishing Protestations*, at 1381–91.

53. Indeed, some scholars use the phrase "plea discount" to describe differential sentencing. See, e.g., Wright, *Trial Distortion*.

54. See Yue Ma, "Prosecutorial Discretion and Plea Bargaining in the United States, France, Germany, and Italy: A Comparative Perspective," 12 *Int. Crim. Just. Rev.* 22, 39–40 (2002).

55. See *Id.* at 41. See also Yue Ma, "A Comparative View of Judicial Supervision of Prosecutorial Discretion," 44 *Crim. L. Bull.* 31 (2008).

56. The difference in post-plea and post-trial sentencing should not only be reduced but quite possibly also set as a fixed amount so that prosecutors cannot offer better deals in weak cases than in strong ones. See, generally, Russell D. Covey, "Fixed Justice: Reforming Plea Bargaining with Plea-Based Ceilings," 82 *Tul. L. Rev.* 1237 (2008). Professor Oren Gazal-Ayal proposes a partial ban in which plea bargaining is prohibited where the concession extended to the defendant is large, as often occurs in weak cases. This partial ban, in Gazal-Ayal's view, would deter prosecutors from filing charges in weak cases at the beginning because of the burdens of trying such cases. See Oren Gazal-Ayal, "Partial Ban on Plea Bargains," 27 *Cardozo L. Rev.* 2295 (2006). See also Wright, *Trial Distortion*, at 111–12.

57. See Givelber, *Punishing Protestations*, at 1398–1408.

58. See *Id.* at 1404. See also Gazal-Ayal, *Partial Ban*, at 2335–37.

59. See Yaroshefsky, *Ethics and Plea Bargaining*, at 30–31.

60. See Brown, *Decline of Defense Counsel*, at 1612, 1625–27; Hashimoto, *Ethical Plea Bargaining*, at 949, 956.

61. See, e.g., Scott & Stuntz, *Plea Bargaining as Contract*, at 1942–43.

62. See Hashimoto, *Ethical Plea Bargaining*, at 951; Kevin C. McMunigal, "Guilty Pleas, *Brady* Disclosure, and Wrongful Convictions," 57 *Case W. Res. L. Rev.* 651, 657–60 (2007). In addition to drug and alcohol abuse, youth and mental illnesses can impair the ability of some criminal defendants to understand or remember the events that led to criminal accusations. See John G. Douglass, "Can Prosecutors Bluff? *Brady v. Maryland* and Plea Bargaining," 57 *Case W. Res. L. Rev.* 581, 582 (2007).

63. According to the American Bar Association's Standing Committee on Ethics and Professional Responsibility, a defendant's consent does not absolve a prosecutor of her disclosure obligations. See *ABA Op. 09-454* at 7.

64. See, e.g., Kevin C. McMunigal, "Disclosure and Accuracy in the Guilty Plea Process," 40 *Hastings L.J.* 957, 1005 (1989). For an argument in favor of changing the procedural rules governing discovery (particularly the Federal Rules of Criminal Procedure)

instead of creating new constitutional rights, see Susan R. Klein, "Enhancing the Judicial Role in Criminal Plea and Sentence Bargaining," 84 *Tex. L. Rev.* 2023, 2042–52 (2006).

65. See McMunigal, *Disclosure and Accuracy*, at 1005–23.

66. See chapter 2, this volume.

67. See, generally, Corinna Barrett Lain, "Accuracy Where It Matters: *Brady v. Maryland* in the Plea Bargaining Context," 80 *Wash. U. L.Q.* 1 (2002); McMunigal, *Disclosure and Accuracy*, at 1005–23. Professor John Douglass has argued that marrying *Brady* and plea bargaining, for various reasons, is an imperfect union. See Douglass, *Can Prosecutors Bluff?*; John G. Douglass, "Fatal Attraction? The Uneasy Courtship of *Brady* and Plea Bargaining," 50 *Emory L.J.* 437 (2001).

68. Model Rules of Prof'l Conduct R. 3.8(d) (2008).

69. See Hashimoto, *Ethical Plea Bargaining*, at 957–58. An ethics opinion issued by the American Bar Association interpreted Rule 3.8(d) as requiring the disclosure of all favorable information to the defense before a guilty plea. See *ABA Op. 09-454* at 6. For a discussion of some other suggested changes to the ethical rules in the area of plea bargaining, see Cassidy, *Some Reflections*, at 104–9.

70. To be sure, rigorous prosecutorial review of potential criminal *charges* at the outset of the process diminishes the likelihood that innocents will ever reach the plea bargaining stage at all. See chapter 2, this volume. A study by Professors Ron Wright and Marc Miller concluded that the "hard screening" of cases early on in the charging process by veteran prosecutors can filter out many weak cases and decrease the risk that cases involving innocent defendants will result in plea bargains. See Ronald Wright & Marc Miller, "The Screening/Bargaining Tradeoff," 55 *Stan. L. Rev.* 29, 94–96 (2002).

71. See Jenia Iontcheva Turner, "Judicial Participation in Plea Negotiations: A Comparative View," 54 *Am. J. Comp. L.* 199, 202–3, 212–13 (2006).

72. *Id.* at 202–3.

73. See Burke, *Prosecutorial Passion*, at 207.

74. See Turner, *Judicial Participation*, at 200. Judges also figure prominently in negotiating settlements to criminal cases in Europe. See Luna & Wade, *Prosecutors as Judges*, at 1462–63.

75. See Turner, *Judicial Participation*, at 207–8.

76. See *Id.* at 204. Professor Colin Miller contends that judicial participation in the plea bargaining process would generate fairer outcomes in part because the prosecutor's initial offer—which Miller argues creates an "anchoring effect"—would not have as much influence on the ultimate sentence. See Colin Miller, "Anchors Away: Why the Anchoring Effect Suggests that Judges Should Be Able to Participate in Plea Discussions," Sept. 5, 2010 (available at http://papers.ssrn.com/sol3/papers.cfm?abstract_id=1672442).

77. See Turner, *Judicial Participation*, at 214, 248–56.

78. At least one of the states that allows for judicial involvement in plea bargains, Connecticut, endorses this practice. *Id.* at 263–64.

79. *Id.* at 261.

80. See Leipold, *Pretrial Process*, at 1154–55. No contest pleas usually apply to low-level offenses. See Bowers, *Punishing the Innocent*, at 1165–66.

81. See North Carolina v. Alford, 400 U.S. 25 (1970).

82. See, e.g., Albert W. Alschuler, "Straining at Gnats and Swallowing Camels: The Selective Morality of Professor Bibas," 88 *Cornell L. Rev.* 1412 (2003); Stephanos Bibas,

"Harmonizing Substantive-Criminal-Law Values and Criminal Procedure: The Case of Alford and Nolo Contendere Pleas," 88 *Cornell L. Rev.* 1361 (2003); Bowers, *Punishing the Innocent*, at 1165–67.

83. See Bibas, *Harmonizing Values and Procedure*, at 1385–86.

84. See Leipold, *Pretrial Process*, at 1155.

85. See Bowers, *Punishing the Innocent*, at 1165–70.

86. See Leipold, *Pretrial Process*, at 1155–56.

87. As Professor Andrew Leipold argues, "if nolo pleas are bad, *Alford* pleas are worse." *Id.* at 1156.

88. *Id.* at 1157. See also Bibas, *Harmonizing Values and Procedure*, at 1403 n. 216.

89. See, generally, Alschuler, *Straining at Gnats*. See also Jenny Elayne Ronis, Note, "The Pragmatic Plea: Expanding Use of the *Alford* Plea to Promote Traditionally Conflicting Interests of the Criminal Justice System," 82 *Temple L. Rev.* 1389, 1406–11 (2010).

90. See Leipold, *Pretrial Process*, at 1164.

PART II. BEYOND A REASONABLE DOUBT?

1. This discussion derives from Daniel S. Medwed, "Anatomy of a Wrongful Conviction: Theoretical Implications and Practical Solutions," 51 *Vill. L. Rev.* 337 (2006).

2. *Id.* at 340.

3. *Id.* at 340–41.

4. *Id.* at 341–42.

5. *Id.* at 342.

6. *Id.*

7. *Id.* at 343.

8. *Id.*

9. *Id.* at 343–44. The lawyers nonetheless chose to present an innocence defense. Five inmates testified that Wong did not commit the crime, but these witnesses did not identify the perpetrator. *Id.* at 344. The report also contained an excerpt from a conversation with another prisoner, Alexander Winston Sylvester, in which Sylvester declared that "after stabbing the black inmate, the Puerto Rican inmate threw the blade down behind him onto the snow. A second Puerto Rican inmate picked up the blade, put it in a pair of gloves and walked up the hillside." Sylvester, after being informed about the consequences of perjury, refused to sign a written statement to this effect. *Id.* at 343–44.

10. *Id.* at 344.

11. *Id.* at 344–45.

12. *Id.* at 345.

13. *Id.*

14. *Id.* at 345–46.

15. *Id.* at 346.

16. *Id.*

17. *Id.* at 347.

18. *Id.* at 347 n.70.

19. *Id.* at 347–48.

20. *Id.* at 348–49.

21. *Id.* at 349.

22. *Id.*

23. *Id.* at 349–50.

24. *Id.* at 350–52.

25. *Id.* at 352–53.

26. *Id.* at 353–54.

27. *Id.* at 354–55.

28. *Id.* at 355.

29. *Id.* at 355–56.

30. *Id.* at 356–57.

31. *Id.* at 364–69.

32. *Id.* at 357.

33. See Berger v. United States, 295 U.S. 78, 88 (1935). See also Bennett L. Gershman, "'Hard Strikes and Foul Blows': *Berger v. United States* 75 Years After," 42 *Loy. U. Chi. L.J.* 177 (2010).

CHAPTER 4. PREPARATION AND EXAMINATION OF WITNESSES

1. See, e.g., Susan Bandes, "Loyalty to One's Convictions: The Prosecutor and Tunnel Vision," 49 *How. L.J.* 475, 484 (2006); Erwin Chemerinsky, "The Role of Prosecutors in Dealing with Police Abuse: The Lessons of Los Angeles," 8 *Va. J. Soc. Pol'y & L.* 305, 320–21 (2001). Many prosecutors understand that conviction rates are an imprecise barometer of overall effectiveness. See, e.g., Lisa M. Budzilowicz, "Holding Prosecutors Accountable: What Is Successful Prosecutorial Performance and Why Should It Be Measured?" 41-*JUN Prosecutor* 22 (2007). Professor Richard Boylan has argued that the cumulative length of prison sentences affects the careers of chief federal prosecutors more than conviction rates per se. See Richard T. Boylan, "What Do Prosecutors Maximize? Evidence from the Careers of U.S. Attorneys," 7 *Am. Law & Econ. Rev.* 379 (2005).

2. Catherine Ferguson-Gilbert, Comment, "It Is Not Whether You Win or Lose, It Is How You Play the Game: Is the Win-Loss Scorekeeping Mentality Doing Justice for Prosecutors?" 38 *Cal. W.L. Rev.* 283, 290 (2001).

3. See Jessica Fender, "Defense Attorney Cites DA Bonuses in Bid for New Prosecutor," *Denver Post*, Mar. 29, 2011.

4. See Evan Moore, "Justice under Fire: 'Win at All Costs' is Smith County's Rule, Critics Claim," *Houston Chronicle*, June 11, 2000. State prosecutors secure convictions in roughly 85 percent of felony cases and 90 percent of misdemeanors. See Eric Rasmusen et al., "Convictions versus Conviction Rates: The Prosecutor's Choice," 11 *Am. Law & Econ. Rev.* 47, 49 (2009).

5. See Daniel S. Medwed, "The Zeal Deal: Prosecutorial Resistance to Post-Conviction Claims of Innocence," 84 *B.U. L. Rev.* 125, 150–53 (2004). See also Judith L. Maute, "'In Pursuit of Justice' in High Profile Criminal Matters," 70 *Fordham L. Rev.* 1745, 1747 (2002); Jane Campbell Moriarty, "'Misconvictions,' Science, and the Ministers of Justice," 86 *Neb. L. Rev.* 1, 23 (2007). Some data suggest that "appointed prosecutors, less worried about poorly informed public opinion, have lower conviction rates." See Rasmusen et al., *Convictions*, at 73.

6. See Medwed, *Zeal Deal*, at 153–54.

7. See Rasmusen et al., *Convictions*, at 51.

8. See Bennett L. Gershman, "The Prosecutor's Duty to Truth," 14 *Geo. J. Legal Ethics* 309, 350 n. 223 (2001).

9. Medwed, *Zeal Deal*, at 154.

10. See Lawton P. Cummings, "Can an Ethical Person Be an Ethical Prosecutor? A Social Cognitive Approach to Systemic Reform," 31 *Cardozo L. Rev.* 2139, 2148–49 (2010); Kay L. Levine, "The New Prosecution," 40 *Wake Forest L. Rev.* 1125, 1187 (2005); Medwed, *Zeal Deal*, at 138–40; Abbe Smith, "Can You Be a Good Person and a Good Prosecutor?" 14 *Geo. J. Legal Ethics* 355, 378 (2001).

11. See, e.g., George T. Felkenes, "The Prosecutor: A Look at Reality," 7 *Sw. U. L. Rev.* 98, 99 (1975).

12. The tension between these conflicting messages creates an "ongoing schizophrenia" for prosecutors to which I have alluded throughout this book. See, e.g., Kenneth J. Melilli, "Prosecutorial Discretion in an Adversary System," 1992 *BYU L. Rev.* 669, 698 (1992).

13. See, e.g., Peter A. Joy, "*Brady* and Jailhouse Informants: Responding to Injustice," 57 *Case W. Res. L. Rev.* 619, 630 (2007); Ellen S. Podgor, "The Ethics and Professionalism of Prosecutors in Discretionary Decisions," 68 *Fordham L. Rev.* 1511, 1531–34 (2000).

14. See Fred C. Zacharias, "Structuring the Ethics of Prosecutorial Trial Practice: Can Prosecutors Do Justice?" 44 *Vand. L. Rev.* 45, 48 (1991).

15. Donnelly v. DeChristoforo, 416 U.S. 637, 648–49 (1974) (Douglas, J., dissenting).

16. See H. Richard Uviller, "The Neutral Prosecutor: The Obligation of Dispassion in a Passionate Pursuit," 68 *Fordham L. Rev.* 1695, 1702 (2000).

17. See, e.g., Paul C. Giannelli, "*Brady* and Jailhouse Snitches," 57 *Case W. Res. L. Rev.* 593, 601 (2007).

18. See, e.g., Maurice Possley & Ken Armstrong, "The Flip Side of a Fair Trial," *Chicago Tribune,* Jan. 11, 1999.

19. See Fred C. Zacharias & Bruce A. Green, "The Duty to Avoid Wrongful Convictions: A Thought Experiment in the Regulation of Prosecutors," 89 *B.U. L. Rev.* 1, 20–21 (2009). Professor Bennett Gershman has explored the range of incentives that prosecutors may have for coaching witnesses, most notably, to eliminate discrepancies in their testimony, conceal embarrassing details in their accounts, or prevent revealing information which might show that the prosecutor failed to comply with his disclosure duties. See Bennett L. Gershman, "Witness Coaching by Prosecutors," 23 *Cardozo L. Rev.* 829, 833–38 (2002).

20. See Gershman, *Witness Coaching*, at 855–59; Peter A. Joy & Kevin C. McMunigal, *Do No Wrong: Ethics for Prosecutors and Defenders* (Chicago: ABA, 2009), 169–70; Richard C. Wydick, "The Ethics of Witness Coaching," 17 *Cardozo L. Rev.* 1, 12–18 (1995); Fred C. Zacharias & Shaun Martin, "Coaching Witnesses," 87 *Ky. L.J.* 1001, 1009–10 (1999).

21. See Model Rules of Prof'l Conduct R. 3.4(b) (2008).

22. See, e.g., R. Michael Cassidy, *Prosecutorial Ethics* (St. Paul, MN: Thomson-West, 2005), 50. The novelist James Fenimore Cooper popularized the phrase "horseshedding," a reference to the nineteenth-century practice of lawyers preparing witnesses in carriage sheds close to rural courthouses. It is often called "woodshedding" or simply "coaching" in modern parlance. See Joy & McMunigal, *Do No Wrong*, at 169.

23. See Cassidy, *Prosecutorial Ethics*, at 48–51; Criminal Justice Standards Comm., Am. Bar Ass'n, Standards for Criminal Justice, Standard 3-3.1(d) (3d ed., 1993) [hereinafter "ABA Standards"]; Bennett L. Gershman, *Prosecutorial Misconduct,* 2d ed. (St. Paul, MN:

Thomson-West, 2007), 450–451. Prosecutors, more generally, must refrain from impairing defense efforts to find and interview witnesses. See Gershman, *Prosecutorial Misconduct*, at 449–55. One controversial issue concerns whether it is ethical for a prosecutor to warn witnesses about the adverse consequences of disclosing certain information to defense counsel. For a discussion of this issue, see Melanie D. Wilson, "Quieting Cognitive Bias with Standards for Witness Communications," 62 *Hastings L.J.* 1227, 1236–46 (2011).

24. See, e.g., Miller v. Pate, 386 U.S. 1, 6–7 (1967). See also ABA Standards, Standard 3-5.6(a).

25. See, e.g., Cassidy, *Prosecutorial Ethics*, at 97–98.

26. See *Id.* at 98–99; Gershman, *Prosecutorial Misconduct*, at 404–5. Prosecutors are also barred from using cross-examination to discredit a witness whom they know is telling the truth. See Joy & McMunigal, *Do No Wrong*, at 14.

27. See, e.g., Gershman, *Prosecutorial Misconduct*, at 416–17.

28. Professor Richard Wydick classifies witness coaching into three "grades." He treats Grade One coaching as overt acts by a lawyer directing a witness to alter her story; Grade Two consists of covert attempts to alter the story; and Grade Three occurs where a lawyer does not knowingly prompt a witness to create a false story, but the lawyer's conversation technique nonetheless affects the witness's account. See Wydick, *Ethics*, at 18–37. According to Wydick, "unlike Grades One and Two, Grade Three witness coaching is not grounds for lawyer discipline or criminal prosecution for subornation of perjury." *Id.* at 37. See also Zacharias & Martin, *Coaching*, at 1010–11.

29. See Gershman, *Witness Coaching*, at 838–44. Children, identification witnesses, and cooperators are highly susceptible to suggestive interviewing. *Id.* at 844–50. See also Wydick, *Ethics*, at 9–12.

30. See Wydick, *Ethics*, at 11.

31. See Gershman, *Witness Coaching*, at 829–30. See also Roberta K. Flowers, "Witness Preparation: Regulating the Profession's 'Dirty Little Secret,'" 38 *Hastings Const. L.Q.* 1007, 1007–10 (2011).

32. The description of this case derives mainly from the Decision and Order overturning Fernando Bermudez's conviction in 2009. See Decision and Order, People of the State of New York v. Fernando Bermudez, Supreme Court of the State of New York, County of New York (Hon. J. Cataldo), Nov. 9, 2009, 3–6 [hereinafter "Bermudez Decision and Order"].

33. *Id.* at 33–45, 52.

34. *Id.* at 7, 12–13.

35. *Id.* at 7, 12, 16, 23–24, 47–49.

36. *Id.* at 14–20.

37. *Id.* at 14–20, 78–79.

38 See Stephanos Bibas, "Prosecutorial Regulation versus Prosecutorial Accountability," 157 *U. Pa. L. Rev.* 959, 997–1000 (2009).

39. See *Id.* at 997–1000, 1007–9; Fred Klein, "A View from Inside the Ropes: A Prosecutor's Viewpoint on Disclosing Exculpatory Evidence," 38 *Hofstra L. Rev.* 867, 878–79 (2010); Scott J. Krischke, Note, "Absent Accountability: How Prosecutorial Impunity Hinders the Fair Administration of Justice in America," 19 *J.L. & Pol'y* 395, 420–24 (2010); Levine, *New Prosecution*, at 1197–98. Professor Stephanos Bibas also advocates frequent performance evaluations and incentive-pay systems as possible ways of encouraging best

practices in prosecutors' offices. See Bibas, *Prosecutorial Regulation*, at 1013–15. Professor Kay Levine recommends changing "standards for promotion within the office to reward prosecutors for time spent on victim services or community education efforts and to discourage a mentality that equated achievement with winning at trial." Levine, *New Prosecution*, at 1197.

40. See, e.g., Wydick, *Ethics*, at 41–44.

41. See Gershman, *Witness Coaching*, at 851–54, 861–62.

42. See Bermudez Decision and Order, 11–12.

43. See Gershman, *Witness Coaching*, at 859–60.

44. See Flowers, *Witness Preparation*, at 1019–27.

45. See Michael L. Rich, "Coerced Informants and Thirteenth Amendment Limitations on the Police-Informant Relationship," 50 *Santa Clara L. Rev.* 681, 689–90 (2010).

46. See, e.g., Myrna S. Raeder, "See No Evil: Wrongful Convictions and the Prosecutorial Ethics of Offering Testimony by Jailhouse Informants and Dishonest Experts," 76 *Fordham L. Rev.* 1413, 1419 (2007). Much of the following discussion related to jailhouse informant testimony comes from my article, Daniel S. Medwed, "Anatomy of a Wrongful Conviction: Theoretical Implications and Practical Solutions," 51 *Vill. L. Rev.* 337, 364–69 (2006).

47. See, e.g., Robert M. Bloom, *Ratting: The Use and Abuse of Informants in the American Justice System* (Westport, CT: Praeger, 2002), 63–64.

48. See, e.g., Jack King, "Twisted Justice: Prosecution Function in America Out of Control," 23-*MAR Champion* 10, 10–11 (1999).

49. See, e.g., United States v. Cervantes-Pacheco, 826 F.2d 310, 315 (5th Cir. 1987) ("It is difficult to imagine a greater motivation to lie than the inducement of a reduced sentence."). There is also little disincentive considering that perjury is hard to prosecute.

50. Raeder, *See No Evil*, at 1419.

51. *Id.*

52. See Brandon L. Garrett, "Judging Innocence," 108 *Colum. L. Rev.* 55, 87 (2008). In one of these three cases, Dana Holland's wrongful conviction, the co-defendant who had been found not guilty by a judge turned out to be the perpetrator. *Id.* at 87 n. 121.

53. Gershman, *Witness Coaching*, at 848–49.

54. See, e.g., Hoffa v. United States, 385 U.S. 293, 311–12 (1966). For a brief history of the use of informants, see Clifford S. Zimmerman, "From the Jailhouse to the Courthouse: The Role of Informants in Wrongful Convictions," in *Wrongly Convicted: Perspectives on Failed Justice*, ed. Saundra D. Westervelt & John A. Humphrey (Piscataway, NJ: Rutgers University Press, 2001), 55, 57–58.

55. See, e.g., Bloom, *Ratting*, at 64–66; Giannelli, *Brady and Jailhouse Snitches*, at 596–97; Zimmerman, *From the Jailhouse*, at 56.

56. See Steven M. Dettelbach, "Commentary: *Brady* from the Prosecutor's Perspective," 57 *Case W. Res. L. Rev.* 615, 616 (2007). See also Stephen S. Trott, "Words of Warning for Prosecutors Using Criminals as Witnesses," 47 *Hastings L.J.* 1381 (1996).

57. See United States v. Dennis, 183 F.2d 201, 224 (2d Cir. 1950). See also Robert P. Mosteller, "The Special Threat of Informants to the Innocent Who Are Not Innocents: Producing 'First Drafts,' Recording Incentives, and Taking a Fresh Look at the Evidence," 6 *Ohio St. J. Crim. L.* 519, 551 (2009); Alexandra Natapoff, "Snitching: The Institutional and Communal Consequences, 73 *U. Cin. L. Rev.* 645, 660–63 (2004); Trott, *Words of Warning*, at 1390–91.

58. Giglio v. United States, 405 U.S. 150 (1972).

59. See, e.g., Thomas A. Mauet, "Informant Disclosure and Production: A Second Look at Paid Informants," 37 *Ariz. L. Rev.* 563, 563–64 (1995).

60. See, e.g., Trott, *Words of Warning*, at 1398–1400.

61. See Bennett L. Gershman, "Litigating *Brady v. Maryland*: Games Prosecutors Play," 57 *Case W. Res. L. Rev.* 531, 538–41 (2007). See also R. Michael Cassidy, "'Soft Words of Hope': *Giglio*, Accomplice Witnesses, and the Problem of Implied Inducements," 98 *Nw. U. L. Rev.* 1129, 1150 n.114 (2004).

62. See Cassidy, *Soft Words*, at 1158–59; Gershman, *Litigating Brady*, at 538–41.

63. See Natapoff, *Snitching*, at 665. The lower courts are divided as to whether only formalized agreements with witnesses must be turned over. See Joy & McMunigal, *Do No Wrong*, at 135–40.

64. For an interesting discussion of the application of general ethical rules to the prosecutorial practice of utilizing jailhouse informants, see Raeder, *See No Evil*, at 1427–39.

65. Samuel R. Gross et al., "Exonerations in the United States, 1989 through 2003," 95 *J. Crim. L. & Criminology* 523, 544 (2005).

66. In a study conducted by the Innocence Project in New York City, 19 percent of the first 250 DNA exonerations in the United States involved cases where informant testimony contributed to the conviction at trial. See Innocence Project, *250 Exonerated: Too Many Wrongly Convicted* (2010), 38–39 (available at http://www.innocenceproject.org/docs/InnocenceProject_250.pdf). See also Giannelli, *Brady and Jailhouse Snitches*, at 595 n. 16.

67. See Medwed, *Anatomy of a Wrongful Conviction*, at 366.

68. *Id.* Professor Alexandra Natapoff challenges the notion that informants are a necessary law enforcement device, suggesting it is unclear whether they provide "net benefits" to crime prevention. See Natapoff, *Snitching*, at 660–63.

69. On Lee v. United States, 343 U.S. 747, 757 (1952).

70. See, e.g., Giannelli, *Brady and Jailhouse Snitches*, at 598.

71. See Natapoff, *Snitching*, at 697–700.

72. See Giannelli, *Brady and Jailhouse Snitches*, at 604–6.

73. Dodd v. State, 993 P.2d 778, 784 (Okla. Crim. App. 2000).

74. *Id.*

75. See Giannelli, *Brady and Jailhouse Snitches*, at 605–6.

76. *Id.* at 608.

77. See Mosteller, *Special Threat*, at 565–70.

78. See chapter 2, this volume; Natapoff, *Snitching*, at 700.

79. See, e.g., George C. Harris, "Testimony for Sale: The Law and Ethics of Snitches and Experts," 28 *Pepp. L. Rev.* 1, 63–64 (2000).

80. To be fair, jurors might look askance at jailhouse informants and at prosecutorial reliance on such "scum." See Trott, *Words of Warning*, at 1385.

81. See, e.g., Joy, *Brady and Jailhouse Informants*, at 646–47; Alexandra Natapoff, "Beyond Unreliable: How Snitches Contribute to Wrongful Convictions," 37 *Golden Gate U. L. Rev.* 107, 112–13 (2006). The Federal Rules of Evidence provide opportunities to conduct pretrial hearings away from the jury when justice demands it. Many states have similar rules. See, e.g., Joy, *Brady and Jailhouse Informants*, at 645–46.

82. See *Report of the ABA Criminal Justice Section's Ad Hoc Innocence Committee to Ensure the Integrity of the Criminal Process, Achieving Justice: Freeing the Innocent, Convict-*

ing the Guilty, ed. Paul Giannelli & Myrna Raeder (2006), 63, 70 [hereinafter *ABA Report on Innocence*]. See also Giannelli, *Brady and Jailhouse Snitches*, at 610; Joy, *Brady and Jailhouse Informants*, at 639; Mosteller, *Special Threat*, at 554.

83. See, e.g., Medwed, *Anatomy of a Wrongful Conviction*, at 368.

84. See Natapoff, *Snitching*, at 701–2.

85. See, e.g., Ian Weinstein, "Regulating the Market for Snitches," 47 *Buff. L. Rev.* 563, 568 (1999).

86. See Medwed, *Anatomy of a Wrongful Conviction*, at 367. See also Emily Jane Dodds, Note, "I'll Make You a Deal: How Repeat Informants Are Corrupting the Criminal Justice System and What to Do about It," 50 *Wm. & Mary L. Rev.* 1063 (2008).

87. See Natapoff, *Snitching*, at 700–701.

88. See, e.g., Joy, *Brady and Jailhouse Informants*, at 638; Raeder, *See No Evil*, at 1417.

89. See Mosteller, *Special Threat*, at 557; Napue v. Illinois, 360 U.S. 264 (1959).

90. Gershman, *Prosecutorial Misconduct*, at 246–47.

91. See I. Bennett Capers, "Crime, Legitimacy, and Testilying," 83 *Ind. L.J.* 835 (2008); Christopher Slobogin, "Testilying: Police Perjury and What to Do about It," 67 *U. Colo. L. Rev.* 1037 (1996).

92. See Capers, *Testilying*, at 868.

93. See, e.g., Steven Zeidman, "Policing the Police: The Role of the Courts and the Prosecution," 32 *Fordham Urb. L.J.* 315, 349–53 (2005).

94. See Raeder, *See No Evil*, at 1437–38.

95. See chapter 1, this volume. A number of commentators suggest that prosecutors should do a better job of screening informants before they appear at trial. See, e.g., Giannelli, *Brady and Jailhouse Snitches*, at 609; Mosteller, *Special Threat*, at 573–74; Raeder, *See No Evil*, at 1438.

96. See *ABA Report on Innocence* at 67–69; Raeder, *See No Evil*, at 1437.

97. See Raeder, *See No Evil*, at 1449.

98. See Natapoff, *Snitching*, at 651, 697.

CHAPTER 5. TEST TUBES ON TRIAL

1. Parts of this chapter derive from Daniel S. Medwed, "Closing the Door on Misconduct: Rethinking the Ethical Standards That Govern Summations in Criminal Trials," 38 *Hastings Const. L.Q.* 915, 938–42 (2011).

2. Anecdotes about the "CSI Effect" are legendary among lawyers in criminal practice. It is unclear, however, whether this phenomenon actually exists. See, e.g., Hon. Donald E. Shelton et al., "A Study of Juror Expectations and Demands Concerning Scientific Evidence: Does the 'CSI Effect' Exist?" 9 *Vand. J. Ent. & Tech. L.* 331, 332–33 (2006).

3. See Paul C. Giannelli & Kevin C. McMunigal, "Prosecutors, Ethics, and Expert Witnesses," 76 *Fordham. L. Rev.* 1493, 1494 n. 7 (2007), citing Joseph L. Peterson et al., "The Uses and Effects of Forensic Science in the Adjudication of Felony Cases," 32 *J. Forensic Sci.* 1730, 1748 (1987).

4. The desire to earn convictions may be one reason why prosecutors use defective scientific evidence, but the story is more complex. See Giannelli & McMunigal, *Prosecutors*, at 1528.

5. See Buckley v. Fitzsimmons, 509 U.S. 259 (1993); Giannelli & McMunigal, *Prosecutors*, at 1495–97; Jane Campbell Moriarty, "'Misconvictions,' Science, and the Ministers of Jus-

tice," 86 *Neb. L. Rev.* 1, 9 (2007); Myrna S. Raeder, "See No Evil: Wrongful Convictions and the Prosecutorial Ethics of Offering Testimony by Jailhouse Informants and Dishonest Experts," 76 *Fordham L. Rev.* 1413, 1422 (2007). For a discussion of what happened to Cruz and Hernandez, see Innocence Project, "Profile of Rolando Cruz" (available at http://www.innocenceproject.org/Content/Rolando_Cruz.php); Innocence Project, "Profile of Alejandro Hernandez" (available at http://www.innocenceproject.org/Content/Alejandro_Hernandez.php).

6. See Innocence Project, *250 Exonerated: Too Many Wrongly Convicted* (2010), 28–29 (available at http://www.innocenceproject.org/docs/InnocenceProject_250.pdf) [hereinafter *250 Exonerated*].

7. See, e.g., Simon A. Cole, "More Than Zero: Accounting for Error in Latent Fingerprint Identification," 95 *J. Crim. L. & Criminology* 985, 986–87 (2005); Innocence Project, "Profile of Stephan Cowans" (available at http://www.innocenceproject.org/Content/Stephan_Cowans.php).

8. See Innocence Project, *250 Exonerated* at 31. See also Brandon L. Garrett, "Judging Innocence," 108 *Colum. L. Rev.* 55, 84 (2008).

9. For instance, 21 percent of the first 250 DNA exonerations derived in part from faulty microscopic hair analysis. See Innocence Project, *250 Exonerated* at 30.

10. See David Grann, "Trial by Fire: Did Texas Execute an Innocent Man?" *New Yorker*, Sept. 7, 2009; Bob Herbert, "Innocent but Dead," *New York Times*, Aug. 31, 2009; Steve Mills & Maurice Possley, "Man Executed on Disproved Forensics: Fire That Killed His 3 Children Could Have Been Accidental," *Chicago Tribune*, Dec. 9, 2004. Willingham has not yet been posthumously exonerated as of July 2011.

11. See Innocence Project, "Experts Question More Massachusetts Arson Convictions" (http://www.innocenceproject.org/Content/Experts_Question_More_Massachusetts_Arson_Convictions.php).

12. See Moriarty, *Misconvictions*, at 6.

13. See, e.g., Keith A. Findley, "Innocents at Risk: Adversary Imbalance, Forensic Science, and the Search for Truth," 38 *Seton Hall L. Rev.* 893, 937–39 (2008); Moriarty, *Misconvictions*, at 8–9. Although forensic disciplines have been derided as lacking a "scientific culture," it is not precisely clear what that term means. See, generally, Simon A. Cole, "Acculturating Forensic Science: What Is 'Scientific Culture,' and How Can Forensic Science Adopt It?" 38 *Fordham Urb. L.J.* 435 (2010).

14. See Moriarty, *Misconvictions*, at 8–9. Professor Erin Murphy has contended that an emerging "second generation" of forensic science, including DNA typing, data mining, location tracking, and biometric techniques, represents an improvement over many of the traditional forensic sciences, but she cautions that they also possess the capacity for misuse. See Erin Murphy, "The New Forensics: Criminal Justice, False Certainty, and the Second Generation of Scientific Evidence," 95 *Cal. L. Rev.* 721 (2007).

15. See Brandon L. Garrett & Peter J. Neufeld, "Invalid Forensic Science Testimony and Wrongful Convictions," 95 *Va. L. Rev.* 1, 9 (2009).

16. See William C. Thompson, "Beyond Bad Apples: Analyzing the Role of Forensic Science in Wrongful Convictions," 37 *Sw. L. Rev.* 1027, 1033–44 (2008). See also Garrett & Neufeld, *Invalid Testimony*, at 64–66.

17. See Moises Mendoza & Bradley Olson, "HPD Fingerprint Unit Is Focus of Criminal Probe," *Houston Chronicle*, Dec. 2, 2009.

18. See "Scathing SBI Audit Says 230 Cases Tainted by Shoddy Investigations," *News & Observer* (Charlotte, NC), Aug. 27, 2010. Rampant problems recently led to the closure of the Nassau County crime lab in New York. The local district attorney ordered the retesting of physical samples in all felony drug cases (roughly 3,000) since 2007. The lab's handling of blood alcohol testing has also come under attack. See Andrew Keshner, "Judge to Oversee Cases Involving Faulty Crime Lab," *N.Y.L.J.*, Mar. 22, 2011.

19. See Brendan J. Lyons, "Probe: Crime Data Faked," *Albany Times-Union*, Dec. 18, 2009; Joel Stashenko, "N.Y. District Attorneys Urged to Review Convictions in Wake of Widespread Evidence Errors," *N.Y.L.J.*, Dec. 21, 2009.

20. Prosecutors, for instance, may have exacerbated the flawed forensic evidence in Sutton's case by diverting the expert testimony at trial in a fashion that contributed to the wrongful conviction. See Robert Aronson & Jacqueline McMurtrie, "The Use and Misuse of High-Tech Evidence by Prosecutors: Ethical and Evidentiary Issues," 76 *Fordham L. Rev.* 1453, 1479–80 (2007); Garrett & Neufeld, *Invalid Testimony*, at 84–85.

21. See Giannelli & McMunigal, *Prosecutors*, at 1497–98; Moriarty, *Misconvictions*, at 6–7; Raeder, *See No Evil*, at 1420–21.

22. See Garrett & Neufeld, *Invalid Testimony*, at 83; Giannelli & McMunigal, *Prosecutors*, at 1498–1500; Raeder, *See No Evil*, at 1421. For a general description of the Robert Miller case, see Innocence Project, "Profile of Robert Miller" (available at http://www.innocenceproject.org/Content/Robert_Miller.php). Not all these scandals involve forensic scientists employed by crime labs. See, e.g., Raeder, *See No Evil*, at 1421.

23. See *Strengthening Forensic Science in the United States: A Path Forward* (Washington, DC: National Academies Press, 2009), 14–33. See also Paul C. Giannelli, "Wrongful Convictions and Forensic Science: The Need to Regulate Crime Labs," 86 *N.C. L. Rev.* 163 (2007); Daniel S. Medwed, "Introduction: Path Forward or Road to Nowhere? Implications of the 2009 National Academy of Sciences Report on the Forensic Sciences," 2010 *Utah L. Rev.* 221, 221 (2010). As Professor Keith Findley points out, several states have experimented with forensic science commissions to provide oversight of state crime laboratories. See Findley, *Innocents at Risk*, at 952–53.

24. See Miller v. Pate, 386 U.S. 1 (1967). See also Bennett L. Gershman, "Misuse of Scientific Evidence by Prosecutors," 28 *Okla. City U. L. Rev.* 17, 17–18 (2003); Giannelli & McMunigal, *Prosecutors*, at 1520–21.

25. See Gershman, *Misuse*, at 21–28.

26. See *Id.* at 22.

27. *Id.*

28. See Giannelli & McMunigal, *Prosecutors*, at 1508–13. One questionable practice involves experts generating reports calculated to offer minimal benefit to the defense before trial and then acting to "spruce up" the reports as trial nears. See Michael J. Saks, "Scientific Evidence and the Ethical Obligations of Attorneys," 49 *Clev. St. L. Rev.* 421, 436 (2001).

29. See Garrett & Neufeld, *Invalid Testimony*, at 53; Gershman, *Misuse*, at 32.

30. See Giannelli & McMunigal, *Prosecutors*, at 1521–23.

31. See Gershman, *Misuse*, at 33–34. Prosecutors have also mischaracterized scientific evidence in their closing arguments, a topic covered in chapter 6. See also *Id.* at 35–38; Giannelli & McMunigal, *Prosecutors*, at 1526–27.

32. See chapter 4, this volume.

33. See Raeder, *See No Evil*, at 1423–24.

34. See Giannelli & McMunigal, *Prosecutors*, at 1528.

35. See chapter 1, this volume; Giannelli & McMunigal, *Prosecutors*, at 1528.

36. See Daubert v. Merrell Dow Pharmaceuticals, Inc., 509 U.S. 579 (1993).

37. For a discussion of how the diffusion of responsibility within the criminal justice system "may disinhibit the prosecutor to pursue his case with increased zealousness and to pursue a conviction," see Lawton P. Cummings, "Can an Ethical Person Be an Ethical Prosecutor? A Social Cognitive Approach to Systemic Reform," 31 *Cardozo L. Rev.* 2139, 2153 (2010).

38. Professor Paul Giannelli has suggested that forensic analysts often suffer from a "motivational" or "role effects" bias—biases that could be offset by insulating crime labs from law enforcement institutions. See Paul C. Giannelli, "Independent Crime Laboratories: The Problem of Motivational and Cognitive Bias," 2010 *Utah L. Rev.* 247 (2010).

39. Melendez-Diaz v. Massachusetts, 129 S. Ct. 2527, 2536 (2009).

40. See Rachel E. Barkow, "Institutional Design and the Policing of Prosecutors: Lessons from Administrative Law," 61 *Stan. L. Rev.* 869 (2009).

41. See, generally, Giannelli, *Independent Crime Laboratories*. In fact, more than a century ago, Judge Learned Hand argued in a law review article for a court-appointed tribunal of neutral expert witnesses to guide juries about scientific and other specialized issues. See Learned Hand, "Historical and Practical Considerations Regarding Expert Testimony," 15 *Harv. L. Rev.* 40, 56 (1901).

42. See, e.g., Gershman, *Misuse*, at 40; Raeder, *See No Evil*, at 1450–51.

43. This would preferably take place before plea negotiations start. See Giannelli & McMunigal, *Prosecutors*, at 1519.

44. These changes would comport with the American Bar Association's recommendations regarding the handling of DNA evidence. See Giannelli & McMunigal, *Prosecutors*, at 1519–20.

45. Defense lawyers in criminal cases often lack the resources to mount their own expert witness challenge to the government's interpretation and presentation of scientific evidence. See Findley, *Innocents at Risk*, at 929–32.

46. Model Rules of Prof'l Conduct R. 1.1 (2008).

47. See Giannelli & McMunigal, *Prosecutors*, at 1529–30.

48. *Id.* at 1530.

49. See, e.g., Gershman, *Misuse*, at 28–29; Moriarty, *Misconvictions*, at 23–24.

50. See Saks, *Scientific Evidence*, at 433.

51. Criminal Justice Standards Comm., Am. Bar Ass'n, Standards for Criminal Justice: Prosecution and Defense Function Standard 3-3.3(a) (3d ed., 1993).

52. *Id.* Standard 3-3.3(b) of the ABA Standards also provides that a prosecutor "should not pay an excessive fee for the purpose of influencing the expert's testimony or to fix the amount of the fee contingent upon the testimony the expert will give or the result in the case." *Id.*

53. See Moriarty, *Misconvictions*, at 24.

54. *Id.* at 28–29. The proposed revisions to the ABA Standards, which have not yet been finalized, recommend that a prosecutor should scrutinize the experience, reputation, and background of an expert witness before retaining her, and also review the scientific standing of her methods and procedures. See Roberta K. Flowers, "Witness Preparation: Regulating the Profession's 'Dirty Little Secret,'" 38 *Hastings Const. L.Q.* 1007, 1017 (2011).

55. See Giannelli & McMunigal, *Prosecutors*, at 1532–36.

56. *Id.* at 1535. See also Saks, *Scientific Evidence*, at 426.

57. See Saks, *Scientific Evidence*, at 428–29.

58. See, e.g., Raeder, *See No Evil*, at 1420, 1438–39.

59. See Saks, *Scientific Evidence*, at 422–23.

60. Daubert v. Merrell Dow Pharmaceuticals, Inc., 509 U.S. 579 (1993).

61. See *Id.*

62. See, e.g., Paul C. Giannelli, "Admissibility of Scientific Evidence," 28 *Okla. City U. L. Rev.* 1, 7–8 (2003).

63. See, e.g., Findley, *Innocents at Risk*, at 896–97, 934–36; Moriarty, *Misconvictions*, at 18–19; D. Michael Risinger, "Navigating Expert Reliability: Are Criminal Standards of Certainty Being Left on the Dock?" 64 *Albany L. Rev.* 99, 143 (2000).

64. See, e.g., Findley, *Innocents at Risk*, at 954–55.

65. *Id.* at 954.

CHAPTER 6. CLOSING THE DOOR ON INNOCENCE

1. Portions of this chapter derive from Daniel S. Medwed, "Closing the Door on Misconduct: Rethinking the Ethical Standards That Govern Summations in Criminal Trials," 38 *Hastings Const. L.Q.* 915 (2011). Prosecutors have a particularly wide berth during rebuttal closing argument where, pursuant to the "Invited Response Doctrine," they may respond directly to the defense closing arguments. See, e.g., Michael Lyon, "Avoiding the Woodshed: The Third Circuit Examines Prosecutorial Misconduct in Closing Argument in United States v. Wood," 53 *Vill. L. Rev.* 689, 699–701 (2008); Rosemary Nidiry, Note, "Restraining Adversarial Excess in Closing Argument," 96 *Colum. L. Rev.* 1299, 1300, 1333–34 (1996).

2. See, e.g., N.Y. Crim. P. L. 260.30 (2002).

3. This is the prevailing federal practice. Fed. R. Crim. P. 29.1 (2002). California abides by this practice as well. Cal. Penal Code 1093(e) (2004).

4. See, generally, John B. Mitchell, "Why Should the Prosecutor Get the Last Word?" 27 *Am. J. Crim. L.* 139, 156–95 (2000).

5. See, generally, *Id.* See also Michael D. Cicchini, "Prosecutorial Misconduct at Trial: A New Perspective Rooted in Confrontation Clause Jurisprudence," 37 *Seton Hall L. Rev.* 335, 341 (2007).

6. See, e.g., R. Michael Cassidy, *Prosecutorial Ethics* (St. Paul, MN: Thomson-West, 2005), 101–7; Nidiry, *Restraining*, at 1306–8. See also Charles L. Cantrell, "Prosecutorial Misconduct: Recognizing Errors in Closing Argument," 26 *Am. J. Trial Advoc.* 535 (2003).

7. Consultants often advise lawyers to craft trial strategies that steadily build toward a powerful closing. See Ryan Patrick Alford, "Catalyzing More Adequate Federal Habeas Review of Summation Misconduct: Persuasion Theory and the Sixth Amendment Right to an Unbiased Jury," 59 *Okla. L. Rev.* 479, 514 (2006). Empirical studies suggest that jurors rely heavily on closing arguments. See Mitchell, *Last Word*, at 150–56.

8. See Todd E. Pettys, "The Emotional Juror," 76 *Fordham L. Rev.* 1609, 1609 (2007). As Professor Todd Pettys points out, "an emotion can prompt us to act if we perceive that the action will either reduce the unpleasant physiological sensations associated with the emotion or sustain the emotion's pleasant physiological sensations." *Id.* at 1624. To that end,

an emotional appeal by a prosecutor during closing argument can spur jurors to reach a guilty verdict to resolve the unpleasant feeling associated with the defendant or with the prospect of finding the defendant not guilty.

9. As the U.S. Supreme Court proclaimed in 1935, prosecutors "may strike hard blows" but not "foul ones." Berger v. United States, 295 U.S. 78, 88 (1935). See also Cassidy, *Prosecutorial Ethics*, at 101–7; Nidiry, *Restraining*, at 1311–14, 1324.

10. See Cassidy, *Prosecutorial Ethics*, at 102.

11. *Id.*

12. *Id.* at 102–3.

13. *Id.* at 103–4.

14. *Id.* at 104.

15. *Id.* at 105. Prosecutors also should not comment on a defendant's silence after arrest and the receipt of Miranda warnings. Doyle v. Ohio, 426 U.S. 610 (1976).

16. See Cassidy, *Prosecutorial Ethics*, at 106.

17. During closing argument, prosecutors may generally refer to current events, well-known quotes, and stories to persuade juries. See Peter A. Joy & Kevin C. McMunigal, *Do No Wrong: Ethics for Prosecutors and Defenders* (Chicago: ABA, 2009), 197–98.

18. As Professor Bennett Gershman notes, "when courts and commentators talk about prosecutorial misconduct, they often are referring to the prosecutor's argument to the jury." Bennett L. Gershman, *Prosecutorial Misconduct*, 2d ed. (St. Paul, MN: Thomson-West, 2007), 462. See also Cicchini, *Prosecutorial Misconduct*, at 341–42.

19. See Brandon L. Garrett & Peter J. Neufeld, "Invalid Forensic Science Testimony and Wrongful Convictions," 95 *Va. L. Rev.* 1, 85–89 (2009).

20. See *Id.* at 87–88; Innocence Project, "Profile of Drew Whitley" (available at http://www.innocenceproject.org/Content/Drew_Whitley.php).

21. See *Id.*

22. The following description of the Deskovic case derives from the Innocence Project's synopsis of his wrongful conviction and a report on the case prepared at the request of Westchester County District Attorney Janet DiFiore. See Innocence Project, "Profile of Jeff Deskovic" (available at http://www.innocenceproject.org/Content/Jeff_Deskovic.php); *Report on the Conviction of Jeffrey Deskovic* (2007) (available at http://truthinjustice.org/Jeffrey-Deskovic-Comm-Rpt.pdf).

23. See *Report on the Conviction of Jeffrey Deskovic* at 1–2.

24. *Id.* See also *Profile of Jeff Deskovic.*

25. *Profile of Jeff Deskovic; Report on the Conviction of Jeffrey Deskovic* at 2–3.

26. See *Profile of Jeff Deskovic; Report on the Conviction of Jeffrey Deskovic* at 2, 10, 20, 23.

27. See *Report on the Conviction of Jeff Deskovic* at 21–22.

28. *Id.* at 22–23.

29. See *Id.* at 23; *Profile of Jeff Deskovic.* See also People v. Deskovic, 607 N.Y.S. 2d 957 (App. Div. 1994).

30. See *Profile of Jeff Deskovic; Report on the Conviction of Jeffrey Deskovic* at 4.

31. See *Report on the Conviction of Jeffrey Deskovic* at 4.

32. See chapter 4, this volume.

33. See Gershman, *Prosecutorial Misconduct*, at 464 n. 12.

34. *Id.*

35. *Id.* at 462.

36. Dunlop v. U. S., 165 U.S. 486, 498 (1897); Gershman, *Prosecutorial Misconduct*, at 465. Judge Learned Hand elaborated on this point, observing that "it is impossible to expect that a criminal trial shall be conducted without some show of feeling; the stakes are high, and the participants are inevitably charged with emotion." U.S. v. Wexler, 79 F.2d 526, 529–30 (2d Cir. 1935).

37. See State v. Frost, 727 A.2d 1, 4 (N.J. 1999), citing State v. DiPaglia, 315 A.2d 385, 395 (N.J. 1974) (Clifford, J., dissenting); Gershman, *Prosecutorial Misconduct*, at 465 n. 15.

38. See Cantrell, *Prosecutorial Misconduct*, at 535 n. 2; Gershman, *Prosecutorial Misconduct*, at 572–76.

39. See Gershman, *Prosecutorial Misconduct*, at 574–76; Nidiry, *Restraining*, at 1323–24. This "guilt-based" approach to harmless error signifies that on many occasions guilt is the "sole criterion by which harmlessness is gauged." Harry T. Edwards, "To Err Is Human, But Not Always Harmless: When Should Legal Error Be Tolerated?" *70 N.Y.U. L. Rev.* 1167, 1171–72, 1187 (1995).

40. A 2003 study by the Center for Public Integrity examined more than eleven thousand appellate decisions involving allegations of prosecutorial misconduct. Only in approximately two thousand of those cases did the judiciary find the purported errors harmful enough to warrant reversal. See Steve Weinberg, "Breaking the Rules: Who Suffers When a Prosecutor Is Cited for Misconduct?" *Harmful Error: Investigating America's Local Prosecutors*, June 26, 2003 (available at http://projects.publicintegrity.org/pm/default.aspx?act=main).

41. See Emily M. West, *Court Findings of Prosecutorial Misconduct Claims in Post-Conviction Appeals and Civil Suits among the First 255 DNA Exoneration Cases*, Aug. 2010 (available at http://www.innocenceproject.org/docs/Innocence_Project_Pros_Misconduct.pdf), 1–2.

42. *Id.* at 2–3.

43. *Id.* at 4.

44. *Id.* at 5.

45. Special thanks to Emily West, Research Director of the Innocence Project, for analyzing the data in more detail and providing me with this additional information. See e-mail from Emily West to Daniel S. Medwed and accompanying attachment, June 20, 2011 (copy on file with author).

46. See, generally, Adam M. Gershowitz, "Prosecutorial Shaming: Naming Attorneys to Reduce Prosecutorial Misconduct," 42 *U.C. Davis L. Rev.* 1059, 1067–70 (2009).

47. See Paul J. Spiegelman, "Prosecutorial Misconduct in Closing Argument: The Role of Intent in Appellate Review," 1 *J. App. Prac. & Process* 115, 119, 169–70 (1999). Professor Adam Gershowitz studied the appellate opinions cited in the Center for Public Integrity's 2003 report on prosecutorial misconduct and found that appellate judges mentioned the errant prosecutor(s) by name in only 517 of the 2,012 cases in which courts reversed the convictions at trial. See Gershowitz, *Prosecutorial Shaming*, at 1069. See also Weinberg, *Breaking the Rules*.

48. See Kathleen M. Ridolfi & Maurice Possley, *Preventable Error: A Report on Prosecutorial Misconduct in California 1997–2009*, Oct. 2010 (available at http://law.scu.edu/ncip/file/ProsecutorialMisconduct_BookEntire_online%20version.pdf), 50.

49. See Gershowitz, *Prosecutorial Shaming*, at 1084–88.

50. Even after a case is reversed on the grounds of prosecutorial misconduct, appellate courts rarely report the offender to disciplinary officials. See, e.g., Ridolfi & Possley, *Preventable Error*, at 48–50.

51. Model Rules of Prof'l Conduct R. 3.4(e) (2008).

52. Criminal Justice Standards Comm., Am. Bar Ass'n, Standards for Criminal Justice: Prosecution and Defense Function Standards 3-5.8 (3d ed. 1993) [hereinafter "ABA Standards"].

53. ABA Standards, Commentary to Standard 3-5.8.

54. *Id.*

55. See, e.g., Garrett & Neufeld, *Invalid Testimony*, at 85–86.

56. One judge has insisted that "the trial court, through the use of admonishment and curative instructions, and even the threat of declaring a mistrial, can prevent and cure most improper argument by prosecutors." See Robert W. Clifford, "Identifying and Preventing Improper Prosecutorial Comment in Closing Argument," 51 *Me. L. Rev.* 241, 268 (1999). See also Nidiry, *Restraining*, at 1325–34. Courts could also keep prosecutors in line by holding them in contempt. See, e.g., In re Little, 404 U.S. 553 (1972); Lyn M. Morton, Note, "Seeking the Elusive Remedy for Prosecutorial Misconduct: Suppression, Dismissal, or Discipline?" 7 *Geo. J. Legal Ethics* 1083, 1089 n. 38 (1994).

57. In the absence of a defense objection to a particular comment during a prosecutor's summation, appellate courts might consider the issue waived and thus "unpreserved" for review on appeal. See, e.g., People v. Friend, 211 P.3d 520, 543–44 (Cal. 2009).

58. See, e.g., Spiegelman, *Prosecutorial Misconduct,* at 171–74.

59. See *Id.*

60. See *Id.*

61. See *Id.* at 169–83.

62. See Cassidy, *Prosecutorial Ethics*, at 101–7; Nidiry, *Restraining*, at 1310–14, 1324.

63. I am not alone in this sentiment. Professor Brandon Garrett, for instance, has criticized harm analysis by appellate courts "based on a discretionary, flexible, and broad examination of all of the evidence before the jury, taking account of any general perception of the guilt of the defendant." Brandon L. Garrett, "Innocence, Harmless Error, and Federal Wrongful Conviction Law," 2005 *Wis. L. Rev.* 35, 61 (2005). Garrett further cautions that courts should be reticent to classify an error as harmless in cases having "the indicia of wrongful convictions." *Id.* at 113.

64. See People v. Deskovic, 607 N.Y.S.2d 957, 958 (App. Div. 1994).

65. A number of scholars have also complained about the harmless error standard and cited it as a factor in prolonging some wrongful convictions. See, e.g., Garrett, *Harmless Error*; Giovanna Shay, "What We Can Learn about Appeals from Mr. Tillman's Case: More Lessons from Another DNA Exoneration," 77 *U. Cin. L. Rev.* 1499, 1542–45 (2009). Others have condemned the harmless error rule for straying from its original purpose—which was to overturn a conviction only where an error affected the verdict—and evolving into a questionable doctrine that invites appellate judges to assess the factual guilt of the defendant as best they can and affirm the conviction where guilt is overwhelming. See, generally, Edwards, *To Err Is Human.*

66. Professor Sam Kamin has recommended forsaking the harmless error doctrine in cases where prosecutors violate clearly established rights. Sam Kamin, "Harmless Error and the Rights/Remedies Split," 88 *Va. L. Rev.* 1, 73 (2002).

67. For instance, as of a decade ago, the average tenure for a prosecutor in the New Orleans District Attorney's Office was two years. Ronald Wright & Marc Miller, "The Screening/Bargaining Tradeoff," 55 *Stan. L. Rev.* 29, 63 (2002).

68. See Gershowitz, *Prosecutorial Shaming,* at 1088–95.

69. *Id.* at 1095–1105.

70. *Id.*

71. See Alford, *Catalyzing,* at 492–95.

72. See Medwed, *Closing the Door.*

73. ABA Standards, Standard 3-5.8(b).

74. Proposed Standard 3-7.8(b) (manuscript currently on file with author).

75. Proposed Standard 3-7.8(c) (manuscript currently on file with author).

76. The current rules caution that "the prosecutor should not make arguments calculated to appeal to the prejudices of the jury" and "should refrain from argument which would divert the jury from its duty to decide the case on the evidence." ABA Standards, Standard 3-5.8(c)-(d).

77. The Task Force's recommendations about rebuttal specify, among other things, that "the prosecutor may fairly respond to arguments made in the defense closing, but should object to defense arguments it believes were improper and seek relief from the court, rather than respond with arguments the prosecutor knows to be improper." Proposed Standard 3–7.8(d) (manuscript currently on file with author).

78. See, generally, Mitchell, *Last Word.*

79. *Id.* at 216.

80. *Id.*

81. *Id.*

82. Proposed Standard 4-7.7(g) (manuscript currently on file with author).

PART III. THE FALLACY OF FINALITY

1. The following description of the Godschalk case derives principally from the Brief of Appellants Appealing the Order of the U.S. District Court for the Eastern District of Pennsylvania Entered August 27, 2001 Compelling Prosecutors to Turn Over Evidence for DNA Testing 3–4 (manuscript on file with author) [hereinafter *Godschalk Brief*]; Godschalk v. Montgomery County Dist. Attorney's Office, 177 F. Supp. 2d 366 (E.D. Pa. 2001); Innocence Project, "Profile of Bruce Godschalk" (available at http://www.innocenceproject.org/Content/Bruce_Godschalk.php); Seth F. Kreimer & David Rudovsky, "Double Helix, Double Bind: Factual Innocence and Postconviction DNA Testing," 151 *U. Pa. L. Rev.* 547, 547–51 (2002).

2. See *Godschalk Brief* at 4; Kreimer & Rudovsky, *Double Helix,* at 547–48; *Profile of Bruce Godschalk.*

3. For a discussion of the problems associated with the use of jailhouse informants, see chapter 4, this volume.

4. See Kreimer & Rudovsky, *Double Helix,* at 548; *Profile of Bruce Godschalk.*

5. See Kreimer & Rudovsky, *Double Helix,* at 548–49; *Profile of Bruce Godschalk.*

6. See *Godschalk Brief* at 5; Kreimer & Rudovsky, *Double Helix,* at 549; *Profile of Bruce Godschalk.*

7. The Innocence Project first tried to refute the confession. A major stumbling block to this effort lay in the prosecution's unwillingness to hand over any portion of the tape from the interrogation. After several years, prosecutors reluctantly released the tape to the Innocence Project, which sent it to an expert for analysis. The expert determined that it

was likely a false confession. See *Profile of Bruce Godschalk*. For a discussion of false confessions and wrongful convictions, see Steven A. Drizin & Richard A. Leo, "The Problem of False Confessions in the Post-DNA World," 82 *N. C. L. Rev.* 891 (2004). For a more skeptical view of this phenomenon, see Paul G. Cassell, "The Guilty and the 'Innocent': An Examination of Alleged Cases of Wrongful Conviction from False Confessions," 22 *Harv. J. L. & Pub. Pol'y* 523 (1999).

8. See Brady v. Maryland, 373 U.S. 83 (1963). For a discussion of prosecutors' constitutional disclosure obligations, see, generally, chapter 2, this volume.

9. See, generally, Godschalk, 177 F.Supp.2d at 368–70; *Godschalk Brief*; Kreimer & Rudovsky, *Double Helix*, at 549–50; *Profile of Bruce Godschalk*.

10. See Kreimer & Rudovsky, *Double Helix*, at 550–51; *Profile of Bruce Godschalk*.

11. See Kreimer & Rudovsky, *Double Helix*, at 550–51; *Profile of Bruce Godschalk*.

12. See Kreimer & Rudovsky, *Double Helix*, at 550–51; *Profile of Bruce Godschalk*; Sara Rimer, "DNA Testing In Rape Cases Frees Prisoner After 15 Years," *New York Times*, Feb. 15, 2002.

CHAPTER 7. PROSECUTORIAL RESISTANCE TO POST-CONVICTION CLAIMS OF INNOCENCE

1. See Daniel S. Medwed, "Actual Innocents: Considerations in Selecting Cases for a New Innocence Project," 81 *Neb. L. Rev.* 1097, 1122 (2003).

2. See, e.g., Larry Cunningham, "The Innocent Prisoner and the Appellate Prosecutor: Some Thoughts on Post-Conviction Prosecutorial Ethics after *Dretke v. Haley*," 24 *Crim. Just. Ethics* 12, 18 n. 58 (2005). Inmates may alternatively be released through the pardon or parole process, which is discussed later in this chapter.

3. See Daniel S. Medwed, "The Prosecutor as Minister of Justice: Preaching to the Unconverted from the Post-Conviction Pulpit," 84 *Wash. L. Rev.* 35, 47 n. 47 (2009).

4. See *Id.* at 37.

5. See Daniel S. Medwed, "Up the River without a Procedure: Innocent Prisoners and Newly Discovered Non-DNA Evidence in State Courts," 47 *Ariz. L. Rev.* 655, 666–69 (2005).

6. See Medwed, *Preaching*, at 36. Several commentators have urged jurisdictions to revamp their rules of appellate procedure to allow for greater review of new evidence during the direct appeal. See, e.g., Keith A. Findley, "Innocence Protection in the Appellate Process," 93 *Marq. L. Rev.* 591, 608–17 (2009).

7. See, generally, Medwed, *Up the River*.

8. See, e.g., Ex parte Thompson, 153 S.W.3d 416, 417 (Tex. Crim. App. 2005).

9. See, e.g., Herrera v. Collins, 506 U.S. 390 (1993).

10. See, generally, Daniel S. Medwed, "The Innocent Prisoner's Dilemma: Consequences of Failing to Admit Guilt at Parole Hearings," 93 *Iowa L. Rev.* 491 (2008).

11. See, e.g., Bruce A. Green & Ellen Yaroshefsky, "Prosecutorial Discretion and Post-Conviction Evidence of Innocence," 6 *Ohio St. J. Crim. L.* 467, 485–86 (2009); Michael Heise, "Mercy by the Numbers: An Empirical Analysis of Clemency and Its Structure," 89 *Va. L. Rev.* 239 (2003).

12. See Green & Yaroshefsky, *Prosecutorial Discretion*, at 502–3; Medwed, *Preaching*, at 37. See also Douglas H. Ginsburg & Hyland Hunt, "The Prosecutor and Post-Conviction Claims of Innocence: DNA and Beyond?" 7 *Ohio St. J. Crim. L.* 771 (2010).

13. See Medwed, *Preaching*, at 61–64. See also Aviva Orenstein, "Facing the Unfaceable: Dealing with Prosecutorial Denial in Postconviction Cases of Actual Innocence," 48 *San Diego L. Rev.* 401, 410–11 (2011).

14. See, e.g., Daniel S. Medwed, "The Zeal Deal: Prosecutorial Resistance to Post-Conviction Claims of Innocence," 84 *B.U. L. Rev.* 125, 129–30 (2004).

15. See Bennett L. Gershman, "Litigating *Brady v. Maryland*: Games Prosecutors Play," 57 *Case W. Res. L. Rev.* 531, 562–63 (2007).

16. See Medwed, *Preaching*, at 48–49; Orenstein, *Facing*, at 413–16.

17. See Medwed, *Preaching*, at 49–53.

18. See *Id.* at 51; Medwed, *Zeal Deal*, at 148–50.

19. Abbe Smith, "Can You Be a Good Person and a Good Prosecutor?" 14 *Geo. J. Legal Ethics* 355, 384 (2001).

20. See Judith A. Goldberg & David M. Siegel, "The Ethical Obligations of Prosecutors in Cases Involving Postconviction Claims of Innocence," 38 *Cal. W. L. Rev.* 389, 409 (2002); Medwed, *Preaching*, at 51; Medwed, *Zeal Deal*, at 148-50. See also Fred C. Zacharias, "The Role of Prosecutors in Serving Justice after Convictions," 58 *Vand. L. Rev.* 171, 226 (2005).

21. See chapter 1, this volume.

22. See Medwed, *Preaching*, at 51–53.

23. See Alafair S. Burke, "Improving Prosecutorial Decision Making: Some Lessons of Cognitive Science," 47 *Wm. & Mary L. Rev.* 1587, 1612 (2006).

24. See Green & Yaroshefsky, *Prosecutorial Discretion*, at 487–90, 494; Medwed, *Preaching*, at 52–53; Medwed, *Zeal Deal*, at 143–44.

25. See Medwed, *Up the River*, at 702-3; see also Keith A. Findley & Michael S. Scott, "The Multiple Dimensions of Tunnel Vision in Criminal Cases," 2006 *Wis. L. Rev.* 291, 309 (2006).

26. See Green & Yaroshefsky, *Prosecutorial Discretion*, at 489–90; Medwed, *Preaching*, at 53. Professor Aviva Orenstein suggests that prosecutors' offices may also be affected by "groupthink," "a dynamic within an organization whereby members of a deeply cohesive group 'minimize conflict and reach consensus without critically testing, analyzing, and evaluating ideas.'" See Orenstein, *Facing*, at 427.

27. See Burke, *Improving Prosecutorial Decision Making*, at 1612–13. The aversion to cognitive dissonance is similar to the "egocentric bias," one's tendency to adopt a flattering view of oneself and to neglect or discount any information that undermines that positive self-image. See Medwed, *Preaching*, at 53.

28. See, e.g., Green & Yaroshefsky, *Prosecutorial Discretion*, at 467–70; David Luban, "The Conscience of a Prosecutor," 45 *Val. U. L. Rev.* 1, 1-14 (2010); Benjamin Weiser, "Doubting Case, a Prosecutor Helped the Defense," *New York Times*, June 23, 2008, at A1; Melanie D. Wilson, "Finding a Happy and Ethical Medium between a Prosecutor Who Believes the Defendant Didn't Do it and the Boss Who Says That He Did," 103 *Nw. U. L. Rev. Colloquy* 65, 66–67 (2008).

29. See Luban, *Conscience of a Prosecutor*, at 1–3; Weiser, *Doubting Case*; Wilson, *Finding*, at 66–67.

30. Luban, *Conscience of a Prosecutor*, at 1–14; Weiser, *Doubting Case*; Wilson, *Finding*, at 66–67.

31. See Green & Yaroshefsky, *Prosecutorial Discretion*, at 475–76; Medwed, *Preaching*, at 50; Zacharias, *Role of Prosecutors*, at 228.

32. See Innocence Project, "After Exoneration" (available at http://www.innocenceproject.org/know/After-Exoneration.php).

33. See Medwed, *Zeal Deal*, at 157.

34. See Medwed, *Preaching*, at 50–51.

35. See Green & Yaroshefsky, *Prosecutorial Discretion*, at 475–76; Medwed, *Preaching*, at 50–51; George C. Thomas III et al., "Is It Ever Too Late for Innocence? Finality, Efficiency, and Claims of Innocence," 64 *U. Pitt. L. Rev.* 263, 290–93 (2003); Zacharias, *Role of Prosecutors*, at 174, 218–19.

36. See Ronald F. Wright, "How Prosecutor Elections Fail Us," 6 *Ohio St. J. Crim. L.* 581, 589 (2009). In the three other states (Alaska, Connecticut, and New Jersey), the state attorney general is elected and then appoints the local chief prosecutors. *Id.*

37. See chapter 4, this volume. See also Sandra Caron George, Note, "Prosecutorial Discretion: What's Politics Got to Do with It?" 18 *Geo. J. Legal Ethics* 739 (2005). Professor Ron Wright suggests that prosecutors cite conviction rates less often than one might assume. See Wright, *Prosecutor Elections*, at 603–4.

38. See Medwed, *Zeal Deal*, at 156.

39. See *Id.*

40. See Daniel S. Medwed, "Innocentrism," 2008 *U. Ill. L. Rev.* 1549, 1558 (2008); Carolyn Smith, "Gundrum Renames Avery Bill," *Badger Herald,* Nov. 15, 2005 (available at http://badgerherald.com/news/2005/11/15/gundrum_renames_aver.php).

41. See Laurel Walker, "Gundrum Defeats Congdon for Waukesha County Judge Seat," *Milwaukee Journal-Sentinel*, Apr. 6, 2010 (available at http://www.jsonline.com/news/waukesha/90061452.html).

42. See Medwed, *Zeal Deal*, at 156–57. Some prosecutors have lost their jobs in subsequent reelections partly because of controversies related to wrongful convictions or office misconduct. See Rachel E. Barkow, "Organizational Guidelines for the Prosecutor's Office," 31 *Cardozo L. Rev.* 2089, 2116 (2010).

43. See Medwed, *Zeal Deal*, at 159–69. A fourth circumstance is when a case "fascinates members of the media, and their investigative reporting presents the possibility of tainting the chief prosecutor's reputation." *Id.* at 159.

44. See Medwed, *Preaching*, at 49–50; Michele K. Mulhausen, Comment, "A Second Chance at Justice: Why States Should Adopt ABA Model Rules of Professional Conduct 3.8(g) and (h)," 81 *U. Colo. L. Rev.* 309, 314–15, 321 (2010).

45. See Green & Yaroshefsky, *Prosecutorial Discretion*, at 481–82; Medwed, *Preaching*, at 49–50; Zacharias, *Role of Prosecutors*, at 173–75. Legal doctrines crafted by the courts to address prosecutorial actions in the post-conviction setting are comparably vague, affording prosecutors ample discretion to proceed as they see fit. See Zacharias, *Role of Prosecutors*, at 208–9.

46. This study was a joint investigation conducted by the Better Government Association and the Center on Wrongful Convictions. See "The High Costs of Wrongful Convictions: A BCA Rescuing Illinois Investigation with the Center on Wrongful Convictions," June 18, 2011 (available at http://www.bettergov.org/investigations).

47. See, e.g., Imbler v. Pachtman, 424 U.S. 409, 427 n.25 (1976).

48. See Zacharias, *Role of Prosecutors*, at 189–91. See also Medwed, *Preaching*, at 54.

49. In 2009 the Supreme Court chastised the Ninth Circuit Court of Appeals "in concluding that the Due Process Clause requires that certain familiar preconviction trial

rights be extended to protect Osborne's postconviction liberty interest." District Attorney's Office for Third Judicial Dist. v. Osborne, 129 S. Ct. 2308, 2319 (2009). The Court went on to note that "Osborne does not claim that *Brady* controls this case . . . and with good reason." *Id.* at 2320.

50. Professor Fred Zacharias has suggested that prosecutors "highlight postconviction justice issues in their manuals and administrative guidelines." Zacharias, *Role of Prosecutors,* at 238.

51. See Stephanos Bibas, "Rewarding Prosecutors for Performance," 6 *Ohio St. J. Crim. L.* 441, 450–51 (2009); Medwed, *Preaching,* at 61–62; Medwed, *Zeal Deal,* at 170–75.

52. Model Rules of Prof'l Conduct R. 3.8(g) (2008). See also Medwed, *Preaching,* at 55–56; Daniel S. Medwed, "Prosecutorial Ethics in the Postconviction Setting from A to Zacharias," 48 *San Diego L. Rev.* 331, 333–34 (2011).

53. Model Rules of Prof'l Conduct R. 3.8(g) (2008).

54. Model Rules of Prof'l Conduct R. 3.8(h) (2008). In seeking to remedy the conviction, "necessary steps may include disclosure of the evidence to the defendant, requesting that the court appoint counsel for an unrepresented indigent defendant and, where appropriate, notifying the court that the prosecutor has knowledge that the defendant did not commit the offense of which the defendant was convicted." Model Rules of Prof'l Conduct R. 3.8 cmt. 8 (2008).

55. According to Professor Niki Kuckes, these amendments are "the most important additions to Rule 3.8 since the adoption of the *Model Code* in 1969." Niki Kuckes, "The State of Rule 3.8: Prosecutorial Ethics Reform since Ethics 2000," 22 *Geo. J. Legal Ethics* 427, 431–32 (2009). Kuckes also suggests that the precise way in which these amendments came to pass—a "ground-up" effort from professional organizations in New York—is encouraging. *Id.* at 461–62.

56. The rules passed in Colorado, Delaware, Tennessee, and Wisconsin were slightly modified versions of Model Rule 3.8(g) and (h). For a discussion of state responses to these rule changes, see American Bar Association (ABA) CPR Policy Implementation Committee, "Variations of the ABA Model Rules of Professional Conduct Rule 3.8(g) and (h)" (available at http://www.abanet.org/cpr/pic/3_8_g_h.pdf); Delaware Lawyers' Rules of Prof'l Conduct 3.8(d)(2) (2010). Idaho has adopted the Model Rule changes verbatim. See Idaho Rules of Prof'l Conduct R. 3-8(g)–(h) (2010).

57. See ABA Implementation Committee, *Variations.*

58. See Medwed, *Preaching,* at 56; Mulhausen, *Second Chance,* at 328–29.

59. See Medwed, *Preaching,* at 56.

60. *Id.* at 56–57.

61. See Green & Yaroshefsky, *Prosecutorial Discretion,* at 471–72, 481–82.

62. See Medwed, *Preaching,* at 57–58.

63. See, e.g., part 1, this volume.

64. Medwed, *Preaching,* at 58–59.

65. *Id.* at 58.

66. *Id.* at 58–59.

67. See *Id.* at 59. See also Zacharias, *Role of Prosecutors,* at 238–39.

68. See Medwed, *Preaching,* at 59–60. See also Zacharias, *Role of Prosecutors,* at 238–39.

69. See Medwed, *Preaching,* at 60.

70. See *Id.* at 60–61; Zacharias, *Role of Prosecutors,* at 200.

71. See Brandon L. Garrett, "Innocence, Harmless Error, and Federal Wrongful Conviction Law," 2005 *Wis. L. Rev.* 35, 101 (2005); Medwed, *Preaching*, at 61; Mulhausen, *Second Chance*, at 327–28.

72. See E-Mail from Kenneth Wyniemko to Daniel S. Medwed, Sept. 9, 2010 (copy on file with author); Jameson Cook, "Suspect in Rape Sentenced to 10–25 Years for Being Sexual Delinquent," *Oakland (Mich.) Press*, Apr. 15, 2010 (available at http://www.theo-aklandpress.com/articles/2010/04/15/news/local_news/doc4bc7e31d1c5e8798473685.txt); "DNA Proves Man Wrongly Convicted of Rape," June 18, 2003 (available at http://www.clickondetroit.com/print/2278757/detail.html); Innocence Project, "Profile of Kenneth Wyniemko" (available at http://www.innocenceproject.org/Content/Kenneth_Wyniemko.php); "Rape Match?" Aug. 27, 2008 (available at http://www.metrotimes.com/printStory.asp?id=13206).

73. See *Profile of Kenneth Wyniemko*.

74. See *DNA Proves Man Wrongly Convicted*.

75. See *E-mail from Wyniemko to Medwed*; *Profile of Kenneth Wyniemko*.

76. See *E-mail from Wyniemko to Medwed*.

77. See Cook, *Suspect in Rape Sentenced*; *Rape Match*.

78. Medwed, *Preaching*, at 61–62.

79. See part 1, this volume.

80. See Green & Yaroshefsky, *Prosecutorial Discretion*, at 494–95; Medwed, *Preaching*, at 62.

81. See Green & Yaroshefsky, *Prosecutorial Discretion*, at 495, 512 n. 259.

82. See *Id.* at 503-4. Watkins's methodology also dovetails nicely with a suggestion by Professors Bruce Green and Ellen Yaroshefsky that prosecutors should take proactive steps to free inmates when their investigations give them reason to believe that the inmate is "probably innocent." *Id.* at 507-8, 516.

83. See Dallas County Dist. Att'y, *Conviction Integrity Unit* (available at http://www.dallasda.com/conviction-integrity.html).

84. Medwed, *Preaching*, at 62-63. See also Jennifer Emily, "Man Exonerated in '79 Dallas Rape Case Says, 'It's a Joy to be Free Again,'" *Dallas Morning News*, Jan. 5, 2011. The Conviction Integrity Unit has an open file policy during the post-conviction process. See "Voices from the Field: An Inter-Professional Approach to Managing Critical Information," 31 *Cardozo L. Rev.* 2037, 2071 (2010). The Dallas prosecutors' office also requires that attorneys preserve their trial notes. *Id.* at 2073–74.

85. *Voices from the Field* at 2070.

86. In the words of Terri Moore, Watkins's first assistant, "Guess who does not get invited to go to lunch?" *Id.* at 2071.

87. Watkins also made a number of changes to the top brass in the office and brought in outsiders. See *Voices from the Field* at 2069. Another idiosyncrasy to the Dallas experience is that the county crime lab had actually retained biological evidence since the 1980s. *Id.* at 2070.

88. Emily, *Man Exonerated*; Barry Scheck, "Professional and Conviction Integrity Programs: Why We Need Them, Why They Will Work, and Models for Creating Them," 31 *Cardozo L. Rev.* 2215, 2250 n. 99 (2010).

89. Medwed, *Preaching*, at 63.

90. See *Id.* at 63–64.

91. Jennifer Emily & Jason Trahan, "Dallas County District Attorney Craig Watkins Defeats Challenger Danny Clancy," *Dallas Morning News*, Nov. 3, 2010.

92. See Medwed, *Preaching*, at 64. Some prosecutors' offices may wish to proceed incrementally, perhaps by focusing on serious crimes. See Green & Yaroshefsky, *Prosecutorial Discretion*, at 516–17.

93. See Office of District Attorney, Harris County, Texas, "First 100 Days" (available at http://app.dao.hctx.net/OurOffice/First100Days.aspx).

94. See James C. McKinley, Jr., "Cleared, and Pondering the Value of 27 Years," *New York Times*, Aug. 12, 2010. By the summer of 2010, the post-conviction review section had received about 185 requests for DNA tests as well as roughly 75 other innocence claims. *Id.*

95. See John Eligon, "Prosecutor in Manhattan Will Monitor Convictions," *New York Times*, Mar. 4, 2010; Medwed, *Prosecutorial Ethics*, at 334; Cyrus R. Vance Jr., "A Conviction Integrity Initiative," 73 *Alb. L. Rev.* 1213 (2010).

96. See Green & Yaroshefsky, *Prosecutorial Discretion*, at 509–11; Medwed, *Preaching*, at 65.

97. See Robbie Brown, "Judges Free Inmate on Recommendation of Special Innocence Panel," *New York Times*, Feb. 18, 2010; Green & Yaroshefsky, *Prosecutorial Discretion*, at 509–11; Medwed, *Preaching*, at 65.

98. See, e.g., George, *Prosecutorial Discretion*, at 757.

99. Thomas M. DiBiagio, "Politics and the Criminal Process: Federal Public Corruption Prosecutions of Popular Public Officials under the Honest Services Component of the Mail and Wire Fraud Statutes," 105 *Dick. L. Rev.* 57, 63 (2000).

100. See Green & Yaroshefsky, *Prosecutorial Discretion*, at 469.

101. See Medwed, *Zeal Deal*, at 156–57.

102. Angela J. Davis, "The American Prosecutor: Independence, Power, and the Threat of Tyranny," 86 *Iowa L. Rev.* 393, 461–62 (2001). See also Ronald F. Wright & Marc L. Miller, "The Worldwide Accountability Deficit for Prosecutors," 67 *Wash. & Lee L. Rev.* 1587 (2010).

103. See, generally, Sanford C. Gordon & Gregory A. Huber, "Citizen Oversight and the Electoral Incentives of Criminal Prosecutors," 46 *Am. J. Pol. Sci.* 334 (2002).

104. For example, the prosecutors' office in Kitsap County, Washington, which is near Seattle, makes extensive data about its operations available to the public. See Wright & Miller, *Worldwide Accountability*, at 1615–16.

105. See Davis, *American Prosecutor*, at 461–62; Medwed, *Zeal Deal*, at 177–78; Wright, *Prosecutor Elections*, at 606–10.

106. See Medwed, *Zeal Deal*, at 155–56, 178; Wright, *Prosecutor Elections*, at 602. See also Stephanos Bibas, "Prosecutorial Regulation versus Prosecutorial Accountability," 157 *U. Pa. L. Rev.* 959, 984 (2009).

107. See Medwed, *Zeal Deal*, at 155–56, 178.

108. See *Id.* at 179. See also Bibas, *Prosecutorial Regulation*, at 988.

109. Wright, *Prosecutor Elections*, at 592–93.

110. A recent study of felony convictions in North Carolina from 1997 to 2009 shows that, during the year in which a prosecutorial incumbent faced a challenger in running for reelection, the proportion of convictions gained from jury trials versus guilty pleas typically increased. Conversely, when chief prosecutors in particular districts ran unopposed throughout this period, the number of convictions obtained through jury trials

declined substantially. See Siddhartha Bandyopadhyay & Bryan C. McCannon, "The Effect of Reelections on Prosecutors," Oct. 12, 2010 (available at http://papers.ssrn.com/sol3/papers.cfm?abstract_id=1641345).

111. See Gordon & Huber, *Citizen Oversight*, at 349.

112. See Medwed, *Zeal Deal*, at 179.

113. See *Id.* at 179–80.

114. See Eric Rasmusen et al., "Convictions versus Conviction Rates: The Prosecutor's Choice," 11 *Am. Law & Econ. Rev.* 47, 73 (2009).

115. See Medwed, *Zeal Deal*, at 180; Wright, *Prosecutor Elections*, at 581–82.

116. See Medwed, *Zeal Deal*, at 152.

117. See, e.g., George, *Prosecutorial Discretion*, at 757.

118. See Medwed, *Zeal Deal*, at 152, 180.

119. See "New Perspectives on Brady and Other Disclosure Obligations: Report of the Working Groups on Best Practices," 31 *Cardozo L. Rev.* 1961, 1999 (2010).

120. See Medwed, *Zeal Deal*, at 180.

121. See *Id.* at 180–81. See also George C. Thomas III, *The Supreme Court on Trial: How the American Justice System Sacrifices Innocent Defendants* (Ann Arbor: University of Michigan Press, 2008), 190–92. For an extensive analysis of the public prosecutorial model as it has evolved over time, see Carolyn B. Ramsey, "The Discretionary Power of 'Public' Prosecutors in Historical Perspective," 39 *Am. Crim. L. Rev.* 1309 (2002). Several observers suggest that abandoning the public prosecutor model is unrealistic—and potentially problematic. See, e.g., Sara Gurwitch, "When Self-Policing Does Not Work: A Proposal for Policing Prosecutors in Their Obligation to Provide Exculpatory Evidence to the Defense," 50 *Santa Clara L. Rev.* 303, 319–20 (2010); Janet C. Hoeffel, "Prosecutorial Discretion at the Core: The Good Prosecutor Meets *Brady*," 109 *Penn. St. L. Rev.* 1133, 1153–54 (2005).

CHAPTER 8. A CLOSER LOOK

1. States do not always provide adequate procedures for appellate review of denials of newly discovered evidence claims. See Daniel S. Medwed, "Up the River without a Procedure: Innocent Prisoners and Newly Discovered Non-DNA Evidence in State Courts," 47 *Ariz. L. Rev.* 655, 708–15 (2005).

2. Because Smith's case is not a sympathetic one, he is an unlikely candidate for a gubernatorial pardon. For an interesting discussion of the clemency process and how it varies from state to state, see Michael Heise, "Mercy by the Numbers: An Empirical Analysis of Clemency and Its Structure," 89 *Va. L. Rev.* 239 (2003).

3. See George "Woody" Clarke, *Justice and Science: Trials and Triumphs of DNA Evidence* (New Brunswick, NJ: Rutgers University Press, 2007), 16–23, 38–41.

4. See Innocence Project, "Profile of Gary Dotson" (available at http://www.innocenceproject.org/Content/Gary_Dotson.php).

5. See *Id.*

6. See Clarke, *Justice and Science*, at 114.

7. See, generally, Office of State Budget and Management (NC), *Cost Study of DNA Testing and Analysis*, Mar. 1, 2006 (available at http://www.osbm.state.nc.us/files/pdf_files/3-1-2006FinalDNAReport.pdf).

8. See, e.g., Aaron P. Stevens, Note, "Arresting Crime: Expanding the Scope of DNA Databases in America," 79 *Tex. L. Rev.* 921 (2001).

9. See Brandon L. Garrett, "Judging Innocence," 108 *Colum. L. Rev.* 55, 119 (2008).

10. See chapter 7, this volume.

11. See *Id.*; Clarke, *Justice and Science*; Seth F. Kreimer & David Rudovsky, "Double Helix, Double Bind: Factual Innocence and Postconviction DNA Testing," 151 *U. Pa. L. Rev.* 547, 555–60 (2002).

12. On rare occasions prosecutors go beyond resistance. Stories have circulated of prosecutors trying to induce defendants to waive their rights to the preservation of DNA evidence and even destroying biological evidence. See Kreimer & Rudovsky, *Double Helix*, at 561–63.

13. See Garrett, *Judging Innocence*, at 120.

14. See *Id.* at 118–19.

15. See *Id.* at 118–20.

16. See part 3, this volume.

17. See chapter 7, this volume. See also Shaila Dewan, "Prosecutors Block Access to DNA Testing for Inmates," *New York Times*, May 18, 2009.

18. See Garrett, *Judging Innocence*, at 117–18.

19. See Innocence Project, "Two to Go: Alaska Becomes 48th State with a DNA Access Law" (available at http://www.innocenceproject.org/docs/IPonline/May2010.php).

20. See, e.g., Innocence Project, "Access to Post-Conviction DNA Testing" (available at http://www.innocenceproject.org/Content/Access_To_PostConviction_DNA_Testing. php); Kathy Swedlow, "Don't Believe Everything You Read: A Review of Modern 'Post-Conviction' DNA Testing Statutes," 38 *Cal. W. L. Rev.* 355 (2002).

21. See Garrett, *Judging Innocence*, at 117.

22. See, generally, Kreimer & Rudovsky, *Double Helix*; George C. Thomas III et al., "Is It Ever Too Late for Innocence? Finality, Efficiency, and Claims of Innocence," 64 *U. Pitt. L. Rev.* 263 (2003).

23. See District Attorney's Office for Third Judicial Dist. v. Osborne, 129 S. Ct. 2308 (2009). Professor Brandon Garrett contends that, although *Osborne* did not announce a freestanding constitutional right to post-conviction DNA testing, the case crafted a qualified procedural due process right. See Brandon L. Garrett, "DNA and Due Process," 78 *Fordham L. Rev.* 2919, 2921 (2010). Indeed, the Court noted that "Osborne does, however, have a liberty interest in demonstrating his innocence with new evidence under state law," but found "nothing inadequate about the procedures Alaska has provided to vindicate its state right to postconviction relief in general, and nothing inadequate about how those procedures apply to those who seek access to DNA evidence." *Osborne*, 129 S. Ct. at 2319–20. In 2011 the Court confirmed in *Skinner v. Switzer* that a state prisoner may claim violation of his federal constitutional right to procedural due process in a Section 1983 action. Justice Ruth Bader Ginsburg, writing for the majority, noted that *Osborne* "left slim room for the prisoner to show that the governing state law denies him procedural due process." Skinner v. Switzer, 131 S. Ct. 1289, 1293 (2011).

24. See *Osborne*, 129 S. Ct. at 2312–43. See also Adam Liptak, "Justices Reject Inmate Right to DNA Tests," *New York Times*, June 19, 2009.

25. See *Osborne*, 129 S. Ct. at 2331 (Stevens, J., dissenting).

26. *Id.* at 2322.

27. See Innocence Project, *Two to Go*.

28. See, generally, Cynthia E. Jones, "Evidence Destroyed, Innocence Lost: The Preservation of Biological Evidence under Innocence Protection Statutes," 42 *Am. Crim. L. Rev.* 1239 (2005).

29. See *Id.* at 1242–46. See also Bennett L. Gershman, "Misuse of Scientific Evidence by Prosecutors," 28 *Okla. City U. L. Rev.* 17, 25–26 (2003).

30. See Innocence Project, "Preservation of Evidence" (available at http://www.innocenceproject.org/Content/Preservation_Of_Evidence.php); Jones, *Evidence Destroyed*, at 1252–57.

31. See Garrett, *Judging Innocence*, at 116–17 n. 236.

32. See Innocence Project, *Preservation of Evidence*; Cynthia E. Jones, "The Right Remedy for the Wrongly Convicted: Judicial Sanctions for Destruction of DNA Evidence," 77 *Fordham L. Rev.* 2893, 2894–97 (2009).

33. See Arizona v. Youngblood, 488 U.S. 51, 56–57 (1988); Jones, *Evidence Destroyed*, at 1246–48.

34. See Jones, *Evidence Destroyed*, at 1246–48.

35. For an interesting discussion of the factors that prosecutors might consider in deciding whether they are ethically obligated to agree to DNA testing in the first place, see Douglas H. Ginsburg & Hyland Hunt, "The Prosecutor and Post-Conviction Claims of Innocence: DNA and Beyond?" 7 *Ohio St. J. Crim. L.* 771, 780–85 (2010).

36. See, e.g., Utah Code 78B-9-301(9) (2010).

37. See, e.g., Daniel S. Medwed, "The Zeal Deal: Prosecutorial Resistance to Post-Conviction Claims of Innocence," 84 *B.U. L. Rev.* 125, 154–55 n. 140 (2004).

38. See, e.g., Kreimer & Rudovsky, *Double Helix*, at 611.

39. See also Judith A. Goldberg & David M. Siegel, "The Ethical Obligations of Prosecutors in Cases Involving Postconviction Claims of Innocence," 38 *Cal. W. L. Rev.* 389, 410–12 (2002).

40. Some statutes suggest that the defendant must show at the outset why DNA testing is "material" to the defense. See, e.g., N.C. Gen. Stat. 15A-269(a)(1) (2010). Professor Kathy Swedlow, for one, has argued that materiality requirements may be unduly burdensome to satisfy upfront. See Swedlow, *Don't Believe Everything*, at 367–70. See also Innocence Project, *Access to Post-Conviction DNA Testing*.

41. See, e.g., Utah Code 78B-9-301(9) (2010).

42. See Utah Code 78B-9-301(2)(g)(ii) (2010).

43. See Utah Code 78B-9-304(1)(a) (2010).

44. See chapter 3, this volume.

45. See, generally, Daina Borteck, Note, "Pleas for DNA Testing: Why Lawmakers Should Amend State Post-Conviction DNA Testing Statutes to Apply to Prisoners Who Pled Guilty," 25 *Cardozo L. Rev.* 1429 (2004). For an argument against extending access to post-conviction DNA testing to those who pled guilty, see J. H. Dingfelder Stone, "Facing the Uncomfortable Truth: The Illogic of Post-Conviction DNA Testing for Individuals Who Pleaded Guilty," 45 *U.S.F. L. Rev.* 47 (2010).

46. See, generally, Swedlow, *Don't Believe Everything*, at 370–72.

47. See Innocence Project, *Access to Post-Conviction DNA Testing*.

48. See Gershman, *Misuse*, at 40.

49. See Lisa Falkenberg, "At Least Dallas County Gives 2nd Chances," *Houston Chronicle*, Apr. 17, 2007; Michael Hall, "The Exonerated," *Texas Monthly*, Nov. 2008.

50. See Jones, *Evidence Destroyed*, at 1262–65.

51. *Id.* at 1257.

52. See Innocence Project, "Evidence Preservation" (available at http://www.innocenceproject.org/fix/Evidence-Handling.php); Innocence Project, *Preservation of Evidence*.

53. See Jones, *Evidence Destroyed*, at 1264–65.

54. See, generally, *Id.* at 1258–60.

55. See Jones, *Right Remedy*, at 2894–97.

56. See *Id.* at 2944–53.

57. See Gershman, *Misuse*, at 25–26.

CHAPTER 9. IN DENIAL

1. See Aviva Orenstein, "Facing the Unfaceable: Dealing with Prosecutorial Denial in Postconviction Cases of Actual Innocence," 48 *San Diego L. Rev.* 401, 410–11 (2011).

2. See, e.g., Bruce A. Green & Ellen Yaroshefsky, "Prosecutorial Discretion and Post-Conviction Evidence of Innocence," 6 *Ohio St. J. Crim. L.* 467, 477–78 (2009). For a discussion about when prosecutors should help a defendant who possesses new exculpatory evidence in overturning his conviction, see Douglas H. Ginsburg & Hyland Hunt, "The Prosecutor and Post-Conviction Claims of Innocence: DNA and Beyond?" 7 *Ohio St. J. Crim. L.* 771, 785–88 (2010).

3. See Orenstein, *Facing*, at 410; Gene Warner & Matt Gryta, "Man Jailed Nearly 7 Years for '84 Rape is Exonerated," *Buffalo News*, June 21, 2010. In 2011 Virginia Attorney General Ken Cuccinelli II and two other prosecutors joined the Mid-Atlantic Innocence Project's effort to exonerate Thomas Haynesworth for a series of crimes that occurred in Richmond in 1984. DNA testing proved Haynesworth's innocence in two rapes, but there was no biological evidence that could be tested in two other attacks for which he was convicted of crimes. Virginia Governor Bob McDonnell also intervened and asked the state parole board to review the Haynesworth matter. The board granted Haynesworth parole. Maria Glod, "Va. Man Imprisoned for 27 Years Gets Parole," *Wash. Post*, Mar. 18, 2011. As of July 2011, Haynesworth's innocence claim is still pending in the Virginia Court of Appeals.

4. See Orenstein, *Facing*, at 412–16.

5. See Daniel S. Medwed, "The Innocent Prisoner's Dilemma: Consequences of Failing to Admit Guilt at Parole Hearings," 93 *Iowa L. Rev.* 491, 523–28 (2008); Daniel S. Medwed, "Innocentrism," 2008 *U. Ill. L. Rev.* 1549, 1560–63 (2008).

6. See Medwed, *Innocent Prisoner's Dilemma*, at 523–24; Medwed, *Innocentrism*, at 1561.

7. See Medwed, *Innocent Prisoner's Dilemma*, at 524; Medwed, *Innocentrism*, at 1561.

8. See Medwed, *Innocent Prisoner's Dilemma*, at 524; Medwed, *Innocentrism*, at 1561.

9. See Medwed, *Innocent Prisoner's Dilemma*, at 525; Medwed, *Innocentrism*, at 1561–62.

10. See Medwed, *Innocent Prisoner's Dilemma*, at 526; Medwed, *Innocentrism*, at 1562.

11. See Medwed, *Innocent Prisoner's Dilemma*, at 525–27; Medwed, *Innocentrism*, at 1562–63.

12. See Medwed, *Innocent Prisoner's Dilemma*, at 527–28; Medwed, *Innocentrism*, at 1562–63.

13. See Innocence Project, "Profile of Bruce Dallas Goodman" (available at http://www.innocenceproject.org/Content/Bruce_Dallas_Goodman.php).

14. See Medwed, *Innocentrism*, at 1563.

15. See, e.g., Adele Bernhard, "A Short Overview of the Statutory Remedies for the Wrongly Convicted: What Works, What Doesn't and Why," 18 *B.U. Pub. Int. L.J.* 403, 403–4 (2009).

16. See Innocence Project, "Compensation for the Wrongly Convicted" (available at http://www.innocenceproject.org/fix/Compensation.php).

17. See Bernhard, *Short Overview*, at 409–11. According to Professor Adele Bernhard, the pardon requirement in particular "can be an insurmountable barrier to recovery for deserving claimants because executive clemency is entirely discretionary." Adele Bernhard, "When Justice Fails: Indemnification for Unjust Conviction," 6 *U. Chi. L. Sch. Roundtable* 73, 102 (1999).

18. See Innocence Project, "Profile of Kennedy Brewer" (available at http://www.innocenceproject.org/Content/Kennedy_Brewer.php).

19. See *Id.*

20. See *Id.*

21. See *Id.*

22. See *Id.*

23. See chapters 7–8, this volume.

24. See, e.g., Alafair S. Burke, "Revisiting Prosecutorial Disclosure," 84 *Ind. L.J.* 481, 495–96 (2009).

25. See Orenstein, *Facing*, at 428.

26. See *Id.* at 428–36.

27. See, generally, *Id.*

28. See *Id.* at 434–36.

29. See *Id.* at 432–34.

30. See Medwed, *Innocentrism*, at 1558.

31. See, e.g., Hilary S. Ritter, Note, "It's the Prosecution's Story, But They're Not Sticking to It: Applying Harmless Error and Judicial Estoppel to Exculpatory Post-Conviction DNA Testing Cases," 74 *Fordham L. Rev.* 825, 837–41 (2005).

32. *Id.* at 837–38. In situations where a person has been exonerated and prosecutors decide to file the same criminal charges against that person, there is an argument that this potentially violates the Double Jeopardy Clause. See Jordan M. Barry, "Prosecuting the Exonerated: Actual Innocence and the Double Jeopardy Clause," Feb. 8, 2011 (available at http://papers.ssrn.com/sol3/papers.cfm?abstract_id=1758161).

CONCLUSION

1. See George C. Thomas III, *The Supreme Court on Trial: How the American Justice System Sacrifices Innocent Defendants* (Ann Arbor: University of Michigan Press, 2008), 182–84.

2. See Erik Luna & Marianne Wade, "Prosecutors as Judges," 67 *Wash. & Lee L. Rev.* 1413, 1510–13 (2010).

3. For example, I mentioned replacing the norm of public prosecutors who operate in their own organizations with a pool of individual criminal law specialists who work on both sides of the fence, a practice that prevailed for years in Great Britain. See chapter 7, this volume; Daniel S. Medwed, "The Zeal Deal: Prosecutorial Resistance to Post-Conviction Claims of Innocence," 84 *B.U. L. Rev.* 125, 180–81 (2004); Thomas, *Supreme Court on Trial*, at 190–92.

4. See Jacqueline Hodgson, *French Criminal Justice: A Comparative Account of the Investigation and Prosecution of Crime in France* (Oxford: Hart, 2005), 75–79; Robert P. Mosteller, "Failures of the American Adversarial System to Protect the Innocent and the Conceptual Advantages in the Inquisitorial Design for Investigative Fairness," 36 *N. C. J. Int'l & Comm. Reg.* 319, 356–58 (2011). In recent years, however, France has expanded the role the prosecutor plays in its system to minimize the delay in processing criminal cases. The upshot, according to Professor Jacqueline Hodgson, "has been a shift of power away from the trial judge and the *juge d'instruction* in favor of the *procureur*, giving her significant dispositive powers." Jacqueline S. Hodgson, "The French Prosecutor in Question," 67 *Wash. & Lee L. Rev.* 1361, 1362 (2010). Currently France may be on the cusp of abolishing the *juge d'instruction* altogether and transferring all investigative power to the *procureur*. *Id.* at 1363.

5. Hodgson, *French Prosecutor*, at 1362 n. 3, 1368–69.

6. See Hodgson, *French Criminal Justice*, at 67, 70–71, 209; Hodgson, *French Prosecutor*, at 1368–69; Mosteller, *Failures*, at 356–58.

7. See Hodgson, *French Criminal Justice*, at 71–72.

8. See Luna & Wade, *Prosecutors as Judges*, at 1461 n. 218.

9. See Thomas, *Supreme Court on Trial*, at 182; Lloyd L. Weinreb, *Denial of Justice: Criminal Process in the United States* (New York: Free Press, 1977), 117–46.

10. See Thomas, *Supreme Court on Trial*, at 182.

11. See *Id.* at 193–98.

12. See *Id.* at 198–202.

13. See *Id.* at 207–14.

14. Letter from Oliver Wendell Holmes to John C. H. Wu, July 1, 1929, reprinted in Oliver Wendell Holmes, *Justice Holmes to Doctor Wu: An Intimate Correspondence, 1921–1932* (New York: Central Book Co., 1947), 53.

15. I am indebted to Professor Anders Kaye for suggesting the gist of this paragraph for my conclusion.

16. Several scholars have called on law schools to provide better ethics education for aspiring prosecutors. See, e.g., Luna & Wade, *Prosecutors as Judges*, at 1513–19; Ellen S. Podgor, "The Ethics and Professionalism of Prosecutors in Discretionary Decisions," 68 *Fordham L. Rev.* 1511, 1532–33 (2000).

17. Robert H. Jackson, "The Federal Prosecutor," 24 *J. Am. Judicature Soc'y* 18, 20 (1940).

18. *Id.*

Index

forensic evidence, 28, 92–102; arson science, 94; bite marks, 92, 101, 162; boot print evidence, 92–93; crime laboratories, 94–96, 98–100, 102; *CSI* Effect, 92, 200n2; defective DNA comparisons, 93, 95; diffusion of responsibility, 98, 203n37; discovery, 99; fingerprinting, 92–93, 95, 101; forensic odontology, 92, 101; hair microscopy, 92, 101, 180n98, 201n9; handwriting evidence, 101; inaccurate expert testimony, 94; judicial screening, 98, 101–102; and prosecutors, 97–102; "second generation" of forensic science, 201n14; serology, 95–96

forensic fraud, 95–96

forensic odontology, 92, 101

forensic science, 28, 92–102; arson science, 94; bite marks, 92, 101, 162; boot print evidence, 92–93; crime laboratories, 94–96, 98–100, 102; *CSI* Effect, 92, 200n2; defective DNA comparisons, 93, 95; diffusion of responsibility, 98, 203n37; discovery, 99; fingerprinting, 92–93, 95, 101; forensic odontology, 92, 101; hair microscopy, 92, 101, 180n98, 201n9; handwriting evidence, 101; inaccurate expert testimony, 94; judicial screening, 98, 101–102; and prosecutors, 97–102; "second generation" of forensic science, 201n14; serology, 95–96

forensic science commissions, 202n23

French criminal justice system, 168, 220n4

Gaertner, Susan, 150

Garrett, Brandon, 94, 149–150

Gell, Alan, 187n85

Gershman, Bennett, 19, 155

Gershowitz, Adam, 116

Giannelli, Paul, 100

Giglio material, 59

Giglio v. United States, 36

Gilchrist, Joyce, 96–97

Giles, James, 1, 7–11, 25, 40; James Curtis Giles, 7–11, 37, 139; James Earl (a.k.a. "Quack") Giles, 8–10, 37

Givelber, Daniel, 62–63

Godschalk, Bruce, 1, 119–121, 150

Gonser, Craig, 138–139

Goodman, Bruce, 159–161

"gradualist" approach to criminal justice reform, 167

grand jury, 16, 18, 35, 70, 173n26, 175n16

Gross, Samuel, 2, 54, 87

groupthink, 27, 210n26

Guilfoyle, Anthony, 55

Gundrum, Mark, 131

Gutierrez, Nelson, 70, 72–75

habeas corpus, 123, 125–126

hair microscopy, 92, 101, 180n98, 201n9

Hand, Learned, 46

handwriting evidence, 101

harmless error doctrine, 110–111, 113–115, 180n103, 184n36, 206n39, 207n63, 207nn65–66

Haynesworth, Thomas, 218n3

Hellerstein, William, 72, 83

Hernandez, Alejandro, 93

Hidalgo, Olmedo, 129, 142

Holmes, Oliver Wendell, 169

"horseshedding," of a witness, 80, 196n22

Houston Police Department Crime Laboratory (HPDCL) scandal, 95

Houston, post-conviction review unit, 141, 169, 214n94

hunt mentality, 79

immunity for prosecutors, 30, 161

improper bolstering of experts, 98

improper pretrial publicity, 18–19, 173n26, 175n24

improper witness coaching, 81–82, 196n19, 196n22, 197n28

ineffective assistance of counsel, 28, 75

informants, in general, 84–85

innocence commissions, 140–141

Innocence Project, of New York, 9–10, 28, 42, 54, 94, 108, 110, 120–121, 136, 152, 155–156, 161, 163–164, 173n15, 199n66, 208n7

Innocence Project, of Texas, 139

innocence project, Thomas M. Cooley School of Law, 138

inquisitorial model of criminal justice, France, 168–169
institutional design theory, 27, 99
Italy, approach to plea bargaining, 62

Jackson, Robert, 87, 170
jailhouse informants, 28, 75, 84–87; corroboration requirement, 89; disclosure obligations, 86; discovery depositions, 88; enhancing reliability of testimony, 87–89; ethical issues, 87, 90, 199n64; greater discovery, 87–88; history of, 198n54; internal remedies, 90–91; judicial oversight, 89–90; jury instructions, 89; Los Angeles District Attorney's Office review of jailhouse informant practices, 90–91, 169; perjury, 85–87; pre-arranged deals, 86; pretrial reliability hearings, 88–89, 199n81; public registries, 89; rationales for use, 86; review committees, 90–91, 200n95; systemic reform, 89–91; "wink and nod" deals, 86, 88;
Jonakait, Randolph, 23
Johnson, Justin Albert, 163
judicial estoppel, 164, 219n31
juge d'instruction, 168
Justice for All Act, 155

Kitsap County (Wa.), 25–26; general charging standards, 25
Kunstler, William, 72

Lawliss, Timothy, 73–75
law school education, emphasis on ethics, 170, 220n16
Legal Aid Society of New York City, 1
Lemus, David, 129, 142
Los Angeles County Jail, 1989 scandal, 85–86
Los Angeles District Attorney's Office, 41; *Brady* Compliance Division, 41, 169; review of jailhouse informant practices, 90–91, 169
loss aversion, 56, 79, 189n20
Lovitt, Robin, 152, 156
Luna, Erik, 167
Lykos, Patricia, 141

Macy, Robert, 116–117
Marino, Achim Josef, 54
Marino, Carmen, 47–48
market theory of plea bargaining, 60
Marlinga, Carl, 138
Marshall, Thurgood, 44
materiality, *Brady* doctrine, 37–39, 43–45, 183n19, 185n55, 186n73; abandonment of, 44–45, modification of, 43–44
McDonnell, Bob, 218n3
McMunigal, Kevin, 100
Melendez-Diaz v. Massachusetts, 99
Melnikoff, Arnold, 97–98
Menon, Jaykumar, 72
Miller v. Pate, 97
Miller, Robert, 96
minister-of-justice principle, 2–4, 36, 38, 56, 78–80, 87, 118, 124, 126, 132–133, 135, 137, 139, 142, 145, 157, 164–165, 169–170
Mitchell, John, 117–118
Model Rules of Professional Conduct, 32; prosecutors and experts, 99–101; Rule 3.4, 111; Rule 3.8(d), 36, 64; Rule 3.8(g)-(h), 134–135; Rule 3.8 and plea bargaining, 59
Morgenthau, Robert, 141–142
Moriarty, Jane, 94, 100
Mosteller, Robert, 88
motion for new trial, in general, 125
motivational bias, 203n38
Munoz, Luis (a.k.a. "Woolu"), 82

Nassau County (N.Y.) Crime Laboratory, closure of, 202n18
Nassau County (N.Y.) District Attorney's Office, single-eyewitness review boards, 29, 169
Natapoff, Alexandra, 89
National Academy of Sciences (NAS) Report, 96
Neufeld, Peter, 9, 94
New Orleans District Attorney's Office, 179n77
New York County District Attorney's Office, Conviction Integrity Program, 141, 169

New York State Police, Forensic Identification Center, 95
Nifong, Mike, 17–19, 21, 29, 48, 175n24
no contest (*nolo contendere*) pleas, 66–67, 193n80
nolo contendere (no contest) pleas, 66–67, 193n80
non-DNA cases, 1–2, 75, 125, 131, 139
North Carolina Innocence Inquiry Commission, 141–142
North Carolina State Bureau of Investigation (SBI), scandal, 95

Ochoa, Chris, 54
open file discovery, 45–50, 64; debate over, 45–48; in Dallas County Conviction Integrity Unit, 213n84; in Milwaukee, 47; in North Carolina, 48, 187nn85–86; methods of enforcement, 48–50; training, 50
Osborne, William, 151

Pacyon, Douglas, 159
Palladium nightclub murder, 128–129
"paper trail," 123
parole process, in general, 126
passion, impact on prosecutorial decisions, 57
"people trail," 123
plea allocution, 53
plea bargaining, 52–68; abolition, 61, 191n47; career goals and plea bargaining, 57–58, 190nn26–28; concern with public perception, 57; differential sentencing, 61–62; disclosure, 59, 63–64; ethical rules, 59–60; explanations for generous plea offers in weak cases, 56–58; Federal Rules of Criminal Procedure, 65; Federal Sentencing Guidelines, 61; internal regulation, 59–60; internal review, 60, 64–65; Italian practices, 62; judicial monitoring, 64–66; legal doctrines, 58–59; loss aversion, 56–57; market theory of, 60; no contest or *nolo contendere* pleas, 66–67; office policies, 58; partial ban, 192n56; passion, 57; plea discount, 62; presumption of correctness, 53; psychological need for

closure, 57; temptation to plead guilty, 53–56, 60, 68; trial tax, 53, 59–65, 67; tunnel vision, 56, 59; work experience, 57
plea colloquy, 53, 66
plea discount, 62, 189n9, 192n53
political considerations, for prosecutors, 78, 130, 143, 214n110; partisan politics, 145; post-conviction, 130–131, 137, 142–145, 154, 163
Pollack, Barry, 83
polymerase chain reaction (PCR), 148–149
post-conviction DNA testing, 145–157; absence of freestanding federal constitutional right to, 151; barriers to testing, 149–153; costs of, 149, 153; DNA databases, 149; evidence preservation, 151–153, 155–157; guilty pleas, 154–155; history and methodology of, 148–149; prosecutorial resistance, 150; prosecutorial review units, 149–151; statutes, 150–151, 154–155
post-conviction innocence claims, in general, 123–157; based on DNA testing, 147–157; ethics, 131–132, 134–135, 164, 217n35; innocence commissions, 140–141; procedural hurdles, 125–126; prosecutorial review units, 135–141; resistance by prosecutors, 123–157; statewide review units, 141
Pound, Roscoe, 109
power of "adjudication," by prosecutors, 60
preservation of evidence, 151–153, 155–157; in Dallas, 155; and guilty pleas, 154–155; preservation statutes, 155–156; in Virginia, 152, 156
presumption of guilt, 24–25, 127
primacy, 104
private prosecutor model, 145, 215n121
probable cause, 14–16, 174n2, 175n31, 175n33, 178n74; as relates to Duke Lacrosse case, 18–19; proposed reforms to, 19–21
procureur, 168, 220n4
Professional Integrity Programs, 42
"prosecution complex," 3, 169, 171n11
prosecutorial agnosticism, 175n33
prosecutorial elections, 144–145
Prosecutorial Misconduct Projects, 116

prosecutorial reliance on forensic evidence, 97–102; cognitive biases, 98; conceal- ment or delayed disclosure, 97, 99, 102; diffusion of responsibility, 98; dubi- ous forensic expert testimony, 97–98; escalation of commitment, 98; ethical obligations, 99–102; exaggeration of expert testimony during closing argu- ments, 106; expert coaching, 100; expert shopping, 101; improper bolstering, 98; willful blindness, 100

prosecutorial resistance to post-conviction innocence claims, 123–165; cognitive biases, 127–129; to DNA testing, 150; eth- ics, 131–132, 134–135, 164, 217n35; finality, 130, 132–134; innocence commissions, 141–142; internal review units, 135–142; North Carolina Innocence Inquiry Commission, 141–142; political consid- erations, 130–131, 137, 142–145; resource constraints, 129–130, 137; revised theory of guilt, 158, 164; statewide review units, 141; ; and theories of punishment, 164

prosecutorial review committees, 4, 21–29, 42; *Brady* material, 42, 185n50; charging decisions, 21–29, 179n86, 180n95; closing arguments, 112; jailhouse informants, 90–91, 200n95; plea bargaining, 60, 64–65; post-conviction innocence claims based on DNA, 149–150; post- conviction innocence claims generally, 135–141; summations, 112

psychological closure, 53

public prosecutor model, 145, 215n121

racial bias, 5, 75

Ramos, Alberto, 30–31

recency, 104

resource constraints, 28, 127, 129, 137

restriction-fragment-length-polymor- phism (RFLP), 148–149

review committees, 4, 21–29, 42; *Brady* material, 42, 185n50; charging decisions, 21–29, 179n86, 180n95; closing argu- ments, 112; innocence claims based on DNA, 149–150; jailhouse informants,

90–91, 200n95; plea bargaining, 60, 64–65; post-conviction innocence claims based on DNA, 149–150; post- conviction innocence claims generally, 135–141; summations, 112

revised theory of guilt by prosecutors, post-conviction, 158, 164

revolutionary approach to criminal justice reform, 167–169

Risinger, Lesley, 83

risk aversion, 53, 64, 154

Robbins, Louise, 93

Roberts, John, 151

Rocky Mountain Innocence Center (RMIC), 160–161

role effects bias, 203n38

Rosen, Richard, 39–40

Ruiz, United States v., 59, 64, 190n36

Santa Clara County (Ca.) District Attor- ney's Office, 133, 169

Scheck, Barry, 9, 42

Schulz, Stephen, 55–56, 60

scientific evidence, 28, 92–102; arson science, 94; bite marks, 92, 101, 162; boot print evi- dence, 92–93; crime laboratories, 94–96, 98–100, 102; *CSI Effect*, 92, 200n2; defec- tive DNA comparisons, 93, 95; diffusion of responsibility, 98, 203n37; discovery, 99; fingerprinting, 92–93, 95, 101; forensic odontology, 92, 101; hair microscopy, 92, 101, 180n98, 201n9; handwriting evidence, 101; inaccurate expert testimony, 94; judicial screening, 98, 101–102; and pros- ecutors, 97–102; "second generation" of forensic science, 201n14; serology, 95–96

Scott, Michael, 22

Second Look Program, Brooklyn Law School, 1, 9, 55, 72, 83

Sedita, Frank, 159

selective information processing, 22, 38, 44, 64, 127, 189n21

serology testing, 95–96

shaming by naming in judicial opinions, 115–116

short tandem repeat (STR) markers, 149

About the Author

DANIEL S. MEDWED is Professor of Law at the University of Utah and a nationally recognized scholar in the field of wrongful convictions. He lives in Salt Lake City with his wife Sharissa Jones and their daughter Mili. He is a graduate of Yale College and Harvard Law School.